The Twentieth Century World

John Ray and James Hag

Hutchinson

London Melbourne Sydney Auckland Johannesburg

To Sarah and Trina

Hutchinson Education

An imprint of Century Hutchinson Ltd
62–65 Chandos Place, London WC2N 4NW

Century Hutchinson South Africa (Pty) Ltd
PO Box 337, Bergvlei 2012, South Africa

Century Hutchinson Australia Pty Ltd
PO Box 496, 16–22 Church Street, Hawthorn, Victoria 3122, Australia

Century Hutchinson New Zealand Ltd
PO Box 40–086, Glenfield, Auckland 10, New Zealand

First published 1986
Reprinted 1987

© John Ray and James Hagerty 1986

Typeset in Linotron 202 Plantin

British Library Cataloguing in Publication Data

Ray, John, *1929–*
    The twentieth century world.——(History for you)
    1. History, Modern——20th century
    I. Title   II. Hagerty, James   III. Series
    909.82   D421

ISBN 0 09 160911 9

Contents

The world in 1900

IF the clock were turned back to the year 1900 you would find a very different world from the one you know. Several important changes have occurred. Nations have risen and fallen in the league table of strength, fame and success. The world's population has more than doubled. In 1900 much of the world was governed by a small number of the most powerful nations. Most countries now govern themselves.

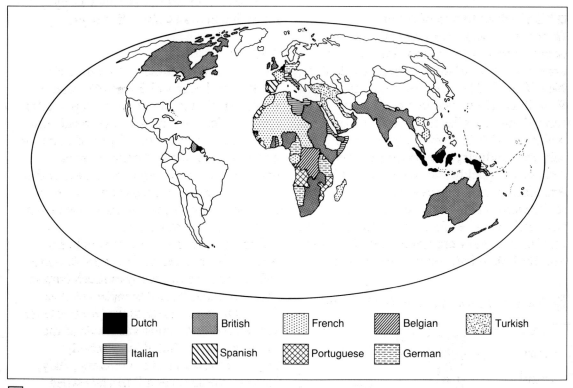

Dutch   British   French   Belgian   Turkish

Italian   Spanish   Portuguese   German

A *A map of the world in 1900 showing those areas ruled by European nations*

● Europe

At the start of the twentieth century, Europe was the world's most powerful continent. It included some of the richest and strongest nations, like Germany and Britain, France and Austria-Hungary. Europe was also the world's most densely populated area, with more inhabitants per square kilometre than any other part. Over one-third of the world's greatest cities were in Europe – London, Paris, Vienna and Berlin.

European nations at that time could show their power in a number of different ways. Some contained great industrial regions where factories turned out millions of manufactured articles to be sold at home and abroad. In others, farming was well developed, usually producing sufficient food for their own people, few of whom were starving, as well as enough to sell to other lands.

Generally, the countries of western Europe were richer than those in the east of the continent. Trade was brisk for nations like Germany and Britain, bringing in millions of pounds each year.

But in 1900, challenging Europe's position, a giant nation was growing very speedily on the further side of the Atlantic Ocean.

● The United States of America

Over the previous half-century millions of people, many of them from Europe, had gone to settle in what was often called 'The New World'. The population had grown to 80 million. They lived in a vast country, three thousand miles from coast to coast, which was rich in farming, forests and minerals. Industry and agriculture were developing quickly and trade was good as American products were carried to all parts of the world. The USA was a young, powerful nation, still attracting thousands of immigrants who were trying to find a better life. By 1900 it had become the world's

greatest producer of manufactured goods, pushing Germany and Britain into second and third places.

Americans kept strong links with Europe in trade and travel. The north Atlantic Ocean was one of the busiest waterways in the world. The fastest crossing was by steamship and took about five days.

● Africa

This was an age of imperialism in Africa. What does that mean? Remember that in 1900, a small number of the most powerful nations ruled over much of the world. An area which was ruled over by another nation was called a 'colony'. All the colonies belonging to one nation were known as that nation's 'empire'. Imperialism is the name given to a nation's plan to find colonies and so build up its own empire.

European nations were keen to build empires for themselves. From 1870, there had been a rush to occupy as much land in Africa as possible, and to make colonies there. This was known as the 'Scramble for Africa'. By 1900 almost the whole of the continent was included in somebody's empire. France, Britain, Germany, Italy, Portugal, Belgium and Spain all owned territories there, which they governed. On the map, those African lands were painted in the colours of the countries which claimed them.

B *The world's population in 1900 and 1980*

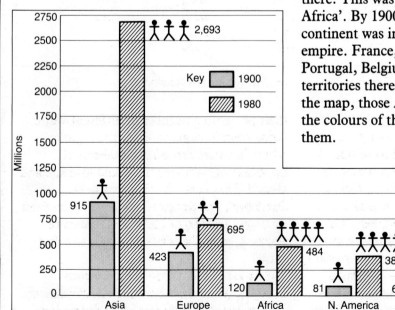

Europeans had gone to Africa for several reasons. They wanted to obtain raw materials like copper and timber for their industries. They wanted to sell some of the goods they produced to the Africans. A few Europeans went to gain prestige – or glory – for their countries. Others travelled to spread the message of Christianity to people who had never heard of it. A few were seeking adventure.

Conquering the Africans was quite easy. Their swords and spears were not as powerful as modern European weapons. As a poet expressed it:

---

1 **Whatever happens, we have got
The Maxim gun and they have not**

(The Maxim gun was an early form of machine-gun.)

By 1914 only two African territories, Liberia and Abyssinia, were independent. Europeans had laid claim to all the rest.

● The Far East and the Pacific

European empires also stretched to countries and islands of the Far East. There too, Britons and Germans, French and Dutch controlled large territories. India, for example, had been part of the British Empire since the mid-eighteenth century. The Dutch East Indies had belonged to Holland since the 1600s.

Far Eastern countries provided raw materials like rubber and tin, tea and rice, so ships sailed regularly to and from Europe, carrying rich cargoes.

Several other nations wanted to gain power in the Far East. One was Japan, which rapidly began to copy Europeans and started to build an empire among countries like China which were not far away. In doing

this the Japanese fought a successful war against the Russians who were also trying to gain territory. A third nation involved was the USA which took a number of Pacific islands and territories that had belonged to the old Spanish Empire in the Far East.

● Diplomacy

In life it's often possible for individuals to settle quarrels before they grow too bad by sitting down and talking about them. This applies to nations as well and is called diplomacy.

There were few wars at the end of the nineteenth century because the leaders of important countries were prepared to discuss their problems rather than fight about them. People in Europe, the world's most powerful continent, enjoyed long periods of peace. In fact there had been no large wars there, involving all the Great Powers (Germany, France, Britain, Austria–Hungary), since

C *The New Century*

the Napoleonic Wars had ended in 1815, almost a century earlier.

But many leaders recognized that if diplomacy broke down, trouble would quickly follow.

● **Everyday life**

It's very strange and difficult for a person of today to think back to the world of 1900. Life then was very different in a number of ways.

For example, there had been little modern technical progress. Motor cars were in their infancy and no powered aeroplane flights had ever been made. Experiments with radio had barely started and television and computers were unknown. Few homes had either electricity or bathrooms.

Women had no vote and only a handful could follow a career. People in Britain could look forward to an average of about fifty years of life, which is twenty years less than at the present day. Yet that was twice as long as an Indian could hope for and Europeans had a longer expectation of life than the inhabitants, say, of South America or Africa.

Life in the twentieth century, which began on 1 January 1901, has altered rapidly. Enormous progress has been made and we now live in a world that is changing faster than ever. □

Exercises

1 Copy and complete these sentences by using words from the **word list.**
   (a) Europe had more . . . per square kilometre than any other continent.
   (b) Germany and Britain grew rich from. . . .
   (c) The greatest producer of manufactured goods was the . . . .
   (d) Liberia and Abyssinia were the only . . . African countries in 1914.
   (e) No powered . . . flight had been made in 1900.

> **word list:** trade; aeroplane; United States; inhabitants; independent

2 Refer to the chapter you have just read and answer the following questions.

   (a) In what ways could European nations show their power in 1900?
   (b) Which nation was developing rapidly in importance at the beginning of the century?
   (c) Give two reasons for Europeans taking overseas colonies.
   (d) Name three nations interested in gaining power in the Far East.

3 Look at cartoon C, The New Century.
   (a) What is Father Time riding?
   (b) What sort of vehicle is 1900 coming in on?
   (c) Explain what you think the person who drew this cartoon was trying to say about The New Century.

4 Explain, in your own words, what the 'Scramble for Africa' was.

Britain and its empire

● **Introduction**

By the early 1900s Britain had set up the largest empire ever known. During the previous century about fifteen million people had left Britain to settle overseas. Many of them had gone to the lands of the empire and they kept strong links with the 'mother country'.

Four of the larger colonies had their own governments and were known as dominions. These were Canada, South Africa, New Zealand and Australia.

Another area of the empire was India, which was an enormous country with millions of people. Some parts were ruled over by local native princes, while others were governed by the British king's representative, called the Viceroy, and a Council of Ministers. India was so valuable in terms of trade that it was known as 'the brightest jewel in the British crown'. India provided such goods as tea and cotton, jute

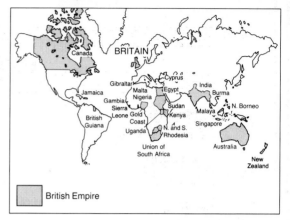

A *The British Empire and dependencies, 1902*

and silk, which were eagerly sought after in Britain. (Jute is used for making sackcloth.)

Some of Britain's remaining colonies were large territories, spread over thousands of square kilometres, while others were ports or small forts for ships or troops. In those areas the local people were usually governed

B *During their state visit to India in 1911, King George V and Queen Mary held a ceremonial court (called a 'Durbar') in Delhi. During this ceremony the Indian princes paid homage to the king and queen. Here, their Majesties come out to show themselves to the multitudes assembled below.*

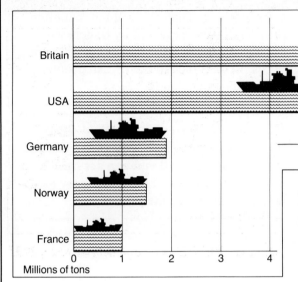

Britain

USA

Germany

Norway

France

5   6   7   8   9   10

0   1   2   3   4
Millions of tons

C *The world's merchant fleets, 1900*

through their king or chief who was advised by British civil servants, or by colonial governors.

● The Royal Navy

The British Empire spread all over the world and was called 'the empire on which the sun never sets'. Because the lands were so widespread, Britain had to build and maintain a strong navy to protect the territories and trade routes. British warships were to be seen on all oceans and the nation had great pride in a navy that was the most powerful in the world.

● Trade

The empire was of great importance in terms of trade. In the late eighteenth century Britain was the first nation to have an Industrial Revolution. This had made it a rich and successful country. The search for raw materials for its industries and for markets where goods could be sold was a main reason why the empire was developed.

But by 1900 Britain was finding greater difficulties in trading. The USA and Germany had grown rapidly as competitors and many countries imposed taxes which made it harder for British traders to sell their goods overseas.

● The family of nations

Many people in Britain were proud of their empire which they treated like a family spread over all the world. For many of them this was a real feeling because they actually had relatives who had emigrated during the previous century and still spoke of Britain as 'home'. Britain was the 'mother country' and they were the children.

● Imperialism

Some writers of the time believed that the British race had a special position in the world. It was their duty to carry British ideas and ways of life to other people. One wrote:

1 Open any map, and glance for one moment at the dominions in which the Union Jack is the standard of the ruling race! Canada, stretching from the Atlantic to the Pacific, the peninsula of India, the continent of Australia, the South of Africa, are only the largest blotches, so to speak, in a world chart blurred and dotted over with the stamp marks of British rule. . . .

Britain and its empire

Wherever the Union Jack floats, there the English race rules; English laws prevail; English ideas are dominant; English speech holds the upper hand.

This was the feeling of imperialism. Many men and women who shared these ideas believed that white people had a duty to look after other parts of the world and help them to develop. It was their task to spread British ideas across the globe.

Other Britons, however, were worried by imperialism. They believed that keeping colonies could be a very expensive business and might lead to trouble, even wars, with other nations. A few felt it was wrong for one race to govern or rule over another one.

Of course, most of the subject peoples (the people who were being ruled over) did not see imperialism as a blessing. They wanted freedom from the control of another nation. They believed that their feelings were being ignored and that the British felt themselves

D *Modern technology, as well as Christianity, was taken to Africa by Europeans. In this nineteenth-century advert, electricity is shown transforming the 'Dark Continent'*

to be superior. They realized too that often their lands were exploited by traders who became very rich while they remained poor.

One wrote a plea to the British people, asking to be left alone:

> **2** **I have no cultivated lands, no silver or gold for you to take. My country is no good to you. . . . All you can get from me is war, nothing else. I have met your men in battle and have killed them. . . .**

● Africa

During the 'Scramble for Africa' Britain had taken a number of territories into its empire. By 1900 more than a dozen of them were under British control and were shown on the map in Britain's colour – red.

But as the new century began the British were at war in Africa with another white race. At the southern tip of the continent lived the Boers, who were descendants of early Dutch settlers. They and the British were fighting over who was to control that area, especially after the discovery of gold and diamonds there.

Everyone expected that the war, which had begun in 1899, would end quickly in a victory for Great Britain, one of the world's most powerful nations. However, the fighting dragged on until 1902. Britain's pride was hurt when its soldiers suffered several humiliating military defeats.

● Australia

Many settlers had left Britain in the nineteenth century to live in Australia. Sheep farming and gold prospecting drew thousands to seek a new life. The country was divided into six colonies but in 1901 they joined together into one nation, as the

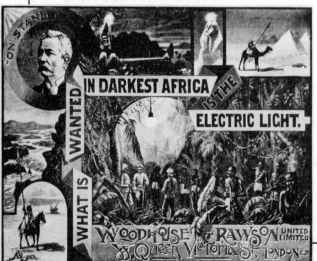

WOODHOUSE & RAWSON UNITED LIMITED
Queen Victoria St., London

'Dominion of Australia'. A reason for doing this was because they feared that Asian people might try to colonize the vast land they had settled in.

In those days Australia had less than four million white inhabitants as well as the Aborigines who were there when the first Europeans arrived.

● New Zealand

New Zealand was further away from Britain than any other part of the empire and the voyage was long and dangerous. By 1900 there was a strong trade with Britain in refrigerated lamb and mutton.

Fewer than one million settlers lived there, together with the Maoris who had inhabited the islands for several centuries. The country was given the title of 'Dominion of New Zealand' in 1907.

● Canada

Canada received many settlers because Britain was comparatively near, across the Atlantic Ocean. In 1889 the Canadian Pacific Railway had linked east and west coasts and large quantities of wheat were exported to Europe by steamship. Thus more British farm-workers were encouraged to emigrate there.

Exercises

1 Copy and complete these sentences.
   (a) The four dominions of the British Empire were. . . .
   (b) In India the King's special representative was called the. . . .
   (c) Britain needed a strong navy because. . . .
   (d) One important reason why the British Empire developed was. . . .
   (e) In 1900 Britain was at war against . . . .

2 The heads (a)–(h) and tails (i)–(viii) of these statements have been mixed up. Write them out correctly.

   (a) The Dominions
   (b) The Boers
   (c) Australia
   (d) The British Empire
   (e) India
   (f) Colonies
   (g) Britain
   (h) New Zealand

   (i) was known as the brightest jewel in the British Crown.
   (ii) was called the empire on which the sun never sets.
   (iii) was further away from Britain than any other part of the empire and became a dominion in 1907.
   (iv) were descendants of early Dutch settlers in South Africa.
   (v) was divided into six colonies but in 1901 became one nation.
   (vi) had their own governments.
   (vii) were governed by colonial governors or by local chiefs advised by the British.
   (viii) owned the world's most powerful navy.

3 Why do you think so many people came to the Delhi 'Durbar'?

4 Read the section on 'Imperialism'. How do pictures B and D show men and women spreading British ideas across the world?

(A *further question appears on page 218.*)

11

The European alliances

● **Introduction**

Although in 1900 there had been no great European war for many years the rumbles of approaching trouble could be heard. The powerful nations of Europe had a number of differences with each other. You know what happens when a group of individuals start arguing. They look round for friends who will help and stick by them if the need arises. To have allies brings a feeling of confidence.

There was a similar situation among the great European nations. As disagreements arose, they searched for partners who would give assistance.

At that time there were six nations mainly involved – France, Germany, Austria-Hungary, Russia, Great Britain and Italy. By 1914 they had formed themselves into two groups, like gangs opposed to each other, and already there had been some small incidents which, fortunately, had been settled by diplomacy.

However, some people wondered how much longer peace would last.

● **The Triple Alliance**

One side, or group of countries was called the Triple Alliance. It consisted of Germany, Austria-Hungary and Italy.

Germany

The strongest of the three was Germany. In fact by 1900 Germany was in many ways the most powerful country in Europe. Germany did not exist as a separate nation until 1871: before then there was a collection of independent states. But in 1870, under the leadership of Prussia, the most powerful state, the Germans defeated France in war and the next year declared themselves to be a new nation.

All of this was achieved under the leadership of Otto von Bismarck, a very clever, sharp-thinking politician. Over the following years he helped to make Germany rich and strong, signing alliances to prevent it from being attacked. For example, he formed the Dual Alliance with Austria-Hungary in 1879 and turned this into the Triple Alliance with Italy three years later. A treaty of friendship was also signed with Russia.

But in 1890 the new German emperor, Kaiser Wilhelm II, dismissed Bismarck and tried to run affairs in his own way. He did not renew the friendship with Russia and soon France and Russia signed their own treaty, promising each other help in the event of an enemy attack.

Germany was a rich, fast-growing industrial power, and it wanted colonies overseas in Africa and the Far East. This made France and Britain suspicious because they already had empires and did not want any rivals. By 1900 Germany had the best trained and equipped army in Europe, which

A *Map of the European Alliances, 1914*

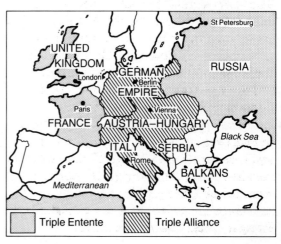

Triple Entente ▢   Triple Alliance ▨

was worrying to its neighbours. Then, to strengthen its position as a colonial power, it started to expand its navy – and that angered Britain.

The German's point of view was that they were being hemmed in – 'encircled' – by France, Russia and Britain, who were trying to prevent Germany from becoming a great world power.

Germany also began to show an interest in south-eastern Europe, aiming to build a railway from Berlin right across to Baghdad in the Middle East. That made Germany an ally of Austria-Hungary.

Austria-Hungary

Austria-Hungary was a great and ancient empire in central Europe. The lands contained people of many different races. Some did not want to belong, and for years had sought independence and the freedom to govern themselves. Yet in 1900 the Austro-Hungarian Empire still existed, ruled over by the Habsburg family. The Emperor, Franz Josef, had been on the throne since 1848 and wanted to hold his empire together.

Serbia, a small, independent country on the border, was a thorn in the Austrian flesh. The Serbs were a Slav nation and did not want to be ruled over by the Austrians. They encouraged other Slavs in the empire to seek freedom. Many Austrians felt that one day there would be a showdown with Serbia.

The Austrians were friendly with the Germans but were great rivals of the Russians. They believed that Russia wanted to take over lands called the Balkans, in south-eastern Europe (page 110). Once, that area had been part of the great Turkish Empire but Turkey had grown weak and now the Balkans was an area that Austria-Hungary itself wanted to control.

Italy

Italy, the third member of the Triple Alliance, was not a very strong power. The Italians had joined in 1882 after a disagreement with France, yet they always had disputes with Austria-Hungary over territory near their borders which both countries claimed. Italy, like Germany, had been a unified country only since the late nineteenth century.

● The Triple Entente

The Triple Entente consisted of three nations – France, Russia and Great Britain.

France

France was a strong military power with a large empire. However, in 1871 the French had been defeated by the Germans who took from them two territories, Alsace and Lorraine. Although many Frenchmen wanted revenge for that defeat they could find no allies until 1892 when they signed an alliance with Russia. Then in 1904 France made an agreement or understanding, called an 'entente', with Britain who had for centuries been its old rival. Both sides

B *King Edward VII of England introduces the British Lion to the French President. A cartoon depicting the Anglo-French 'entente'*

C *Cartoon to show Britain pursuing its policy of 'splendid isolation'*

settled some small disagreements over colonies, then looked ahead to how they might help each other if ever that most terrible event happened – war with Germany.

Russia

Russia was the largest of all powers, but was backward. Russians were interested in the Balkans for two main reasons. First, some of the people there were of the Slav race like themselves and shared the same religion. So Russia took the side of little Serbia in its quarrels with the enormous Austria-Hungary. Second, as Turkish power grew weak in that area the Russians did not want any unfriendly power to control the Balkans,

especially the Dardanelles, where their trade routes passed from the Black Sea to the Mediterranean. Therefore they were worried when Germany and Austria-Hungary showed interest in that part of the world.

Friendship with France was the result. Then, in 1907, Russia made an agreement with France's new friend, Britain, a country with whom it had never been particularly friendly in the past.

Britain

For many years at the end of the nineteenth century Britain had not wanted alliances with any foreign nations. It was the world's most important trading nation with an enormous empire – the 'empire on which the sun never sets'. While other countries were signing pacts and gaining allies the British stood alone, with a policy known as 'splendid isolation'. Britain was an island, with the largest of all navies and felt no need for friends.

However, as Germany grew in power, Britain became worried. The British had always been friendly with the Germans – Queen Victoria had married one – and at that time there was even talk of making an alliance with them. But German naval building after 1900 upset the British who then turned to their old enemy, France, in friendship. In 1907 Britain went a step further and made a friendly agreement with Russia.

The Foreign Secretary, Sir Edward Grey, described the British position in 1911:

1 . . . **After discussions lasting a long time, the result was the Anglo-French Agreement of 1904. This agreement at once removed all risk of quarrel between the United Kingdom and France, and by**

removing that, brought the two nations very rapidly to realize that there was no reason why they should not be the best of friends. . . . Then . . . the same policy was pursued with Russia. . . . So that cause of quarrel disappeared, and, consequently, we and Russia have now become very good friends in diplomacy.

● **Will it work?**

By the early 1900s the two sides, or teams, or gangs, had been formed. Germans found it hard to believe that Britain and France, who had disliked each other, could now be allies. They twice tested out the strength of the friendship by causing small incidents against French power in North Africa. How would Britain react?

The two incidents occurred in Morocco, first in 1905, then in 1911. Each time Germany questioned France's rights in that area. The Kaiser soon discovered that Britain was prepared to stand by its new friend. The British government spoke out clearly in support of the French, following up with more military and naval talks about how the two countries could help each other.

By that time many people realized that in future it would take only a small spark to set Europe alight. Then the great armies and navies would be sent into action. ☐

Exercises

1 Copy and complete these sentences.
   (a) If nations are in trouble they look around for allies because. . . .
   (b) Germany became a separate nation in. . . .
   (c) At the end of the nineteenth century Germany wanted. . . .
   (d) The Austro-Hungarian Empire contained people of. . . .
   (e) By 1914 six nations had formed two major. . . .

2 Using the information in the chapter say what event took place in the following years: 1871, 1879, 1882, 1890, 1892, 1904, 1907.

3 Copy map A. Underneath, make a list of the countries in each alliance. Then write a few sentences explaining *how* and *why* each alliance was formed.

4 (a) Why did France and Britain become allies after being enemies?
   (b) Why did Britain drop the policy of 'splendid isolation'?
   (c) How did the Germans test the 'entente'?

5 (a) Look at picture C and write down who the figures represent at: V, W, X, Y and Z.
   (b) Explain what 'splendid isolation' was.

6 You are a reporter for a British newspaper. The year is 1911. You have just interviewed Sir Edward Grey about the alliance with France and Russia. Write a short report for your newspaper reporting your conversation.

The armed forces

● Introduction

When two groups or gangs are about to have a fight they ask themselves some questions. Who is the strongest on their side? Which one of their enemies is the most powerful? Have any of their friends got weaknesses? What is the best way of tackling their opponents?

All of these questions were asked by the Triple Alliance and the Triple Entente well before 1914. In fact, the commanders of armies and navies on both sides had been making these estimates and laying their plans over the previous fifteen years. Both sides were ready, even keen to get on with what everyone expected would, when it happened, be a short, sharp war.

The leaders of the six main nations knew that at the stroke of a pen they could call up millions of men to go to battle, if necessary to give their lives for their native land. So who did have the greatest power and the best chances?

● Armies

Most of the nations involved were on the mainland of Europe so their armies were of the greatest importance in any war. Armies were made up of many divisions, each division consisting of about 17,000 men. Most of these were infantry divisions of foot soldiers mainly armed with rifles although some were cavalry, mounted on horseback, still hoping to charge with lance and sabre.

Each European army except one consisted of conscripts. These were all the ordinary young men of a nation who had to do military training for a period of two or three years in peacetime, so they could be ready to fight. The exception was Britain, which kept a small army of full-time professional soldiers.

INFANTRY– foot soldiers	
CAVALRY– horsemen	
ARTILLERY– gunners	

A *Fighting branches of the army*

The Triple Alliance

The Austro-Hungarian army was strong and could raise a million men to fight. A disadvantage was that its forces consisted of nearly a dozen different nationalities and its generals were not the best in Europe.

The army knew it could beat Serbia, that troublesome small Slav country but feared the might of giant Russia who had promised to help the Serbs in any trouble.

The Triple Alliance relied heavily on the German army which was probably the best in Europe with a reputation for efficiency and success. It had defeated the French in 1870 and was led by excellent generals who had trained their men well. When the army was ready for action the Germans could put over one and a half million men on to the battlefield. They were particularly strong in artillery, the big guns firing high explosive shells.

For years the German General Staff had realized that war was coming and had planned carefully for it. One special worry for them was fighting on two fronts at once. This meant that they would have to contend with the Russians in the east and the French in the west.

The Triple Entente
In the west, the French army was ready for war, with over a million men. Many of its soldiers were longing for the day when they could take on the Germans again and revenge the defeat of 1870. Their generals believed in attack as the best form of fighting. For that reason they had worked out a plan for striking into Germany right from the start of a conflict. They reckoned

that the force of their advance could carry them all the way to Berlin.

Across Europe to the east lay the giant Russia with the largest army of all. Including reserves, they could raise over six million men. However, the men were poorly led and very badly equipped. Nevertheless, they were prepared to launch a crushing attack on Austria-Hungary and Germany from the east, using their vast army like a steamroller.

The smallest army was Britain's. As an island, Britain was protected by the navy so had no need to train and keep dozens of divisions of soldiers. However, after the end of the Second Boer War in 1902, the British army was reorganized into a small but highly efficient force. Arrangements were made with the French before the war that in case of trouble about 120,000 soldiers would be shipped to France right away to help.

● **The naval race**
In the ten years before 1914 there was a kind of shipbuilding competition between Britain and Germany. Often this is called 'The Naval Race' and it was one of the strongest

B *A British boy soldier, 1914*

C *German soldiers and their equipment*

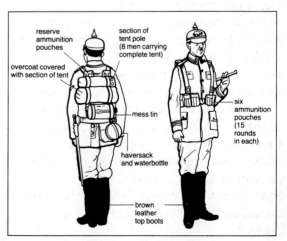

reasons for Britain joining the Triple Entente.

As an island Britain had built up the strength and quality of the Royal Navy over many generations. It needed a powerful navy to protect its shores and to guard trade routes to and from its empire all over the world.

So when the Kaiser and his Minister of Marine, Admiral von Tirpitz, started to build a large fleet, the British reacted sharply. The Kiel Canal, opened in 1895, was widened eleven years later so that German battleships could pass from the North Sea to the Baltic. The Germans believed that a big fleet could be used to stop the Royal Navy from blockading their ports in the event of war. The Kaiser said:

1 . . . **Germany is a young and growing empire. She has a world-wide commerce which is rapidly expanding. . . . Germany must have a powerful fleet to protect that commerce and her manifold [many] interests in even the most distant seas. She expects those interests to go on growing, and she must be able to champion them manfully in any quarter of the globe.**

In 1906 Britain launched HMS *Dreadnought* as the world's first all big-gun battleship. Germany soon replied by building its own Dreadnoughts. The race was on.

Sir John Fisher was responsible for reorganizing the Royal Navy and making it

D *A German battleship of the World War One period*

E *The navies in 1914*

	Britain	Germany
Battleships	62	35
Battlecruisers	8	5
Cruisers	102	41
Destroyers	300	144
Submarines	78	28

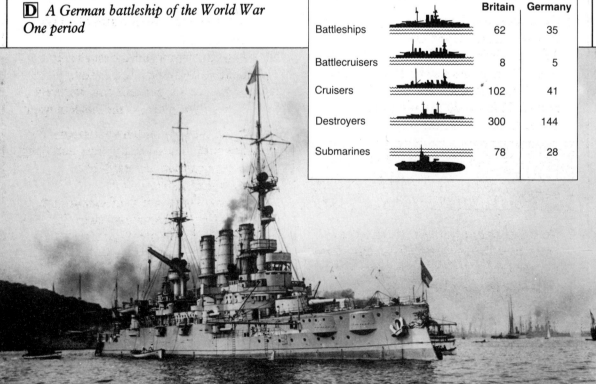

into an efficient fighting force. When Winston Churchill became First Lord of the Admiralty in 1909, he pressed on with the building. In a speech, he commented:

> 2 **This island has never been and never will be lacking in trained and hardy mariners bred from their boyhood up in the service of the sea. The purposes of British naval power are essentially defensive. We have no thoughts . . . of aggression and we attribute no such thoughts to other great powers. . . . The British Navy is to us a necessity and from some points of view the German Navy is to them more in the nature of a luxury. . . .**

The race continued until 1914. By then both navies were extremely powerful.

● **Air Forces**

No successful powered aeroplane flight was made until the Wright brothers' triumphant attempt in 1903. Flimsy aircraft before 1914 were not thought of as fighting weapons. A French general commented: 'Aviation is good sport, but for the army it is useless.'

But some generals saw the value of aircraft – it would be possible to fly over the enemy and bring back reports on their movements. At sea, admirals wanted to use giant airships to do the same job. So in 1914 the armed services of the major nations had some aeroplanes available for use. □

Exercises

1 Copy and complete this paragraph using words from the **word list**.
The . . . defeated the . . . in 1870 and many Frenchmen longed for. . . . The . . . Army did not want to . . . on . . . fronts. This would mean fighting . . . in the east and . . . in the west.

> **word list:** French; two; Russia; Germans; fight; revenge; German; France

2 Read through the chapter to find the answers to the following questions. Write the answers in your book in complete sentences so that they are useful for revision.
   (a) Who was the German Minister of Marine?
   (b) When was HMS *Dreadnought* built?
   (c) Which Great Power's army had no conscripts?
   (d) Which country did the Austrians believe they could beat easily?
   (e) What use did generals and admirals believe aeroplanes could have in war?

3 What did the chapter tell you about . . .
   (a) the questions asked by army and navy commanders before 1914?
   (b) the German army?
   (c) the weaknesses of the Russian army?
   (d) why Germany wanted a large fleet?
   (e) why Britain needed its navy?

4 Compare what the Kaiser and Churchill said about their navies.

5 'A nation with powerful armed forces is less likely to be attacked than a country without them.' Do you agree? Give reasons for your answer.

Sarajevo and war

● Introduction

By 1914 many Europeans were wondering where a war might break out. Would it be an incident on the frontier between France and Germany? Or a quarrel over territory between Austria-Hungary and Russia? Or a naval misunderstanding between Germany and Britain?

In the event the spark that set off the war was lit on a street in a little-known town called Sarajevo, in the Balkans. A quarrel followed between Serbia and Austria-Hungary and in spite of all the efforts of diplomacy, over the following month Europe marched to battle.

● Murder at Sarajevo

Sarajevo was in Bosnia, a province, or area, of the Austro-Hungarian Empire where the people were of the Slav race. Many of them wanted to be separated from the empire and united with Serbia, the small Slav nation just across the border. The Serbians also wanted this and therefore there had been bad feeling between them and the Austrians for many years.

The Archduke Franz Ferdinand was heir to the throne of Austria-Hungary. He decided to visit Bosnia to watch army manoeuvres which were being held near Sarajevo. His wife, the Countess Sophie, went with him and they arrived in the town on Sunday, 28 June 1914.

But waiting for them were six young men, members of a terrorist organization called the Black Hand. They were Serbs who hated the Austrians and were set on a desperate course. They were going to kill the Archduke. On that hot Sunday two attempts were made on Franz Ferdinand's life.

In the first a small bomb was thrown at his car, but the explosion injured other people instead. The thrower of the bomb, named Cabrinovic, was captured by the police, while the Archduke was driven on to the Town Hall for a reception.

After the reception, on the return journey through the streets of Sarajevo two shots were fired into the royal car by a nineteen-year-old student, Gavrilo Princip. The first hit Franz Ferdinand in the throat; the second caught Sophie in the stomach. They were rushed back to the Town Hall for medical treatment but it was too late. Both died shortly afterwards.

Later, Princip said:

> **1** I aimed at the Archduke. . . . I do not remember what I thought at that moment. I only know that I fired twice, or perhaps several times, without knowing whether I had hit or missed.

The next day, *The Times* newspaper contained this report:

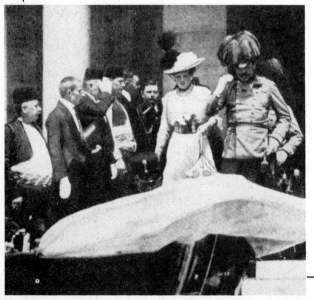

A *Moments before the murder*

B *The arrest of Cabrinovic*

2 The Austro-Hungarian Heir Presumptive the Archduke Francis Ferdinand, and his wife, the Duchess of Hohenburg, were assassinated yesterday afternoon at Sarajevo, the capital of Bosnia. The actual assassin is described as a high school student, who fired bullets at his victim with fatal effect from an automatic pistol as they were returning from a reception in the Town Hall.

● **The last days of peace**
The Austrians soon discovered that the six young assassins had been trained over the border in Serbia, and had been sent to Sarajevo shortly before the Archduke's visit. This news filled the Austro-Hungarian government with bitter anger and they were eager for revenge. This was their chance to hit back at Serbia, the country that had been troublesome for so long. But they knew that Russia would step in to help the Serbs. They could do nothing without the help of their ally, Germany.

What would Germany do?
On 5 July Germany told the Austrians that they could rely on their help. The Austrians immediately prepared a list of demands (an 'ultimatum') which they handed to the Serbian Government on 23 July. The words were accusing:

3 . . . It becomes plain from the evidence and confessions of the criminals of the outrage of 28 June, that the murder was planned in Belgrade, that the murderers received the arms and bombs with which they were equipped from Serbian officers . . . that, lastly, the transportation of the criminals and their arms to Bosnia was arranged and carried out by leading Serbian frontier officials. . . .

The note went on to demand such points as punishment for those involved in the murder plot and a promise not to stir up further trouble over Bosnia. The Serbs agreed to all points except one. They refused to allow Austrian officials into their country to make investigations. Austria-Hungary therefore claimed that Serbia had rejected its demands. Fighting started on 28 July, when an Austrian gunboat shelled the city of Belgrade.

● **Help!**
Once trouble started, the great countries were pulled into war one by one. They all kept the promises made to their friends, except Italy which decided to remain neutral.

As the Austrians threatened Serbia, Russia began to arrange its troops along the Austro-Hungarian border. Then Germany stepped in, ordered the Russians to stop and declared war on them on 1 August.

At the same time the French called up their army along the frontier with Germany. The German Government realized that war with France was now inevitable and declared war on 3 August.

● Great Britain

There was a powerful group in Britain that wanted no part in a general European war. Sarajevo and the Balkans were hundreds of miles away and these people hoped that Britain would stand aside. British interests lay overseas in the empire and not in Europe. However, Britain was a member of the Triple Entente and others felt it was a point of honour to stick to the agreement.

The event that shifted the balance of opinion was the German invasion of neutral Belgium on their way to attack France. A treaty of friendship between Belgium and Britain had existed since 1839 and now the Germans had marched into the lands of a small, innocent nation.

The Foreign Secretary, Sir Edward Grey, explained this to the House of Commons, as a listener reported:

4 When he turned to Belgium he seemed to have the whole House with him. For the first time he was cheered. He quoted the words of the Treaty by which we were bound to defend her neutrality; he read the appeal from the King of the Belgians to King George. If Belgium fell, Holland and Denmark would follow. If France were beaten to her knees in a life-and-death struggle while we stood aside, if we allowed the whole of Western Europe opposite to us to fall under the domination of a single Power. . . .

Britain demanded that the Germans should leave Belgium, which of course they would not. At midnight on 4 August 1914 Britain declared war on Germany. Sir Edward Grey looked out from his window that night and said to a friend:

5 The lamps are going out all over Europe; we shall not see them lit again in our lifetime.

C *French reservists in Paris go to join their regiments*

Sarajevo and war

Young men from Edinburgh to Cardiff, from London to Belfast wondered what the future held for them as they went to join the army. They rushed in their thousands to volunteer for the forces.

Nearly all believed they'd be home by Christmas.

D *British recruiting poster*

TO THE

YOUNG WOMEN OF LONDON

Is your "Best Boy" wearing Khaki? If not don't YOU THINK he should be?

If he does not think that you and your country are worth fighting for—do you think he is WORTHY of you?

Don't pity the girl who is alone—her young man is probably a soldier—fighting for her and her country—and for YOU.

If your young man neglects his duty to his King and Country, the time may come when he will NEGLECT YOU.

Think it over—then ask him to

JOIN THE ARMY TO-DAY

Exercises

1 Copy and complete the following sentences by adding a word from the **word list.**
   (a) An incident at . . . led to war.
   (b) The Austrians looked to the . . . for help.
   (c) The . . . . were drawn into the war one by one.
   (d) The German invasion of . . . brought . . . . into the war.
   (e) . . . of men . . . for the armed forces.

   word list: Germans; thousands; Belgium; Sarajevo; Great Britain; volunteered; Great Powers

2 The timetable of war: dates and events have been jumbled here. Match them correctly and put them in order.
   (a) German declaration of war on France *4 August 1914*
   (b) Austro-Hungarian gunboat shelled Belgrade *1 August 1914*
   (c) Britain declared war on Germany *28 July 1914*
   (d) The murder at Sarajevo *3 August 1914*

   (e) Germany declared war on Russia *28 June 1914*

3 In your own words explain why:
   (a) the Archduke was visiting Sarajevo;
   (b) the Black Hand gang wanted to kill him;
   (c) the Austrians needed Germany's help;
   (d) some people in Britain did not want to go to war;
   (e) Sir Edward Grey thought Britain had to go to war.

4 Look at pictures A and B and then complete these exercises.
   (a) In which year were the photographs taken?
   (b) Name the man and woman walking down the steps.
   (c) Name the man being arrested.
   (d) How do these pictures relate to the other pictures in this chapter?

5 *Discussion:* Look at picture D. Do you think it was right to tell women to persuade their young men to go into the army?

(A further question appears on page 218.)

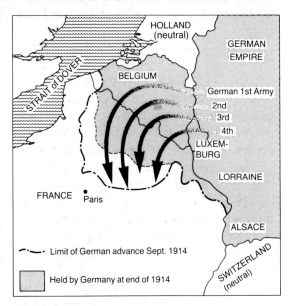

A *The Schlieffen Plan, 1914*

● The Schlieffen Plan

German generals had planned for a war long before the fighting started. One of them, von Schlieffen, had drawn up a scheme when he was Chief of Staff between 1892 and 1906. He knew that Germany had to avoid battling on two fronts at once – against Russia in the east and France and Britain in the west. So he planned a quick knock-out blow against France. As soon as France was out of the war, the Germans could take their time over defeating Russia.

The Schlieffen Plan involved sweeping through neutral Belgium, into northern France, then swinging round to cut off Paris.

On paper the plan was excellent. Part of it said:

⚡ 1 **Germany must strive, therefore, first, to strike down one of the allies while the other is kept occupied; but then, when** the one antagonist [enemy] is conquered, it must, by exploiting [using] its railroads, bring a superiority of numbers to the other theatre [area] of war, which will also destroy the other enemy.

● The early stages

The German invasion of Belgium brought Britain into the war and an army of 100,000 men, called the 'British Expeditionary Force', was quickly transported to France.

But nothing seemed able to stop the German advance. They quickly crushed Belgium and pushed their way forward. They were only 24 km from Paris before being held up in fierce fighting at the Battle of the Marne. Exhausted and disappointed, the Germans fell back. By October 1914

B *The Western Front*

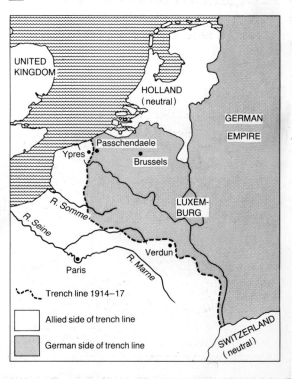

both sides were digging in and formed a line of trenches stretching over 644 km from the Channel coast to the Swiss border. This line became known as the Western Front.

● The trenches

Over the next four years the Western Front developed into the area of greatest land fighting ever known. Men dug into the ground with picks and shovels to escape the constant hail of fire from the enemy's guns. They lived and died there in the mud and hard-baked earth.

An officer described the scene:

2 . . . Paddling about by day, sometimes with water above the knees; standing at night hour after hour on sentry duty, while the drenched boots, puttees and breeches became stiff like cardboard with ice from freezing cold air. Rain, snow, sleet, wind, and a general discomfort all added their little bit to the misery of trench life . . . manual labour and sentry duty night and day with insufficient sleep; never warm, never dry; dog-tired and weary in body and mind.

In the past, cavalry (horsemen) and infantry (foot soldiers) had charged into battle but now a new type of war started in which attackers could easily be stopped by bullets fired from well protected defenders. Generals on both sides had little idea of how to fight under these conditions. Sometimes they threw whole divisions of men 'over the top', across no man's land, only to have them cut to pieces by fierce fire from the enemy trenches. Five thousand men's lives might be spent to gain an advance of a quarter of a mile – which was then lost next day in a counter-attack. Casualty lists grew enormous. Armies passed through what one soldier called the 'sausage machine' – fed with live men and churning out corpses.

● Weapons of war

Great advances had been made in the development of weapons during the later part of the nineteenth century.

C *A trench*

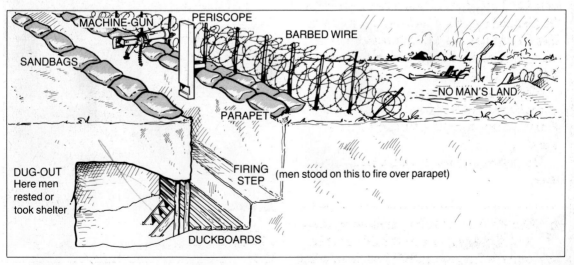

The main weapon was the breech-loading rifle which enabled a man to fire between five and ten shots before reloading. A development of this weapon – the machine-gun – was much heavier but even more deadly, firing several hundred rounds a minute. It killed thousands of men.

In close trench fighting, small-scale weapons such as bayonets, hand grenades and trench mortars were used to drive the enemy back.

Many generals also used heavy shell-fire from wheeled guns to attack the other side. The battle areas became pitted, blasted and cratered, resembling the surface of the moon.

The guns fired from behind the front lines and men listened intently to the whistling approach of the shells.

● Deadlock

The war had little movement. There was deadlock as each side waited for the other to give way – which it did not.

Two new weapons were introduced in an attempt to overcome the stalemate. One was poison gas, first used in 1915. It was contained in gas-shells or released from canisters when the wind was in the right direction. Thousands of men were killed or made ill by the gas – but still the trench line held.

Cavalry were obviously of no use in the front-line, but in 1916 Britain introduced an 'armoured horse' – the tank. These lumbering mechanical monsters crushed barbed wire and crossed trenches. But they were not fast or mobile enough to break the deadlock.

● The great battles

Trench warfare reached a peak of intensity in 1916 and 1917. At Verdun the Germans launched a huge attack to sap strength from the French. But the plan went wrong.

Heavy fighting went on for months as neither side would give way. Total casualties there are unknown, but it is possible that one million men were killed or wounded in the struggle.

In an effort to relieve their French allies the British army began an offensive (an attack) in the valley of the River Somme. For eight days, 1,500 guns bombarded the enemy positions, but the Germans merely withdrew from their front-line trenches or went deep underground into safe dug-outs.

On 1 July, British infantry went over the

D *A wartime advertisement*

top, towards the German trenches. They in turn faced heavy bombardment. On the first day of the battle alone they suffered 60,000 casualties.

Only the smallest advances were made by both sides.

In the next year they tried again. Not surprisingly there were similar disastrous results. French attacks in April were led by General Nivelle, who hoped to sweep the Germans out of his native land. Instead, the French army suffered such heavy casualties that some units refused to fight and the offensive ground to a halt.

Later in the year a British attack was launched in the north, towards the Channel coast. The hope was that the Germans would be worn down, then exhausted. But after some early successes, heavy rain fell and the offensive foundered in a sea of mud in the area of Passchendaele.

By the end of 1917 the trench line had not been broken and the end of the war seemed far away. ☐

Exercises

1 Refer back to the chapter you have just read and complete these sentences.
   (a) In his plan, von Schlieffen aimed to. . . .
   (b) Attacks on the Western Front brought heavy casualties because. . . .
   (c) Poison gas and tanks were introduced because. . . .
   (d) The Battle of the Somme was launched because. . . .
   (e) By the end of 1917 the trench line. . . .

2 Copy the map of the Schlieffen Plan and the map of the Western Front into your book. Underneath each, write a few sentences to explain what the map shows.

3 Complete this paragraph by using words from the **word list.**
   From the early part of the war . . . faced each other in lines of. . . . Thousands of men lived and died in them as . . . side could make successful. . . . The power of modern . . . held them up. In places like

. . . and Passchendaele the . . . were enormous. At the end of 1917 . . . still seemed far away

word list: peace; armies; Verdun; neither; advances; casualties; trenches; weapons.

4 Read the chapter carefully and then write a paragraph on each of these:
   (a) the weapons used on the Western Front;
   (b) the difficulty in capturing the opposing trenches. You may illustrate your answer.

5 (a) Look at picture D. How are the trenches presented here?
   (b) Now look at document 2. What are the trenches really like?
   (c) Why do you think people in Britain had little idea of the true condition of the trenches?

War on the other Fronts

● The countries involved

In any quarrel between two groups of people, some join in later than others. Before the war ended, Turkey and Bulgaria joined the countries of the Triple Alliance. Italy, however, changed sides in 1915 and joined the Triple Entente nations.

Nine other nations went to war against Germany and Austria-Hungary. They were Belgium, China, Greece, Italy, Japan, Portugal, Rumania, Serbia and the USA. Also, many men from the British Empire went to fight for what they called their 'mother country', from places as far as India and Canada, New Zealand and Australia, South Africa and the Pacific Islands.

● The Eastern Front

The Germans had a great fear of having to fight on two fronts at the same time. They had devised the Schlieffen Plan so that they could conquer the French quickly, *then* turn to deal with the Russians. On the other side, the French and the Russians intended to attack Germany from both sides at once, thus splitting German forces.

At first, Russian armies attacked in the east, entering East Prussia in August 1914. But poor planning and shortages of equipment soon brought them difficulties. The Germans sent two little-known generals, Hindenburg and Ludendorff, to the Eastern Front and their armies gained some stunning victories against bigger numbers.

Throughout 1915 the fighting continued and slowly the Russians were driven back by German and Austro-Hungarian troops. Russian soldiers fought with great bravery but they lacked basic equipment. Their Chief of Staff commented:

A *Russian prisoners with their Austrian guards. Many Russians deserted or surrendered due to lack of weapons and equipment.*

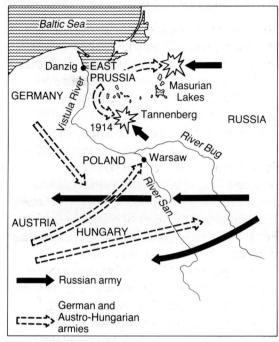

B *The Eastern Front, 1914*

The war seemed to drag on for ever and thoughts of rebellion came to some minds.

● The Dardanelles

When Turkey joined the war as Germany's ally at the end of 1914, the other side tried to force her out by attacking the Dardanelles. British, Australian and New Zealand troops landed at Gallipoli in April 1915. As well as defeating the Turks, they also hoped to open a sea route to Russia through the Black Sea. But they met fierce resistance and were soon in trouble. The Turks fought well, some under the command of German officers who organized the defence.

C *The Dardanelles, 1915*

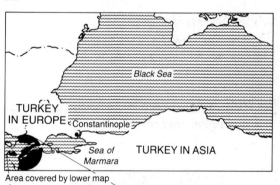

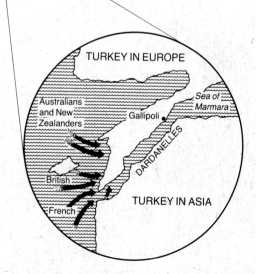

> **In several infantry regiments which have taken part in the recent battles at least one-third of the men had no rifle. These poor devils had to wait patiently under a shower of shrapnel, until their comrades fell before their eyes and they could pick up their arms. It's a perfect marvel under the circumstances that there was no panic. . . .**

In 1916 came one last offensive against the Austrians, who were saved only by the arrival of German troops. Although they started brilliantly the Russians ran low on ammunition and came to a halt.

By then the Russian people and their army were deeply discontented with a government that was leading them badly. How much longer could they be expected to fight and die in their thousands?

The whole operation came to a halt because the Turks could not be defeated, even after more troops were landed in August. The weather was cruel, varying from burning heat in summer to snow in winter. At last, the attack was given up and the Royal Navy evacuated the troops by sea in the following January.

Winston Churchill, who had organized much of the campaign, took much of the blame for failure and lost his position as First Sea Lord.

● Mesopotamia

In another attack on the Turks British troops were landed in Persia, hoping to advance to the city of Baghdad. Under the command of General Townshend, the force had some early successes. But in December 1915 10,000 men were trapped in the town of Kut and surrounded by the Turks. No one could relieve them and at the end of April 1916 they surrendered. It was the greatest blow suffered by the British army since the American War of Independence in 1781.

The prisoners were treated badly and hundreds died during their captivity.

● The Italian Front

The Triple Entente nations persuaded Italy to change sides and join them through the secret Treaty of London, signed in 1915. This promised Italy territories on the border of Austria-Hungary that the Italians claimed belonged to them. On 23 May 1915 Italy entered the war.

For two years the war was fought between Italy and Austria, with few advances or retreats. But the Italian army lacked good organization and suffered a severe defeat in October 1917. A combined German and Austrian force attacked the Italians and

gained a great victory at Caporetto. The Italians lost thousands of men and hundreds of guns as they retreated seventy miles, but the line held when British and French troops arrived to help from the Western Front.

Towards the end of the war the Italians were more successful and won the Battle of Vittorio Veneto in 1918.

● Salonika

The war had started when Austria-Hungary attacked Serbia. The Serbs fought with great bravery and spirit until the end of 1915, when the power of German, Austrian and Bulgarian troops were finally too much for them. In an effort to help the Serbs, four British and French divisions were landed in nearby neutral Greece, at Salonika. This gave the Triple Entente nations a foothold in the Balkans, but the troops did little and made no advances until the last stages of the war.

● The Desert Campaign

British forces attacked the Turks in several parts of the Middle East. From their bases in

D *The War on other Fronts*

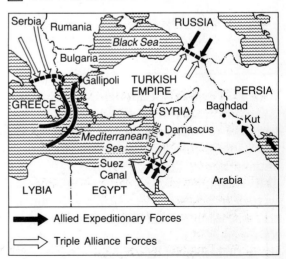

Allied Expeditionary Forces

Triple Alliance Forces

Egypt they pushed their enemy back through Palestine and Syria which lay in the Turkish (or Ottoman) Empire. Finally, in October 1918, the British and Empire forces, under General Allenby, entered Damascus. Within a few weeks Turkey asked for an armistice (a temporary peace agreement).

Fighting also took place in the desert areas of Arabia, where the Arab tribes were encouraged to rebel against their Turkish masters. An English officer, T. E. Lawrence, was appointed military adviser to the Arabs and organized many of their attacks.

● **German colonies overseas**

Unlike the Royal Navy, the German navy was unable to protect all the lands of its empire in 1914. German colonies were attacked at the start of the war. A German naval base in China was captured by the Japanese. In the Pacific, New Guinea and Samoa were taken over. This also happened in Africa, where Togoland, Cameroon and South-West Africa were occupied. However, in East Africa, local troops led by German officers fought with great courage and skill and remained undefeated at the end of the war.

Exercises

1 Copy and complete these sentences.
  (a) The Germans devised the Schlieffen Plan because. . . .
  (b) The Allies attacked the Dardanelles because. . . .
  (c) In Mesopotamia the British Army
     . . . .
  (d) The Italians joined the Allies because
     . . . .
  (e) In 1914 the German navy could not
     . . . .

2 (a) Write out the names of the Triple Entente nations.
  (b) Which other countries joined the war on the side of the Triple Entente nations?
  (c) Write out the names of the Triple Alliance nations.
  (d) Which countries supported the Alliance?
  (e) Which country changed sides?

3 (a) Give one reason why the Russians were defeated.
  (b) Explain why it was necessary for the Germans to defeat the Russians.

4 (a) Why were Allied troops landed at Gallipoli?
  (b) What obstacles did they face?
  (c) What were the results of the Dardanelles campaign?

5 Look at picture A. Imagine you are one of the Russian prisoners in the picture. Describe in a few sentences how you feel and what you are thinking as you sit there surrounded by Austrian guards.

6 Write briefly about the following using, where possible, maps to illustrate your explanation:
  (a) the Eastern Front;
  (b) the Desert Campaign;
  (c) the Italians versus the Austrians;
  (d) the German colonies.

War at sea and in the air

● The navies

In 1914 Britain had the world's strongest navy, with about 600 ships. The main striking power, called the Grand Fleet, was stationed in Britain, facing east. Britain's main rival at sea was Germany which had built up a large High Seas Fleet before 1914. Admirals of the Royal Navy hoped for a great naval battle in the North Sea. Some believed it would come when the Germans tried to invade England's east coast.

In 1914 sea battles between German and British fleets were fought off South America. At Coronel the British were defeated and in the Falkland Islands the German ships were overpowered.

A *Naval vessels*

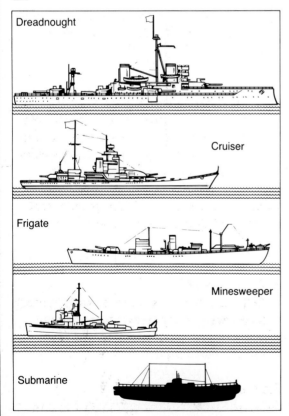

Dreadnought

Cruiser

Frigate

Minesweeper

Submarine

● Jutland

In May 1916 the only great naval battle of the war occurred, when the two main fleets met off Jutland Bank in the North Sea. The Germans' plan was to destroy part of the British fleet, but British Naval Intelligence had decoded their secret messages and so the Grand Fleet was prepared for the attack.

The battle, on 31 May, was confused. Information failed to reach commanders and both sides made mistakes. However, the Germans quickly sank three British battle-cruisers.

A German officer reported what happened to HMS *Queen Mary*:

> **1** First of all a vivid red flame shot up from her forepart. Then came an explosion forward which was followed by a much heavier explosion amidships, black debris of the ship flew into the air, and immediately afterwards the whole ship blew up with a terrific explosion. A gigantic cloud of smoke arose, the masts collapsed inwards, the smoke cloud hid everything and rose higher and higher. Finally nothing but a thick, black cloud of smoke remained where the ship had been.

Fighting went on into the night but the High Seas Fleet escaped. The Royal Navy was left in command of the North Sea, but had suffered heavier losses.

Who won? There's still argument, but an American newspaper headline summed it up:

> **2** The German Fleet has assaulted its jailer, but it is still in jail.

● The U-boat campaign

After Jutland, the Germans realized that further sea battles could bring disaster to their fleet. So they decided to concentrate on undersea warfare. From early 1917 they ordered unrestricted submarine attacks on all ships entering European waters.

The U-boats (the name given to German submarines) had great success at the start. They sank dozens of merchant ships which were carrying valuable cargoes of food and military equipment. At one time there was even the chance that the people of Britain would face starvation, so rationing was strict.

However, counter-measures were taken. Merchant ships had to sail in escorted convoys, so protection was given. A method was found of discovering where submarines were lurking below the surface, then depth charges (underwater bombs) were dropped overboard on them. In this way the U-boat attacks were held at bay.

One important result of Germany's campaign was not to its liking. The Americans were angry that neutral ships were being sunk and on 18 March 1917 sent this note to the German government:

---

3 **Unless the Imperial Government should now immediately declare and effect an abandonment of submarine warfare against passenger and freight-carrying vessels, the Government of the United States can have no choice but to sever [cut off] diplomatic relations with the Central Empires [Germany and Austria-Hungary] all together.**

● The blockade

Although there were few sea battles between

B *The German people nurse their 'baby', the U-boat. Pictures of the Kaiser and Admiral Tirpitz smile their approval.*

the great surface fleets of both sides, the war at sea was crucial in the defeat of the Triple Alliance. The Royal Navy carried out a long, slow blockade against Germany and its allies. British ships blocked their trade routes, preventing them from getting food, raw materials, and supplies. Their people went hungry and their industry suffered heavily.

● Aircraft in 1914

In 1914 each nation had only a small number of aeroplanes. Many commanders did not trust these new gadgets, which could be unreliable.

Reconnaissance

Aircraft were first used for reconnaissance

Triplane

Biplane

Monoplane

C An artist's impression of the different types of aeroplane

revolvers and rifles were used, but soon machine-guns were introduced and planes fell from the skies.

Both sides built up squadrons which hunted together over the war zone, where their short, savage battles were called 'dog-fights'. They organized tactics which were developed so that pilots could help each other in combat. The Germans had the 'Flying Circus', a squadron of expert flyers under Baron von Richthofen, and these airmen scored many successes.

Aces

A pilot was called an 'ace' after he had shot down five enemy machines. Richthofen was the most successful 'ace' of the war, shooting down 80 British and French aircraft before he was killed. Among other 'aces' were Georges Guynemer of France and Mick Mannock of Britain.

People at home treated these aces like film stars of a later generation, wrongly believing that they lived lives of glamour.

(reporting on enemy movements) or spotting the fall of shellfire for their own artillery. As they showed their value in this work, those who had sneered at aeroplanes now changed their tune. One British general wrote:

4 **They have furnished me with complete and accurate information which has been of incalculable value in the conduct of operations. . . .**

Air fighting

Air fighting started when planes from each side met over the battlefields. At first,

Zeppelins

Giant airships filled with hydrogen gas were called Zeppelins, after their German inventor. The Germans used them in attacks on England, where they dropped bombs on towns and cities. War from the air, with civilians as targets, was a new and disturbing form of fighting.

London provided a close and easy target. Anti-aircraft guns and searchlights were placed round the city but could not prevent the raids. Then fighter planes were brought into action to attack the giants. Some spectacular sights were seen at night when Zeppelins caught fire and fell burning from the skies.

War at sea and in the air

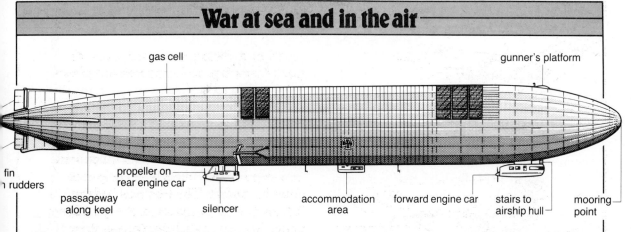

gas cell

gunner's platform

fin
rudders

propeller on
rear engine car

passageway
along keel

silencer

accommodation
area

forward engine car

stairs to
airship hull

mooring
point

D *A German airship – a Zeppelin. These attacked eastern and south-eastern English towns. Many British civilians were killed and wounded.*

Exercises

1 Copy and complete these sentences using the words in the **word list**.
   (a) The Royal Navy's main force was called the . . . Fleet.
   (b) A . . . charge would be used against . . . .
   (c) Contests between aeroplanes were called. . . .
   (d) An aeroplane with two sets of wings was a. . . .

> **word list:** depth; Grand; dog fights; submarines; biplane

2 Match each item in the left-hand column with the correct item from the right-hand column.
   (a) Cape Coronel   (i) Unterseeboot (U-boat)
   (b) site of a battle   (ii) convoy
   (c) a submarine   (iii) torpedo
   (d) U-boat's weapon   (iv) Jutland
   (e) protecting merchant ships   (v) a German victory

3 Draw a diagram of either a U-boat, a biplane, or a Zeppelin. Label your diagram and underneath, write in a few sentences what you know about it.

4 (a) Look at picture B. Explain in your own words what it shows.
   (b) What was the U-boat campaign?
   (c) Why did the U-boat campaign start?
   (d) What were the results of the campaign?

5 Using all the information and source material in this chapter, do *one* of the following:
   (a) Imagine that you are a pilot in a dog fight. Describe what happens to you and your comrades.
   (b) Imagine that you are a British sailor at Jutland. Describe your experience.
   (c) Imagine you are a civilian in London during a Zeppelin raid. Describe what happens.

6 Write a paragraph explaining why World War 1 was so different from previous wars.

The Home Fronts

● **Off to war**

People nowadays can look back and see the devastation caused by wars during the 20th century. They do not rush gladly into a fight between nations and often look back with amazement at the enthusiasm for war that was shown in 1914. Perhaps that generation would have been more subdued if they had known what lay ahead.

On both sides men went to fight for their country's cause. They were sure that their motives were just – and that the enemy's were unjust. A German newspaper in August 1914 declared:

1 . . . We have wished so much for this hour. . . . The sword which has been forced into our hand will not be sheathed until our aims are won and our territory extended as far as necessity demands.

A month later the British Prime Minister said:

2 . . . Responsibility for all the . . . sufferings which now confront the world belongs to one Power, and one Power only, and that Power is Germany.

A *Women at work in a munitions factory during the First World War*

Waves of patriotism (love of your own country) swept across all nations. In Britain it even caused a group of women called the Suffragettes who were campaigning for the right to vote, to stop their fight and turn against the new enemy. Their newspaper announced:

3 This paper has always sought to rouse women to a sense of their personal dignity and importance and of their rights as individuals, so quite naturally and logically, in the present crisis, our appeal is to the patriotism of women. The supreme reason why we fought for the vote is to make British civilization even finer. . . . A woman's deepest instinct and her reason tell her that Prussia stands for all that is deadly to woman's spirit in the world. We will not be Prussianized!

Most people expected the war to be over quickly. A few months of heavy fighting, they believed, would finish up with one side victorious and the other in full retreat. The conclusion would come with the French in Berlin or the Germans in Paris.

Just here and there were people who thought things would take longer – they were called pessimists.

4 . . . three years will do to begin with. A nation like Germany, after having forced the issue, will only give in after it is beaten to the ground. That will take a very long time. No one living knows how long.

That was the view of Field-Marshal Kitchener, Britain's military leader. He knew that the tough, well-equipped armies

B *Women at work heaving coal during the First World War*

and navies of determined nations would not be beaten easily. And, of course, he was right.

● **Women at war**

The nations at war all used women to help in the struggle. They were not sent to the front line, although nurses were never far behind it, but were asked instead to take over the work of men who had joined the fighting services. Within a short time, each country's war effort depended heavily on the work of its women.

Many well-to-do women volunteered for hospital work. They acted as nurses, both near the front line and in their own countries where soldiers were sent to convalesce (recover from an injury or illness). They raised money, made bandages, cooked and knitted.

The first effect of the war on some poorer women was to bring unemployment, because the trades in which they worked, such as dressmaking, lost their demand. Before long, however, other jobs became available. Delivery girls, riding bicycles, worked for shops. The Post Office used women to deliver letters. Railway companies employed women ticket-collectors, porters, even guards on trains. 'Clippies' (women bus conductors) were seen on buses, collecting fares, while thousands of women learned to drive vans and cars.

Some of the most valuable work was seen in factories, especially those producing arms and ammunition. A French general summed up the women's value in this way when he said:

---

5 If the women in war factories stopped for twenty minutes, we should lose the war.

C *Women serving in a grocer's shop during the First World War*

A crisis occurred for Britain in 1915 when a shortage of shells threatened the British Army on the Western Front. Lloyd George was appointed to be Minister of Munitions and his appeals for all-out production were met by thousands of women who began factory work.

In Germany and Austria-Hungary, as well as in France and Britain, women showed their equality with men. Some did heavy work, moving large loads, delivering coal or sweeping streets. Thousands worked on the land, or in offices. The men whose jobs they filled went off to fight.

● Other effects

Women who stayed at home faced the difficult task of bringing up their families alone. Yet some women welcomed this new 'freedom'. Service allowances were paid to them directly and they had the chance of working and earning their own money. For many, it was a break from the constant breeding of children.

But in spite of the new-found freedom, with the use of make-up, smoking in public and shorter skirts, there was still worry. Casualties on the front line were so high. Families dreaded the sight of the telegram or the official letter which could be delivered to their door. It might tell them that a husband, son or brother had been wounded – or killed in action.

● Rationing in Britain

As the U-boat campaign sank more and more ships there were shortages of food in Britain. Rationing was introduced for some foods, such as fats and eggs. There were also shortages of other foods and fuel, so long, patient queues formed for them. A newspaper reported in 1917:

The Home Fronts

6 The usual week-end potato and coal scenes took place in London yesterday. At Edmonton 131 vehicles were lined up at the gates of a coal depot at nine o'clock in the morning, while the crowd numbered several hundreds. There were also bread and potato queues of such a length that the police had to regulate them. . . .

● **The blockade**

The Royal Navy's blockade of Germany and Austria-Hungary was like a slow strangulation. There were shortages of basic foods and people living in towns and cities were particularly affected. Hunger and lack of nourishment gradually had an effect, because they affected people's will to fight on.

Some people in the Central Powers (Germany and its allies) faced starvation. A German politician wrote in 1917:

6 The bread ration was reduced this spring. The potato supply has been insufficient. During the past months labourers had to live on dry bread and a little meat. Under-nourishment is spreading. Conditions making for health are impaired. When we face this situation, we have to say: Our strength is almost spent!

By 1918 many Germans and Austrians were ready to make peace.

Exercises

1 Copy and complete the following sentences using the words in the **word list**.
   (a) Patriotism means a . . . of your own. . . .
   (b) Most people in 1914 believed that the war would. . . . . . .
   (c) During the war thousands of . . . went out to. . . .
   (d) The German U-boat campaign led to . . . in Britain.
   (e) Germany and Austria-Hungary suffered from the. . . .

   word list: blockade; quickly; work; love; rationing; women; end; country

2 Make a list of the jobs women did during the war.

3 Design a poster calling for women to help as either (a) nurses, or (b) munition workers.

4 (a) How did the U-boat campaign affect Britain?
   (b) How did the Royal Navy's blockade affect Germany? Illustrate your answers.

5 Using the documentary extracts and pictures in the chapter write a newspaper column entitled 'Women and the War'.

6 Explain why some people had these views:
   (a) 'the war will be over quickly';
   (b) 'any nation not using its women to replace men at work will lose this war';
   (c) 'the Royal Navy is doing more than the Army to defeat the Germans'.

The end of the war

● The blockade

In the days before fast air travel Americans felt very separated from other nations and they did not want to become involved in other nations' problems.

But gradually the USA *was* drawn in. The British blockaded German ports to prevent supplies from reaching their enemy. This policy offended those Americans who wanted freedom of the seas.

The Germans used a different blockade, which lost them many friends in the USA. The sinking of the liner *Lusitania* by a German submarine in 1915 killed 128 Americans, and a number of other ships were also torpedoed on their way to Europe. Several were American and each sinking brought the USA closer to war.

● American trade and industry

By 1914 the USA was the world's greatest manufacturing country. As Germany and Britain could not trade freely, American industry benefited from the First World War. The Americans stepped in to take many overseas markets, as well as supplying the Allies.

● The USA goes to war

Early in 1917 the Germans tried to stir up trouble between Mexico and the USA, so that the Mexicans would become Germany's allies and attack the Americans. British Intelligence discovered this and passed the information to President Wilson of the USA. A wave of anger swept through the American nation.

This anger increased after 1 February 1917 when the Germans began an unrestricted, all-out U-boat campaign, sinking any ship of any nation which traded with the Allies.

On 6 April 1917 President Wilson addressed Congress (the American parliament) and asked them to declare war on Germany. He said:

A *'A Trophy': British soldiers capture a German trench. A drawing by J. Walford*

1 The new policy has swept every restriction aside. Vessels of every kind, whatever their flag, their character, their cargo, their destination, their errand, have been ruthlessly sent to the bottom without warning and without thought along with those of the belligerents [the fighting nations]. Even hospital ships carrying relief to the sorely bereaved and stricken people of Belgium . . . have been sunk. . . .

The Americans then entered the war.

● The Yanks are coming!
The tired nations, Britain and France, who had suffered heavy casualties looked forward to thousands of young Americans taking part in the struggle for victory. But the USA had only a small army. It took months to equip and train men, then sail them to Europe. At first, only a small trickle of Americans arrived in France, but later the figure grew to a flood. The soldiers were commanded by General John J. Pershing.

The Germans knew that the Americans would alter the balance on the Western Front. So in the spring of 1918 they launched one last great offensive, hoping for victory.

● Ludendorff's offensive
When Russia collapsed in the east, dozens of German divisions were released to fight on the Western Front. General Ludendorff was put in command of an all-out offensive to crush the French and British before American help arrived.

The great offensive began on 21 March 1918, aimed at a weak part of the British line. German forces soon broke through and advanced several kilometres, unheard of on the Western Front!

As the situation grew desperate, General Foch was made Commander-in-Chief of all Allied forces, British and French. By early May some Germans had advanced 48 km and a fear grew that they might even reach Paris.

However, the all-out effort was expensive to the Germans. They halted, lacking the power to make the final breakthrough.

A German general wrote:

2 Our advance became slower and slower . . . it was all in vain; our strength was exhausted.

● August 1918
By August the Allies were strong enough to launch an offensive. That month became a

B *Soldiers and civilians celebrate the armistice in London*

time of disaster for the German Army, as General Ludendorff commented:

> **[3] August 8th was the blackest day of the German Army in the history of this war. This was the worst experience that I had to go through. . . . Retiring troops, meeting a fresh division going bravely into action, had shouted out things like 'Blackleg' and 'You're prolonging the war.'**

His army was cracking up.

● The armistice

In the autumn Germany was near defeat. Its allies were being beaten, there were revolutions at home and some of its servicemen did not want to fight. Bulgaria gave in on 29 September and the Turks on 30 October. Then the Austrians surrendered.

On 8 November some German officers asked to see Marshal Foch. They wanted an armistice.

On 11 November Allied Headquarters issued an order:

> **[4] Hostilities will cease at 11.00 hours today, Nov. 11th. Troops will stand fast on the line reached at that hour which will be reported by wire to Advance GHQ (Headquarters). Defensive precautions will be maintained.**

Thus at eleven a.m. – the eleventh hour of the eleventh day of the eleventh month – the fighting stopped. In the front line, men crouched in the trenches, waiting for the end. Many looked back to memories of comrades dead and wounded.

In the Allied capitals civilians went wild with excitement. Paris, New York and London were filled with cheering crowds who welcomed the end of bad times.

● The cost of the war

'They shall grow not old as we that are left grow old,' wrote the poet Laurence Binyon. He was talking of roughly eight and a half million dead men, mostly from France and Germany, Russia and Austria, Britain and

C *The casualties of war*

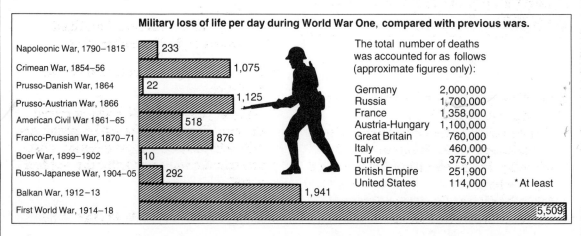

Military loss of life per day during World War One, compared with previous wars.

War	Deaths per day
Napoleonic War, 1790–1815	233
Crimean War, 1854–56	1,075
Prusso-Danish War, 1864	22
Prusso-Austrian War, 1866	1,125
American Civil War 1861–65	518
Franco-Prussian War, 1870–71	876
Boer War, 1899–1902	10
Russo-Japanese War, 1904–05	292
Balkan War, 1912–13	1,941
First World War, 1914–18	5,509

The total number of deaths was accounted for as follows (approximate figures only):

Germany	2,000,000
Russia	1,700,000
France	1,358,000
Austria-Hungary	1,100,000
Great Britain	760,000
Italy	460,000
Turkey	375,000*
British Empire	251,900
United States	114,000

* At least

The end of the war

Italy. The total of wounded was about twenty million.

Such figures are staggering. A simpler way of looking at them is this. The dead would have filled Wembley football stadium eighty times over; the wounded would have filled it two hundred times.

Today all over Europe you will see war memorials to the dead. The misery of the wounded is still remembered by their families.

In material terms, thousands of homes and buildings were destroyed or damaged. People sat back and started to count the cost.

Exercises

1 Copy and complete the following sentences by using words from the **word list**.
   (a) At the end of 1917 France, . . . , Germany and Austria- . . . were all becoming . . . by the war.
   (b) On 21 March 1918 the . . . . . . a great. . . .
   (c) The general commanding the Germans was called. . . .
   (d) By . . . 1918 the Allies started to push the . . . back.
   (e) The . . . . . . on 11 November 1918.

word list: war; launched; Britain; Ludendorff; Germans; August; exhausted; offensive; ended; Hungary; Germans

2 (a) Why were both sides growing tired by the end of 1917?
   (b) Why did the Germans launch a last offensive on the Western Front?
   (c) Why did the German offensive grind to a halt?
   (d) Why did the Germans ask for an armistice in November?

3 Look at picture A then copy and complete the grid (yours will be bigger).

Letter	I can see
A	British soldiers attacking a German trench
B	A wounded German soldier
C	

4 Read the documents, then answer these questions.
   (a) What does document 3 tell you about the Germany army?
   (b) How can you tell from documents 2 and 3 that the German army is nearing the end?
   (c) What order was issued to Allied troops on 11 November 1918?

5 How did civilians react to news of the armistice?

6 Imagine you are a soldier who survived the war. Using the information in this and other chapters on the war describe what you felt like when you knew the war had ended.

(A further question appears on page 218.)

The Treaty of Versailles

● **The treaties**

A war ends in two stages. First of all an armistice is signed to fix the time and conditions for the fighting to stop. After that, both sides have discussions then sign a peace treaty. By that stage they hope that their quarrel is settled.

Between June 1919 and August 1920 five separate treaties were made with the Central Powers (Germany and its allies), who had surrendered. All were signed near Paris and each one takes its name from the place where the representatives met.

● **The background to Versailles**

After the end of the war a new horror swept over Europe. There was an outbreak of a deadly influenza, known as Spanish 'flu, which killed millions of people. In fact, it has been estimated that more lives were taken by the illness than were lost in the previous four years of fighting. The victims were ordinary people, suffering from undernourishment and hardship and they were to be found in all countries.

Thus the leaders of the nations met in an atmosphere of death and tragedy.

● **The Treaty of Versailles**

In November 1918 the Kaiser had abdicated (resigned) and Germany ceased to be a monarchy, with a King and emperor. Instead, a republic was set up under the leadership of Fritz Ebert, in the city of Weimar. That government sent its representatives to Versailles to learn the terms of the treaty.

What they learned was harsh.

Their nation lost some territory, as map C shows. East Prussia was separated from the rest of Germany so that the Poles could be given access to the Baltic Sea by receiving part of West Prussia. Alsace and Lorraine were handed back to France. The Saar coalfields were taken over by the French for fifteen years.

All of Germany's overseas colonies were taken and given to other nations to care for.

No fortifications were allowed in the Rhineland and Allied troops were to be stationed there for fifteen years. Most of the German navy and its merchant ships had to be handed over. The German Air Force was disbanded. The army was to be limited to 100,000 men.

The Germans were to pay damages, called reparations, to other nations and a committee was set up to assess the amount. In April 1921 they came up with the figure of £6,600,000,000.

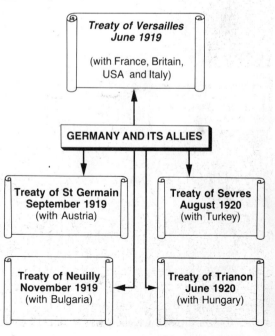

A *The five treaties*

Treaty of Versailles
June 1919
(with France, Britain, USA and Italy)

GERMANY AND ITS ALLIES

Treaty of St Germain
September 1919
(with Austria)

Treaty of Sevres
August 1920
(with Turkey)

Treaty of Neuilly
November 1919
(with Bulgaria)

Treaty of Trianon
June 1920
(with Hungary)

● The War Guilt Clause

What particularly upset the Germans was the War Guilt Clause (Article 231) of the treaty. This made them accept the sole blame for causing the war – and in their view that was unjust. The clause said:

> **1** **Germany accepts responsibility for causing all the loss and damage to which the Allied and Associate Powers and their nationals have been subjected in consequence of the war imposed on them by the aggression of Germany and her allies.**

The German delegates were not allowed to discuss the terms of the treaty. They were told they had to sign, which they did, in the Hall of Mirrors at Versailles on 28 June 1919. That was five years to the day after the shootings at Sarajevo, which had set the terrible war in motion.

A British diplomat described the scene:

> **2** **Through the door at the end appear two huissiers [escorts] with silver chains. They march in single file. After them come four officers of France, Great Britain, America and Italy. And then, isolated and pitiable, come the two**

B *The Treaty of Versailles – leaders and their aims. Germany was not invited to join the discussions, so had to wait to learn the terms of the treaty*

United States of America represented by President Woodrow Wilson. He wanted nations to solve their problems by discussion rather than war. He thought that a spirit of forgiveness towards the Germans was the way to achieve this.

France represented by Georges Clemenceau, nicknamed 'the tiger'. He wanted Germany punished and made too weak to threaten France again.

Britain represented by Prime Minister Lloyd George. He was in a difficult position. On a personal level he agreed with many of President Wilson's ideas, but he knew that many British people thought he should 'make Germany pay'.

Italy represented by Prime Minister Orlando. He wanted extra land for his country at the expense of Austria-Hungary.

German delegates, Dr Muller, and Dr Bell. The silence is terrifying. . . . They keep their eyes fixed away from those two thousand staring eyes, fixed upon the ceiling. They are deathly pale. . . . It is all most painful.

● The new map

After Versailles and the other treaties were signed, the map of Europe had a new look (map D).

The old empire of Austria-Hungary disappeared. Both Austria and Hungary were made into separate states, while the new Yugoslavia included the old Serbia and many Slav people. Czechoslovakia was another country made from the empire.

The Turks lost some of the land they had owned in Europe. The city of Istanbul (the old Constantinople) and some land to the west was all that remained.

The new Russian Communist government was not represented at the Peace Conference. Nevertheless, four new countries were formed from the western part of Russia. They were Finland, Latvia, Estonia and Lithuania.

● Good and bad

The men who made the treaty believed that they'd done a good job. It was right that countries like Belgium and France should be repaid for the damage done to their lands. And by taking so much strength from Germany's armed forces they believed that the Germans would not be able to wage war again, or threaten their neighbours.

C *The loss and gain of land, 1919*

D *Europe after the Versailles settlement, 1919*

The Treaty of Versailles

They had recognized also the independence of those people who wanted to govern themselves, by creating new nations, like Yugoslavia.

But the treaty was a bitter pill for the Germans to swallow. Rightly or wrongly they believed they'd been treated unfairly and punished for what was not their fault. The amount of reparations, they claimed, was ridiculously high and could never be paid.

There are two points of view on the treaty, so each side has to be examined carefully. But it was detested by many Germans. And by an Austrian who had fought with the German army and vowed never to accept its terms.

His name was Adolf Hitler.

● **The League of Nations**

One of President Wilson's suggestions was to set up a League of Nations. Its task was to help nations to cooperate in peace, rather than fight wars. The League had an Assembly and a Council where discussions could be held. A Court of International Justice was created to hear arguments between nations.

However, from the start the League had weaknesses. No nation could be forced to obey its rulings, because it had no army. The main stumbling block was that in spite of President Wilson's pleas, his own country would not join. Other important nations, like Russia, Germany and Japan left after several years.

Exercises

1 Look at picture B.
   (a) Write down the names of the people labelled A, B, C and D.
   (b) Which country did each one lead?
   (c) What aims did each one have when they all met at Versailles?

2 Copy and complete this grid (yours will be bigger).

<table>
<tr><th colspan="3">The Peace Treaties</th></tr>
<tr><th>Treaty</th><th>Date</th><th>Countries concerned</th></tr>
<tr><td>Versailles</td><td>June 1919</td><td>Germany, Italy, France, Britain, USA</td></tr>
<tr><td>St Germain</td><td></td><td></td></tr>
</table>

3 (a) Copy map D.
   (b) Underneath, write a list of the countries which gained land as a result of the treaties (map C will help you).
   (c) Which countries *lost* land as a result of the treaties?

4 (a) What was the League of Nations?
   (b) Why was it set up?
   (c) Why did it have weaknesses?

5 Read documents 1 and 2. Do you think Germany was treated harshly at Versailles? Write a short paragraph in answer to this question. Here are some topics you might like to include: colonies, navy, air force, army, reparations, lost territory, war guilt.

(*A further question appears on page 218.*)

Russia, 1900 – 17

A *Russian Peasant Huts, 1900*

● Russia in 1900

In 1900 Russia was a nation with great troubles. Many of the people were poor peasants with little political freedom. For example, they had no vote and could not own land freely. Thus they were years behind most of the other inhabitants of western Europe.

Much of the control of Russia lay in the hands of one man – the Tsar. He was an emperor who was treated by his people almost like a god and his word was law. Tsar Nicholas II had come to the throne in 1894 and believed firmly that he should be a father-figure for his nation, deciding its policies at home and abroad with the advice of a small group of ministers.

One of the Laws of the Russian Empire showed the position he held in his nation. It stated:

---

1 **The Emperor of all the Russias is an autocratic [most powerful] and unlimited monarch. God himself commands that his supreme power be obeyed. . . .**

The Tsar believed that to be true and so did millions of his subjects.

However, during the last twenty years of the nineteenth century, industries had developed quickly in some parts of Russia. Factories were built to produce iron and steel, railways, cotton and other manufactured goods. Their workers were not peasants living in the countryside and they wanted rights. They were seeking the vote, higher wages and the freedom to belong to trade unions.

To achieve their aims they formed political parties, like the Social Revolutionary Party (later split into the Bolsheviks and the Mensheviks), the Liberals and the Social Democratic Party. Soon there were strikes, but the Tsar's government sent in secret agents to find the leaders. Anyone taking part in industrial action might be arrested and imprisoned or exiled, so political parties had to operate secretly.

● The ideas of Karl Marx

Some of these 'underground' politicians believed in the ideas of Karl Marx. Marx (1818–83) was a German Jew who lived in Paris, Brussels and London, where he wrote books setting out his ideas. He divided society into two classes. First came the capitalists, who were owners of factories, land and wealth. Second were the workers (the proletariat) who were employed by the capitalists.

Marx claimed that capitalists controlled governments for themselves. They set out to use workers to make money, while paying them little. One day, he said, workers would rebel, abolish capitalism and share out wealth. This would be communism and he claimed that all would benefit.

A keen follower of Marx's ideas was Vladimir Ulyanov, known as Lenin, a member of the Social Revolutionary Party. In 1900 he left Russia to live in Switzerland and waited for the day when he could bring his ideas back to his native land.

● The Russo-Japanese War, 1904–5

Disaster came in 1904 when Russia went to war with Japan. The two nations had quarrelled for several years over Manchuria and Korea, territories in the Far East which both wanted to control.

When talks broke down, the Japanese made a sudden attack on the Russian fleet at Port Arthur. After that, the Russians suffered continual defeats. On land their armies were beaten, while their fleet was wiped out in 1905 at the Battle of Tsushima. Soon Russia had to ask for peace and Japan had proved to be an important power.

Who was to blame for the defeat? Russian forces were brave, but badly led, so there was an outcry against the government. There

B *The Japanese fleet attacking the Russians at Port Arthur*

were several strikes and sailors of the Black Sea Fleet mutinied.

● Bloody Sunday

On Sunday 22 January 1905, while the war was still on, thousands of people marched in a procession to the Tsar's Winter Palace in St Petersburg (later called Petrograd; later still Leningrad). Led by a priest, Father Gapon, they were protesting for better working conditions and more political freedom.

They were met by a hail of bullets from soldiers protecting the Palace. Scores of people were killed or wounded. The incident led to great anger among the workers and a greater determination to gain reforms.

● The Duma

Under pressure, the Tsar agreed to call a Duma (Parliament) and some wage-earners were given the vote. However, over the next few years the Tsar paid little attention to what his parliament wanted. If he did not like their suggestions he could dismiss them. Some voters and candidates were imprisoned if they did not agree with government policies.

So by 1914 ordinary Russians did not have much control over the running of their country. Thousands of them disliked the Tsar and his supporters. They waited for a day when a revolution would overthrow them.

● Russia at war, 1914–17

When Russia went to war in 1914 it was with the largest army of any nation taking part. It was expected that the Russian 'steamroller' would flatten Germany from the east. But bad leadership and organization soon led to disasters. The 'steamroller' went into full retreat.

There were shortages of everything except

C *Peasants and workers fight on street barricades during the revolution of 1905. The revolutionaries were treated very harshly and this caused much bitterness*

D *The Russian 'steamroller' army*

men, who became 'cannon fodder' in the early campaigns. The Russian soldiers showed great bravery, but suffered terrible casualties. Their mass attacks against German and Austrian positions were often devastated by enemy artillery fire. Yet, because of shell shortages, their own guns were sometimes limited to firing only five rounds per day!

There was trouble also for civilians at home in Russia. There, the shortages of food and everyday goods meant that many people suffered badly. Many Russians became angry with a government that appeared unable to govern.

The Tsar appointed himself as Commander-in-Chief of his army in an effort to put matters right, but things only got worse. In 1916, after heavy Russian attacks, the Austrians were very weak, yet the Russians lacked the leadership to carry them to victory.

Inside the nation, the Tsarina (the Tsar's wife) was given a strong hand in governing the counry. But she was under the influence of a strange monk, or 'holy man' named Rasputin. He claimed that he could cure her son who was suffering from a rare blood disease. So the government was filled with corruption and ordinary people had little faith in their leaders. The stage was set for a great change. ☐

Exercises

1 Copy and complete these sentences using the words in the **word list.**
   (a) In 1900 Russian people had little political. . . .
   (b) The . . . was the most powerful man in Russia.
   (c) The Tsar's wife, the . . . , was under the influence of a monk called. . . .
   (d) . . . . . . divided society into capitalists and workers.
   (e) After the 1905 Revolution the Tsar agreed to call a. . . .

word list: Karl Marx; Tsar; Duma; Rasputin; Tsarina; freedom

2 Explain what you can see in picture B *or* picture C. What had happened before the event portrayed took place and what were the results of it?

3 (a) Who was the Tsar and what power did he have?
   (b) How was Russia changing in the late 19th century?
   (c) What did the Russian people want?

4 (a) Who was Karl Marx?
   (b) What were some of the ideas that Marx believed in?
   (c) Why do you think Marx's ideas were popular with some Russians?

5 (a) Imagine you are a Russian officer in 1916. Write a list of reasons why your country should stay in the war against Germany.
   (b) Imagine you are a Russian woman in 1916. Write a list of reasons for *not* staying in the war.

The year of the revolution, 1917

A *Angry Russian troops march through Petrograd in early 1917. On the banner are the words 'Liberty', 'Equality' and 'Fraternity' – words used by French revolutionaries in 1789.*

● The March revolution

In March 1917 matters came to a head in Russia. In Petrograd a riot began among people queueing for bread and soon spread through the city. There were strikes by some workers and several army units mutinied. The Tsar quickly abdicated (resigned) and a provisional, or temporary, government was set up. Its leader was Alexander Kerensky, a Socialist, who became Prime Minister in July. He wanted to create an elected government (democracy) in Russia. Also, Russia decided to stay at war with Germany. That was a great relief to Britain and France who feared that their ally might pull out.

The British Prime Minister, Lloyd George, sent a letter to the provisional government:

1 It is with sentiments of the most profound satisfaction that the people of Great Britain and of the British Dominions across the seas, have learned that their Ally Russia now stands with the nations which base their institutions upon responsible Government. I do not doubt that . . . the Russian people will be strengthened in their resolve to prosecute the war. . . .

● Lenin

The Germans had been watching these events and now turned them to their own advantage. For some time they had been in touch with Lenin and other revolutionaries who lived in exile in Switzerland. They learned that if ever these men came to power in Russia they would be prepared to make peace.

So in the spring of 1917 the German authorities provided a special train to take Lenin and his followers back to Russia. It arrived with them in Petrograd on 3 April. Lenin addressed the crowd which had come to the station to greet him and obviously hoped that what was happening in Russia would spread across the world:

2 **Dear Comrades, soldiers, sailors and workers! I am happy to greet in your persons the victorious Russian revolution, and greet you as the vanguard of the world-wide proletarian [working-class] army. . . . The hour is not far distant when . . . the peoples will turn their arms against their own capitalist exploiters. . . . The world-wide Socialist revolution has already dawned. . . . Germany is seething. . . . Any day now the whole of European capitalism may crash. The Russian revolution accomplished by you has prepared the way and opened a new epoch [age]. Long live the world-wide Socialist revolution!**

Who was this man with revolutionary ideas? Lenin was born in 1870, the son of a civil servant. One of his brothers was hanged for plotting against the Tsar in 1887 and afterwards Lenin worked tirelessly for a revolution to overthrow the Tsar and set up a Communist state. Because of these ideas his life was in danger from the Russian authorities and he'd had to live abroad after 1900.

Now he was being offered the opportunity to put his ideas into practice, but first of all

he had to overthrow Kerensky's government. One thing that gave him hope was that the Russian army did not give the provisional government the support it asked for. Thousands of soldiers wanted to go home. Kerensky's government was losing its grip.

● **The November revolution**
Throughout Russia councils of workers, called soviets, were set up and some began to take land from landlords and give it to peasants. Lenin tried to gain control of many of these soviets. Also, one of Lenin's fellow Bolsheviks, named Trotsky, built up an army of Red Guards who were loyal to the cause of revolution.

By the end of 1917 the situation in Russia had grown worse. There was hunger and prices had risen dramatically. It appeared that Kerensky's government was no improvement on the Tsar's. In the front line troops still suffered badly.

In November, Lenin and the Bolsheviks saw their chance. They launched a second revolution, starting in Petrograd. Trotsky's

B *Lenin addressing a crowd*

soldiers took over important parts of the city, including the government buildings and Lenin announced that the nation was now led by the Communists – and he was the leader!

He then set out two points of his policy. One was that land was given to all peasants. The other was that Russia was pulling out of the war.

● Making peace

Very soon the new Russian Bolshevik government asked the Germans for an armistice, which was signed on 2 December 1917. Then, for several months the two sides

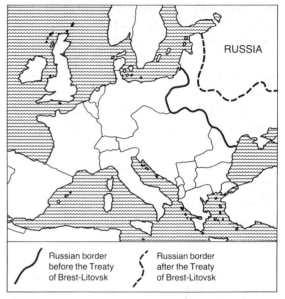

RUSSIA

Russian border before the Treaty of Brest-Litovsk	Russian border after the Treaty of Brest-Litovsk

D *The treaty of Brest-Litovsk*

sat round a conference table to hammer out the details of what each should give – and take. A treaty was signed in March 1918 at the town of Brest-Litovsk – and Germany took most! A large part of European Russia, including one-third of its inhabitants, was taken inside the new German frontier.

Some of the Bolshevik leaders who made peace stated:

3 We cannot and must not continue a war which was begun by Tsars and capitalists. . . . Russia . . . declares the present war with Germany, Austria-Hungary, and Bulgaria at an end. Simultaneously Russian troops receive the order for demobilization on all fronts.

C *An English cartoon*

● The allies react

Britain and France were extremely angry at what had happened. Their ally had taken

The year of the revolution, 1917

itself out of the war without consulting them. The benefits of making Germany fight on two fronts at once had disappeared at a stroke. Scores of German divisions were now freed to move westwards and fight on the Western Front.

General Ludendorff, the German commander, held a conference in November 1917 at which he told his officers:

4 The situation in Russia . . . will, as far as can be seen, make it possible to deliver a blow on the Western Front in the New Year. The strength of the sides will be approximately equal.

Our general situation requires that we should strike at the earliest possible moment, if possible at the end of February or beginning of March, before the Americans can throw strong forces into the scale. We must beat the British.

These considerations did not affect Lenin. Once he had started the revolution rolling he was determined that it should not be allowed to stop. □

Exercises

1 Copy and complete these sentences.
   (a) In Petrograd people rioted and army units. . . .
   (b) Kerensky became Prime Minister of Russia when. . . .
   (c) The Germans helped Lenin get back to Russia because. . . .
   (d) Trotsky was the leader of. . . .
   (e) The peace treaty between Germany and Russia was. . . .

2 Study cartoon C very carefully and answer these questions.
   (a) What do figures A, B, and C represent?
   (b) What is meant by 'German Gold'?
   (c) What did figure C want to happen in Russia?

3 Imagine that you were at the station in Petrograd to greet Lenin on 3 April 1917. Write an entry in your diary for that day recording his arrival, his speech, his background, and what you hoped he would achieve in Russia.

4 What was a 'soviet'? How were these different from earlier types of government in Russia? Did Lenin support soviets?

5 Read the section 'Making peace' and study map D.
   (a) Why was peace signed between Russia and Germany?
   (b) Which country gained territory?
   (c) What were Bolshevik reasons for making peace?

6 Write a few sentences on the following:
   (a) the British view of the provisional government in Russia;
   (b) the German view of revolution in Russia;
   (c) the British view of the Treaty of Brest-Litovsk;
   (d) the military advantages which Germany gained after Brest-Litovsk.

Russia's time of trial

● Reactions, 1918

Many Russians did not approve of the Bolshevik revolution in their country at the end of 1917. They grew even angrier when Lenin's government pulled out of the war by signing the Treaty of Brest-Litovsk early in the following year. Some of these people were loyal to the Tsar and the landowners. Others were supporters of Kerensky's government which they felt had been unfairly overthrown. Together, these groups were generally called the 'White' Russians and they soon started fighting the 'Reds'. That was the outbreak of one of the most terrible civil wars seen in the twentieth century.

The former allies of Russia sent troops to help the 'Whites'. To them the Bolsheviks ('Reds') were dangerous men who would encourage revolutions in other countries of the world. Also, if the Bolsheviks could be overthrown, perhaps Russia could be persuaded to re-open its war against Germany. So detachments from France, Britain, Italy, the USA and Japan arrived. Eventually the Poles too invaded western Russia.

But the efforts of the invaders were disjointed and Russia is such a vast country that they had little success.

● The royal family

Great changes came to the Tsar and the royal family when the revolution broke out. At first they were kept together as prisoners in a palace. Then they were moved on and, in April 1918, were shifted to Ekaterinburg (later called Sverdlovsk). They had become a burden to the new government who did not know what to do with them.

The final details of what happened to them are not known clearly. It is believed that on 16 July 1918 they were all taken to a cellar by local Bolsheviks, where they were shot. Such a murder attracted little notice at a time when thousands were dying.

● Trotsky and the Red Army

At the heart of the success of the Bolsheviks was the Red Army, led by Leon Trotsky, the Commissar for War. Trotsky was a shrewd and ruthless man. He travelled round Russia in a war train, encouraging and helping, threatening and bullying those under his command. Thus he could be taken close to the centre of military operations and raise the spirit of the fighting men. He later commented:

---

1 **When they were aware of the train just a few miles behind the firing line, even the most nervous units would summon up**

A *The Russian royal family in captivity, 1917*

B *A Russian cartoon showing Lenin sweeping away kings, priests and the wealthy*

all their strength. . . . Often a commander would ask me to stay for an extra half-hour so that news of the train's arrival might spread far and wide.

Trotsky used a ruthless secret police, the Cheka, to stamp out opposition wherever the Bolsheviks took control. Anyone from the bourgeoisie (middle class) who opposed his will was treated harshly.

His orders were carried out – and opposition was gradually overcome. People were scared of what they called 'The Red Terror'.

Trotsky used some officers who had been in the Tsar's armies, because of their experience as soldiers. He also made sure that every regiment contained dedicated

Bolsheviks who believed fervently in the revolution and could explain their ideas to the rest of the troops.

In general, Russian peasants supported the Red Army for two very simple reasons. They stood for a new order and a fresh start in a backward nation. And ordinary labourers who had seized wealth and land from richer people did not want to hand it back.

By 1921 the Red Army was successful and the 'White' Russians were defeated. Some fled abroad, while others settled to accept the new life. The Allies withdrew their troops from Russia and another stage of the revolution was achieved.

● **The new government**
At one time the Tsar and his supporters in Russia had an almost absolute power over ordinary people. This power allowed for little personal freedom. There was no parliament of the type found in Britain. Those attempting to oppose the authorities would find themselves imprisoned – or lose their lives.

The new Bolshevik government introduced by Lenin and his supporters was not much different. Power had passed from one set of hands to another. Lenin and his followers claimed to be interested far more in the welfare of peasants and workers, but the methods used were at least as ruthless as before. Lenin's policy was clear. First of all, opponents must be overthrown by the workers. When that had been done the Bolsheviks would govern – alone. Votes in democratic elections did not matter to them because they did not agree that there should be more than one political party. They had a different view of democracy from that held in the west.

They took steps to control the state. For

example, the Church's wealth and lands were taken over. Industry and land became state-controlled. Newspapers unfriendly to the Bolsheviks were suppressed.

By 1921 a Communist dictatorship was in power.

● Famine, 1918–21

One of the worst effects of the civil war in Russia was the famine that it brought. As fighting raged across the land peasants had difficulty in cultivating crops. In some areas the transport system broke down so that food could not reach workers in towns and cities. It has been estimated that in 1921–2 over five million people died and millions of others suffered from malnutrition.

Armed groups were sent out into the countryside by the government. Their task was to take food supplies from peasants and distribute them to the towns. But the problem was that not enough was being grown.

● Life for ordinary Russians

The state became the new landlord in the countryside. A decree of 1917 took over the ownership of the soil:

---

3 The right of private ownership of land is abolished forever. . . .

All citizens . . . who are willing to till the land, either by themselves or . . . in collective groups, are entitled to its use . . . .

The land is to be divided equally among the toilers according to needs or labour capacity, depending on local conditions. Each community is to decide for itself . . . whether its land is to be held collectively or as individual homesteads.

Later, peasants were allowed to keep any surplus grain and sell it at a profit.

In factories, groups of workers took over the control of industry which had once

C *Victims of the famine*

belonged to private owners. They became responsible for such matters as production and wages. But they found that the Bolsheviks were opposed to trade unions. 'You don't need to bargain for your wages and conditions now that we are the government,' suggested the Bolsheviks. 'We stand for the workers.'

● **Lenin's last days**

So much of the change in Russia was achieved by Lenin's leadership. He was an outstanding personality who never relaxed in his determined drive to bring Communism to Russia. Only in that way, he believed, could the mass of peasants and city workers hope to have a higher standard of living.

From 1922 Lenin suffered a series of strokes and had to cut back on the amount of work he tackled. In the next year more strokes almost paralysed him, then on 21 January 1924 he died. Millions of Russians mourned him and his body was embalmed and placed in a glass coffin in Red Square, Moscow. Today, thousands file past the corpse every year, paying homage to the founder of their revolution.

In 1924 the problem which was uppermost in people's minds was: 'Who would succeed Lenin?' Would it be the confident, but arrogant Trotsky? Or the powerful, but rude Stalin?

Exercises

1 Copy and complete these sentences.
 (a) Russia's allies wished to overthrow the Bolsheviks because. . . .
 (b) On 16 July 1918, the Russian royal family. . . .
 (c) During the civil war, Leon Trotsky . . . .
 (d) Russian peasants generally supported the Reds because. . . .
 (e) Today, Russians pay homage to the memory of Lenin by. . . .

2 What would be your thoughts if you were a member of the Russian royal family in 1918? (clues: prison, loss of power, no palace, loss of wealth, the new rulers, fear)

3 Explain in your own words:
 (a) 'The Red Terror';
 (b) Lenin's policy towards his opponents;
 (c) the effects of the civil war on ordinary Russians.

4 (a) Explain what is happening in cartoon B.
 (b) Read the sections 'The new government' and 'Life for ordinary Russians' and make a list of changes made by the Bolsheviks.
 (c) Is the cartoon an accurate reflection of what the Bolsheviks did in Russia?

5 Write out these sentences and then say which are fact and which are opinion:
 (a) Russia's wartime allies were generally opposed by the 'Red' Russians.
 (b) The Russian royal family were shot to prevent them coming back to power.
 (c) The Red Army would not have been successful without Trotsky's war train.
 (d) Russian peasants gained no more freedom under the Bolsheviks than they had under the Tsar.

(*A further question appears on page 218.*)

Stalin and Russia till 1939

● **Stalin v Trotsky**

When Lenin died in 1924 there were two main rivals for his position. One was Joseph Stalin, who came from Georgia, in southern Russia. The other was Leon Trotsky, a Jew and founder of the Red Army. Each tried to draw supporters to his way of thinking. Each man had a different idea of how the Communist revolution should develop next.

Trotsky believed in international revolution and wanted uprisings of workers to spread throughout the world, in all other countries. He was disappointed that this had not happened in 1917–18, when Russia had led the way.

Stalin saw things in a different light. He believed in 'socialism in one country'. By that he meant that Russia had got to be built up first into a strong state. Its heavy industry had to be expanded and it had to make use of its vast resources. A few years after this time he summed up his ideas:

> **1** We are fifty or a hundred years behind the advanced countries. We must make good the lag in ten years. Either we do it or they crush us.

Stalin was General Secretary of the Communist Party and soon he used his power there to remove rivals – including Trotsky. First Trotsky was expelled from the government, then from the party. By 1928 Stalin was the new dictator of Russia. (A dictator is a leader of a country who has total control over everything and everybody in that country.) In that year Trotsky left Russia and finally went to live in Mexico. But even there he was not safe. Stalin sent an agent to murder him, which he did in 1940, by embedding an ice-pick in his head.

A *Trotsky (extreme left) and Stalin (extreme right) at a parade in Moscow. They had very different ideas about how Russia should develop after the revolution*

B *The flag of the USSR*

● Five Year Plans

A great problem faced Stalin. He was master of the largest country on earth. It had endless wealth. All of this, he believed, had to be developed quickly, or those countries that disliked Communism could attack and overwhelm a new state.

The badge adopted by the Communists was the hammer and sickle. In trying to give Russia a modern industry Stalin was developing the hammer. Coal mines were sunk, oil wells drilled and rivers dammed for their power. He set high production targets for workers to reach in what were known as the Five Year Plans.

Scores of thousands of men and women were moved to distant areas of Russia (now known as the USSR – Union of Soviet Socialist Republics) and there they had to build, then work in, growing industrial cities. Hours were long and they received little pay or other rewards for their labours. Often their homes were overcrowded, food was short and there were no luxury goods. All were working for the future. Few dared to argue or criticize – because the secret police held the nation in a tight grip.

In addition there were thousands of prisoners who were drafted to the new areas from all over Russia. Often their crimes were slight, but they could be sentenced to five or ten years in a gulag (labour camp) where hundreds were worked to death.

Production certainly increased and Russia rapidly became an industrialized nation, overtaking countries like Britain.

The name 'Stalin' means 'man of steel' and the Russian leader showed a hard,

ruthless quality in achieving his aims. For him the needs of the State came before people's comfort – even before their lives. No one knows exactly how many thousands of lives were taken by the Five Year Plans.

● Down on the farm

What of the sickle in the Russian Communist badge?

For all Russians, in town or country, the supply of food was a constant problem. Although they lived among millions of acres of good farming land the peasants could not produce enough for everyone to eat. Stalin was a planner and in 1927 he wrote:

---

2 **The way out is to unite the small and dwarf peasant farms gradually but surely, not by pressure but by example and persuasion, into large farms based on common, co-operative collective cultivation of the land. . . . There is no other way out.**

Thus, over the next few years millions of peasants were forced to live on collective farms where all of their crops and animals

C *Industrial production in million tonnes*

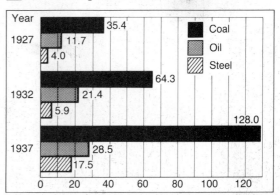

Year		
1927	Coal	35.4
	Oil	11.7
	Steel	4.0
1932	Coal	64.3
	Oil	21.4
	Steel	5.9
1937	Coal	128.0
	Oil	28.5
	Steel	17.5

could be taken for use by the state. Production actually went down because the new ways were unpopular.

Any small farmer who had done reasonably well for himself, had saved money, or employed a few labourers was called a kulak. Stalin treated them as enemies of the nation and stamped them out by sending thousands to forced labour camps.

To the person in a free society, such an existence sounds terrifying. But the average Russian peasant felt better off than in the days of the Tsar, and therefore accepted the new rulers quietly. They grew their grain and tended cattle for their new masters.

● The purges

Even among those who had been close to Stalin during the years of revolution, there grew the feeling that the party Secretary had too much power and was moving too fast.

D *A French cartoon, 1935. The banner reads, 'We are happy'*

Stalin and Russia till 1939

This was a challenge to Stalin's authority and he met it with his usual ruthlessness. Between 1935 and 1936 thousands of opponents were 'removed', that is killed. The world was amazed because many had been loyal Bolsheviks from the time of the revolution and some were men of high position.

What was more puzzling at the time was that many of them came to court and pleaded guilty, confessing openly to crimes against the state. We know now that they had been in the hands of the secret police for months and had been 'brainwashed'. No wonder they were eager to confess! The same happened in the Red Army, where about one-fifth of the officers were shot.

The 'Show Trials' of the late 1930s proved that Stalin was absolute and complete dictator of Russia. There was only one political party – the Communists – and even in their ranks no one could afford to differ from the leader.

● Russian foreign policy

In Stalin's time a barrier existed between Bolshevik Russia and the rest of the world. There was little freedom for foreigners to travel into the Communist state and few Russians were allowed out. Most other governments feared that Communism might spread to their own lands, so relations with Moscow were cool.

Hitler came to power in Germany in 1933 as a bitter opponent of the Bolsheviks and as his forces were built up in size Russia was obviously one of his targets. That was a puzzle for governments of countries like Britain and France. They disliked Hitler but Stalin's Russia seemed an equal threat. They refused to join with Russia in a pact against Hitler.

Inside Russia, Stalin's policy of industrializing led to massive production of guns, tanks and aeroplanes. He was determined to have a show of strength against any aggressor.

Exercises

1 Draw the flag of the USSR and explain the symbols on it.

2 Copy and complete this grid (yours will be bigger).

Stalin wanted	Trotsky wanted
Socialism in one country	International revolution

3 Describe what is happening in cartoon D and explain what it means.

4 List the ways in which Stalin modernized the USSR in the 1920s and 1930s. (Clues: Five Year Plans; coal mines; production targets; collective farms)

5 Using diagram C to help you, draw a graph to show how the production of coal, oil, and steel increased in the USSR between 1927 and 1937.

6 (a) What were the purges?
  (b) List two results of the purges.

(A further question appears on page 218.)

Mussolini in Italy

● Italy in 1918

Italy came out of the First World War worse off than it had gone in. You will remember that, although part of the Triple Alliance, the Italians changed sides in 1915 and joined the Triple Entente powers, Britain, France and Russia. They did this hoping to gain some disputed lands from Austria-Hungary.

But in 1918 the costs of war had been high. Italy had suffered great losses in dead and wounded. The country was heavily in debt and there was mass unemployment. In some areas there were violent fights between Communists and their opponents.

At the Peace Conferences of 1919–20, the Italians were disappointed not to get all of the territory they had been promised, especially on the coast of the Adriatic Sea. Many felt they had been used by the Allies, then treated shabbily.

● Benito Mussolini

In this situation Benito Mussolini began to make a name for himself. Born in 1883, he had been a journalist and socialist before the First World War. He served in the Italian army and came home, like thousands of others, disappointed in what his nation had gained from it. Everywhere there was disorder, with Communists fighting others. So in March 1919 he formed a new party – the Fascists. He was supported by many ex-servicemen and by businessmen and landowners who feared the Communists.

Men and women flocked to join. One ex-serviceman later said:

> [1] **When I came back from the war I, like so many others, hated politics and politicians, who, it seemed to me had betrayed the hopes of the fighting men and had inflicted on Italy a shameful peace and on those who worshipped heroism a series of humiliations. . . . It is certain, I believe, that without Mussolini three-quarters of the Italian youth coming home from the trenches would have become Bolsheviks. They wanted a revolution at any cost.**

A *Mussolini's Fascist blackshirts march on Rome in 1922. Mussolini went by train.*

Mussolini's men, dressed in black shirts, took as their badge the fasces, a symbol of authority in Ancient Rome. This gave them the name of Fascists.

Street violence followed between Fascists and Communists, with the police and army usually standing aside. In the first half of 1921 alone about 250 Communists were killed. Mussolini believed that such strong-arm methods were needed – and there were plenty of Italians who approved of what he was doing.

A few Fascists, including Mussolini, were elected to Parliament. In 1922 they felt strong enough to make a bid for power.

● The march on Rome

At the end of October 1922, when the Communists called for a general strike, Mussolini demanded a strong government to stop it. If not, he declared, his Fascists would march on Rome and take over power. In the capital there was confusion over what would happen next until the king, who feared the Communists, asked Mussolini to form a government.

He travelled down from Milan – by train – and collected together a government made up of several parties. He became the leader. For years afterwards the Fascists tried to give the impression that the march on Rome was like a great military operation of popular feeling – which it never was.

● Mussolini's Italy

Over the following years Mussolini took complete power in his country. He achieved his position by the usual methods of dictators. Opponents were beaten up, imprisoned or killed. In 1926 all opposition parties were banned together with newspapers that criticized what *Il Duce* (The Leader) was doing.

Everywhere people were begged or ordered to make Italy great, to restore the glories of Ancient Rome. Mussolini saw himself as a kind of twentieth-century Caesar, making his nation great. He believed in order and discipline, hard work and obedience. The country became a police state and justice was reorganized – to suit the Fascists.

Some advances were made in Italy. Swamps were drained, roads laid down and hospitals erected. It was said that Mussolini made the trains run on time! *Il Duce* did have admirers in other lands which had their own problems.

In 1929 Mussolini made an agreement, called a Concordat, with the Roman Catholic Church in Italy. For years there had been differences between the Papacy and the Italian government, but this agreement settled them. Vatican City, the home of the

B *An Italian painting showing how wonderful life was under Mussolini's rule*

Mussolini in Italy

Pope, became a separate state inside Rome and the Papacy was given a large sum of money. In return the Italian government allowed people freedom of worship.

Mussolini became a popular figure inside his own country. He was a showman and could make fine speeches, waving his arms about and rousing crowds to chant, *'Duce! Duce!'* He was hardly a modest man, as you can gather from reading his autobiography:

> **2** **I love all sports; I drive a motor car with confidence; I have done tours at great speed, amazing not only to my friends but also to old and experienced drivers. I love the aeroplane; I have flown numberless times. When I was kept busy by the cares of power, I needed only a few lessons to obtain a pilot's licence. I fell once from a height of fifty metres but that did not stop my flying.**

Such was the man who was the world's best-known dictator until the rise of Adolf Hitler.

● **Italian foreign policy in the 1930s**

Soon after Hitler came to power in Germany in 1933 he began a friendship with Mussolini. Following Hitler's pattern, Mussolini began a more aggressive foreign policy during the 1930s.

The glories of Ancient Rome had included a large empire and Mussolini tried to copy this for his new Italy. The country first chosen as his victim was Abyssinia (now called Ethiopia) which bordered two Italian colonies in Africa. The Italians had never forgotten a humiliating defeat handed out to them by the Abyssinians in 1896 and Mussolini believed that success there would increase Italy's prestige. A small border incident in that area gave him his chance in 1935. Italian forces armed with tanks, artillery, aircraft and poison gas overwhelmed tribesmen of a poorly equipped nation.

C *Hitler and Mussolini – two Fascist dictators and partners in the Rome-Berlin Axis*

Mussolini in Italy

The Emperor of Abyssinia, named Haile Selassie, made appeals for help but the League of Nations, set up to prevent this type of dispute, did little to stop the Italians. The Abyssinians were soon conquered.

From the next year, Italy was drawn closer to Nazi Germany and its policies. Mussolini sent men to help fight against the government forces in the Spanish Civil War. Germany and Italy formed a union called 'The Axis'. Mussolini claimed that Europe would revolve on an axis of Germany and Italy in the fight against Communism, to prevent its spread from Russia.

Hitler and Mussolini met several times and the Italian leader became a pawn for his partner. He supported Hitler's claims at Munich in 1938 and the Nazi leader felt a debt of gratitude to him after that.

In the following year the two leaders signed 'The Pact of Steel', promising to help each other in time of war. But on the side of the Italians there was delusion over their real strength. Mussolini claimed he could 'mobilize eight million bayonets' and 'blot out the sun with aircraft'. In reality his forces were disorganized and weak.

The weaknesses were shown up in 1939, just before the outbreak of the Second World War. Mussolini tried to show off his power by invading the small country of Albania. So much went wrong with the adventure that people said the Albanians could have won if they'd had a good fire brigade!

The tragedy for Italy was that Mussolini, the dictator, was in power. No one could tell him he was wrong, let alone remove him. ☐

Exercises

1 Copy and complete these sentences by using the words from the **word list**.
  (a) The Italians joined the . . . powers in 1915 because they hoped to . . . land belonging to . . . – . . . .
  (b) . . . became leader of the . . . blackshirts.
  (c) In . . . King . . . . . . asked Mussolini to become . . . Minister.
  (d) Mussolini became the . . . of Italy.

> **word list:** Austria-Hungary; dictator; Victor Emmanuel; Prime; Fascist; Entente; gain; 1922; Mussolini

2 Write sentences in your book to explain what the chapter said about the following:
  (a) Italian disappointments after 1918;
  (b) which Italians joined the Fascists;
  (c) the march on Rome;
  (d) *Il Duce*.

3 Describe picture B and explain how the artist is showing that life is better under the Fascists.

4 Write a short paragraph explaining how Mussolini strengthened his control of Italy. Use the following points: violence; police state; Concordat; employment.

5 Write a short speech for Mussolini to deliver to his followers explaining why Italy has to invade Abyssinia and why Italy has to join the Axis with Hitler's Germany.

(A further question appears on page 218.)

Germany in the 1920s

● **The Weimar Republic**

When the German army was defeated in 1918 the Kaiser abdicated as Emperor and went to live in Holland. The Germans then made their first experiment in democracy, setting up a government with an elected President and ministers. This government, which met at Weimar, is usually called the Weimar Republic.

But in the years immediately after the war Germany was filled with troubles. There was regular street fighting between Communists and groups of Nationalists. (Nationalists believe in their country above all others.) Both sides hated the Weimar government, accusing them of cowardly behaviour in signing the Treaty of Versailles. But they hated each other more! The police stood by as groups killed and injured each other in violent attacks.

In this atmosphere during 1921 the news was given to the Germans of how big their reparations bill was to be in payment for the First World War. The figure was £6,600,000,000 in goods and money. This enormous sum stunned and angered the nation. To the French and Belgians in particular, however, this was no more than simple justice, because of the damage caused to their countries by Germany during the war.

● **Trouble in the Ruhr**

Before long the Germans fell behind with their repayments and told the Allies that they could not keep up with reparations, either in goods or cash. The French and Belgians were angry at this and sent in troops to the industrial area of the Ruhr in western Germany. There they took over factories and coal mines, saying they would take their own reparations.

However, the industrial workers of the Ruhr would not co-operate with their old enemies. They went on strike, refusing to

A *German 'Communists' in Lohberg, April 1920*

produce or move goods. There were a few outbreaks of violence as French troops clashed with German workers. But the main result was that German industry and trade came to a halt. There was mass unemployment, goods were in short supply and prices went up like a rocket.

● Inflation

When a country suffers badly from inflation, wages and prices go up and up. Prices increase because there are few goods. Then wages go up to meet the higher prices, but that causes prices to rise again, because of the extra cost of higher wages. And that causes workers to ask for higher wages and . . . on it goes!

This form of inflation hit Germany in 1923 and caused some of the most terrible economic troubles ever seen. Before long, the main unit of German currency – the mark – was worthless. In January 1919, nine marks had been equal to one American dollar. By January 1922 it took 192 marks to equal the dollar. That figure had risen to more than 4,600,000 in September 1923 and to the unbelievable figure of 4,200,000 million two months later!

The money supply was out of control and those on fixed incomes, or pensions, or with savings found that their money was worthless.

Here is a description of workers of the time on pay day:

1 They all stood outside the pay windows, staring impatiently at the clock, slowly advancing until at last they reached the window and received a bag full of paper notes. According to the figures inscribed on them, the paper notes amounted to 700,000 or to 500 million or to

Hände weg vom Ruhrgebiet!

B *Savage-looking France with her hands on the factories of the Ruhr. This German poster claims 'Hands off the Ruhr' in response to France's invasion of 1923*

380 billion or to 18 trillion marks – the figures rose from month to month, then week to week, finally from day to day. With their bags, the people moved quickly forwards to the doors, all in haste, the younger ones running. They dashed to the nearest food store, where a queue has already formed. . . . When you reached the store, a pound of sugar might have been obtainable for two millions; but by the time you got there, all you could get for two millions was half a pound.

Germany in the 1920s

This bad state of affairs in Germany caused many people to wonder how their nation could get out of this fearful mess. They were prepared to listen to anyone with a plan.

● The Munich *putsch*

Several groups of Germans were particularly angry over what was happening in their country. One group consisted of the Nazis, a small party in Bavaria, whose members had ideas of bringing great changes to Germany. They believed that the German Army had never been beaten but had received 'a stab in the back' from trouble-makers at home. They hated Jews and Communists and they wanted to put power into the hands of one man. This was their leader, a former army corporal named Adolf Hitler.

Nazi anger boiled over in November 1923 when Hitler led a small *putsch* (rebellion) in the city of Munich. He aimed to overthrow the government, telling his listeners:

> **2 The Bavarian government is removed . . . the government of the November criminals and the Reich President are declared removed. A new national government will be formed this very day, here in Munich. . . . I propose that until accounts have finally been settled with the November criminals, the direction of policy in the national government will be taken over by me. . . . The task of this provisional government is to organize a march on that sinful Babel, Berlin, and save the German people. . . . Tomorrow will see either a National Government in Germany, or us dead.**

The revolt was a gigantic failure. As the

C *Wash baskets full of paper money being loaded on to hand carts, Berlin, 1923. People papered their rooms with worthless banknotes*

Germany in the 1920s

Nazis marched through the streets of Munich, Hitler and the First World War hero, General Ludendorff, were in the procession. But armed police were waiting for them. Shots rang out and fourteen Nazis fell dead. In the confusion the uprising broke up. Hitler was arrested and brought to trial. There he was sentenced to prison for five years.

In court, he said:

> **3 I believe that the hour will come when the masses, who today stand in the street with the swastika banner, will unite with those who fired upon them. . . . The army we have formed is growing from day to day. . . . I nourish the proud hope that one day the hour will come when these rough companies will grow to battalions, the battalions to regiments, the regiments to divisions . . . that the old flags will wave again. . . .**

● **Recovery**

At this time the Weimar Republic had a new Chancellor, or leader, named Gustav Stresemann. He realized that strong steps were needed to get his country out of the mess it was in. A new currency (money) was introduced and all the old, worthless notes were called in and destroyed. Germany made an effort to give reparations and, in return, the Belgians and French withdrew their troops from the Ruhr.

Americans started to invest money in Germany. Factories and docks, aerodromes and public buildings were put up all over the country and unemployment dropped. At last wealth began to return to business and industry and so to ordinary people.

Stresemann also improved Germany's relations with other countries. In 1925 the Locarno Pact was signed, with France, Belgium and Germany agreeing to respect each other's frontiers.

Exercises

1 Match these phrases correctly and write the sentences in your book.
   (a) The Kaiser abdicated and . . . prices and wages go up and up.
   (b) Americans started to invest . . . a type of revolt.
   (c) The Germans soon fell behind . . . money in Germany in the 1920s.
   (d) The Munich *putsch* was . . . went to live in Holland.
   (e) Inflation occurs when . . . on the payment of reparations.

2 (a) Which troops can be seen in picture A? Who hated them?
   (b) Explain what you can see in cartoon B. Outline the events leading up to France's action.
   (c) Explain what the men in picture C are doing. What is inflation?

3 Explain why these dates were important to Germans: 1918; 1921; 1923; 1925.

4 (a) Who were the Nazis?
   (b) What did Hitler hope to achieve in the Munich *putsch?*
   (c) What happened in the Munich *putsch?*
   (d) What happened to Hitler?

The USA in the 1920s

● The USA in 1918

The First World War left most European nations exhausted and heavily in debt. The country which had lent them money was the USA. America had not entered the war until the later stages and, being free from the battles and destruction that had ruined other nations, came out of the war richer than it went in. In 1918 America was owed about $13,000 million. Its industry was busy supplying goods to markets all over the world. America was about to start an age of great wealth and was, without doubt, the richest country anywhere.

● Isolationism

President Woodrow Wilson was a shrewd man. He believed that because the USA had grown so strong it would have to become involved in the affairs of other lands. That was why he was so keen for America to join the League of Nations. But many Americans disagreed with him. Europe, they believed, consisted of troubled nations and the USA should not let itself be mixed up with them. America should go back to its old policy of isolation, minding its own business.

So Woodrow Wilson received little support from Congress (the American Parliament). The USA never joined the League of Nations and the presidents of the 1920s generally steered clear of taking part in international affairs.

● The 'Roaring Twenties'

A country's trade and industry can boom or slump. Boom time occurs when trade is brisk, there is plenty of employment and heavy demand for goods. In the 1920s the USA had a great boom and the age is often called the 'Roaring Twenties'.

A *Film poster illustrating the good life of the 1920s.*

Wages rose for millions of Americans and prices were steady, or even fell. Ordinary people had far more to spend. Often they spent money on goods that had once been luxuries and soon had the highest standard

B *A wooden shack in the southern USA, 1925. Poverty has not disappeared.*

From 1925 the American building industry enjoyed a boom. In particular they pioneered skyscrapers so that people could live and work in cities, where the cost of land was expensive. Over a few years, the skyline of some cities changed completely.

American banks and businesses made huge loans to Europe. There, where money was in short supply, investment from the USA was welcomed – and it brought good profits to the investors. Many ordinary Americans were excited at the thought of making money from business, so they invested by buying shares in firms in their own country, hoping 'to make a quick buck'.

The good times seemed to have no end. Thus the Republican Presidential candidate in 1928, Herbert Hoover, was able to claim:

> **1 Our experiment in human welfare has yielded a degree of well-being unparalleled in the world. . . . We are nearer to the ideal of abolition of poverty and fear from the lives of men and women than ever before in any land.**

And at the time most people believed him.

● The movies

With more money to spend and leisure time to spend it in, the USA developed a new form of entertainment – the cinema. Silent moving films had been shown in the early years of the twentieth century, but in the 1920s the town of Hollywood on the west coast developed as the centre of the world of motion pictures.

Soon cinemas sprang up in the USA, then in many other countries. Actors and actresses became 'stars' whose names were

of living of anyone in the world. They bought cars and radios, refrigerators and cookers. These goods could be obtained through hire-purchase and there were plenty of people ready to lend the money.

The USA led the world in the production of motor cars and this item became part of the property of many American workers at a time when some workers in Europe could barely afford a bicycle. There were eight million cars in the USA in 1920; ten years later the number was twenty-three million. Factories using methods of mass-production turned out thousands of motor cars every day – and just as many buyers were waiting to snap them up.

known across the world – Gloria Swanson and Greta Garbo, Rudolf Valentino and Charlie Chaplin.

In 1928 came a giant step forward when the 'talkies' were introduced. The first one was 'The Jazz Singer', starring Al Jolson. A new age in entertainment began.

● Gangsters

On 17 January 1920 the 'Age of Prohibition' began in the USA. This meant that the sale of alcoholic drinks was banned by law. The various groups who had pressed hard for this law believed that it would make America into a better, cleaner place. Drinking no beer and no hard liquor would improve the nation.

In reality, troubles followed. Criminals moved in to provide drink in illegal clubs – and to get rid of any rivals and opponents. Working in groups, they were known as 'gangsters' and the most notorious and efficient was Al Capone, of Chicago. He travelled round in a seven-ton car, protected

C *Beer being poured away during the 'Age of Prohibition'. The smuggling and selling of illicit beer increased*

by armour plating and bullet-proof glass and had his enemies 'bumped-off' with sub-machine guns.

Prohibition certainly failed to stop people drinking alcohol. At last, the government bowed to common sense and the Act was removed at the end of 1933.

● The great crash

The boom time for American industry and trade ended suddenly in 1929. It was followed by a slump so great that over the following years most of the rest of the world was affected.

Looking back now we can see that the signs were there before the trouble happened. American farmers produced too much food and could not sell it abroad as they had once done. Those countries that owed money to the USA found that the Americans would not take their goods – so how could they raise large sums to pay off their debts? And the buying of shares caught the United States in a fever grip. All would be well if the buyers kept going, but what would happen if they faltered and lost confidence?

They did just that in 1929.

Early in October many investors started to sell their shares, hoping to cash in while the price was still high. The idea caught on! The fever for buying now became a fever for selling which gathered pace. The centre of the New York business world is the Stock Exchange, on Wall Street. There, on Tuesday, 29 October 1929, 16,410,030 shares were traded in one day, many of them at rock-bottom prices. Families that had owned shares worth, say, $20,000 in the morning found that they would fetch barely $1,000 by the evening.

The results were devastating all over America. Businesses became bankrupt and

The USA in the 1920s

D *Unemployed men queue for food in New York, 1929. Their slogan was 'In Hoover we trusted, now we are busted'*

workers lost their jobs. This in turn affected people like shopkeepers, who could find no one to buy their goods. People could not repay debts such as mortgages.

By the end of 1929 disaster and tragedy hit the USA as the number of unemployed rose sharply.

Where could the nation go from here? ☐

Exercises

1 Copy and complete these sentences.
  (a) The USA did well in the First World War because. . . .
  (b) Woodrow Wilson wanted the USA to . . . .
  (c) In economics a 'boom time' means . . . .
  (d) Among the cinema stars of the 1920s were. . . .
  (e) The Great Crash in Wall Street was . . . .

2 List the reasons why the 1920s were called 'The Roaring Twenties'.

3 (a) Why was prohibition introduced?
  (b) What were the results of prohibition?

4 Imagine you are a man in the 'Rescue Society' queue (picture D). Tell the man next to you how you lost your money in the Wall Street crash.

5 Read through the chapter carefully and look at all the pictures. Does the poster in picture A contrast with the other pictures? Explain your answer.

The New Deal

A *Roosevelt meets a miner during the 1932 election. Pictures of Roosevelt showed his smiling face and broad shoulders rather than his paralysed legs*

● The depression and its effects

Many Americans had grown so used to the good times of the 1920s, when there was plenty of work and profits were high, that they could hardly believe a great depression had hit their nation at the end of 1929. But the truth was brought home to them in the following year when the level of unemployment soared. Prices of goods fell but then share prices and the profits of industry went down with them, so trade slumped. Banks closed – about five thousand of them in two years – and shopkeepers put up their shutters.

In 1929 about 1.5 million Americans were without work. In the next year this number grew to 4.3 million, then to 8 million in 1931. But that was not the end. There were well over 12 million unemployed in the USA in 1932 – almost one quarter of the labour force (those eligible for work).

Life for these people became a perpetual struggle to survive – they had lost the dignity and hope that having a job brings. Mothers and fathers scraped, saved and scrounged to give their children food, often neglecting themselves to do so. In some areas whole families packed up their belongings and trekked off to another part of the country, seeking work. Soup kitchens were set up in cities to give food to the unemployed who stood and waited in the breadlines.

● Franklin Delano Roosevelt (FDR)

The Republicans who were in power could do little to stem the tide of trouble. They hoped that business and trade would pick up of their own accord and that boom time would return. President Hoover took some measures, such as cutting taxes, but they were not enough.

The stage was set for a very remarkable American to offer himself as Presidential candidate for the Democratic Party at the election of 1932. His speeches offered hope for the future. In one he said:

> **1** **I pledge you – I pledge myself to a new deal for the American people. . . . Give me your help, not to win votes alone, but**

to win in the crusade to restore America to its own people.

Later he promised:

> [2] **We Americans will rise from destruction; we Americans will conquer despair; we Americans are facing new things. With confidence we accept the promise of a New Deal.**

The speaker was Franklin Delano Roosevelt. He was born in 1882, came from a wealthy background and trained as a lawyer. He entered politics as a Senator for the Democratic Party at the age of 28 and soon made progress as a politician. During the First World War he was Assistant Secretary for the navy.

After the war he was struck by a personal tragedy. In 1921 he suffered from polio which paralysed his legs, but Roosevelt fought back against the disease. Although he could never walk without help and spent much of his time in a wheelchair, he kept in touch with politicians, sending them three thousand letters a year.

In 1928 he went back to politics and was elected Governor of New York State, so his fine voice was heard again at rallies. People respected the courage and determination he showed in overcoming illness. Thus in the 1932 election the Democrats chose him to stand against Herbert Hoover, the Republican, for the position of President.

He attacked the government's record, claiming they had done too little to stem unemployment. During one speech he said:

> [3] **There are two theories of prosperity and of well-being. The first theory is that if we make the rich richer, somehow they will let a part of their prosperity trickle down to the rest of us. The second theory – that if we make the average of mankind comfortable and secure, their prosperity will rise upward, just as yeast rises up, through the ranks.**

Roosevelt was a fine public speaker and the American public took to him. He won a landslide victory with a majority of more than twelve million votes.

● **The New Deal**
The main task facing the new President was to provide work for the unemployed and get

B *Tree planting as part of the work of the New Deal*

business going again. The Federal Government in Washington, that is the country's central government, started to play a big part in this. It made large loans of money to the government of each state of the USA. Then, using that money, they in turn started employment schemes. Camps were set up, organized by the army, where young men could find work. They planted trees, built roads through forests and developed large areas of the countryside. Elsewhere, bridges were built, together with schools and hospitals. Farmers were helped with mortgages and given the chance of having modern machinery and electricity on their farms.

The New Deal was introduced in two stages. Between 1933 and 1935 steps were taken to tackle the financial crash and mass unemployment. Then, from 1935–9, laws were passed to give greater social security to working people and bring them more rights.

Roosevelt's New Deal had a mixed reception. Some Republicans claimed that the President was taking too much power and interfering too much in business. But for millions of Americans he had brought some hope when there was despair and had helped to provide work.

● **The Tennessee Valley Authority (TVA)**
The best-known work of the New Deal was to set up what was called the Tennessee Valley Authority. The scheme covered an area across seven states where agriculture was backward or in need. The TVA built power stations and dams so that electricity could be brought there and soil erosion controlled. Many farmers were able to improve their methods and increase output.

● **Recovery**
A proof of Roosevelt's success was that in the next two elections for the Presidency he was returned each time. In fact, in 1936 he gained the greatest of all American election

C *Men repairing roads under the Works Progress Administration (WPA)*

victories, winning 46 states out of the 48 which then made up the USA.

He had an easy style with the American people and made broadcasts to them in what he called 'fireside chats'. His message was simple, straightforward and appealing. For example, at the 1936 election he reminded his audience:

4 In the spring of 1933 we faced a crisis which was the ugly fruit of twelve years of neglect. . . . Do I need to recall to you the fear of those days – the reports of those who piled supplies in their basements, who laid plans to get their fortunes across the border. . . . Do I need to recall the law-abiding heads of peaceful families who began to wonder, as they saw their children starve, how they would get the bread they saw in the bakery window?

The laws passed to help people appealed to Roosevelt's high ideals. Aid was given to the blind and the crippled. An old-age pension scheme was brought in for those over 65. Child labour was stopped.

By 1939 the 'illness' of unemployment was not cured – eight million people were still without regular work. But Roosevelt had done something and conditions were better than they had been seven years earlier. □

Exercises

1 Copy and complete these sentences using the words from the **word list**.
   (a) The Great . . . led to . . . in the USA.
   (b) F.D. Roosevelt belonged to the . . . Party.
   (c) In 1932 Roosevelt defeated . . . in the Presidential election.
   (d) The New . . . was an attempt to create. . . .
   (e) TVA stood for . . . Valley. . . .
   (f) By 1939 unemployment in the USA had been. . . .

   word list: Tennessee; lowered; Deal; employment; Authority; Depression; unemployment; Democratic; Hoover

2 (a) Draw a graph to show the unemployment figures in the USA in the following years: 1929, 1930, 1931, 1932, 1939. You will find the figures in the chapter.
   (b) Give reasons why unemployment rose and then fell.

3 Write a paragraph explaining what the New Deal was and how people reacted to it.

4 (a) Describe what is happening in pictures B and C.
   (b) How do these pictures show that President Roosevelt tried to improve conditions for people in the USA?

5 You are a reporter for an American newspaper. You have been asked to write an account of the work and character of F.D. Roosevelt in the 1930s. Read the chapter again and then write your report.

(*A further question appears on page 218.*)

Japan and China in the 1930s

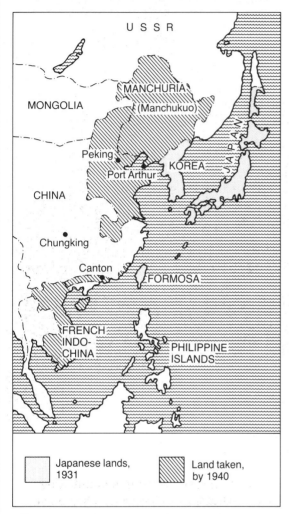

Japanese lands, 1931

Land taken, by 1940

A *Japanese expansion*

● **The background – Japan**

In the twentieth century Japan has developed possibly faster than any other nation in the world. Until 1853, when an American naval expedition sailed to Japan and brought its inhabitants into contact with Western ideas, Japan had been an isolated country with some customs that left it in the Middle Ages. However, after the contact was made it developed quickly. Japanese leaders followed Western ideas, introduced industry and science to their nation and quickly became a leading country in the Far East.

The Japanese population increased at a great rate. Between 1850 and 1910 it almost doubled, rising from twenty-seven million to fifty million. As map A shows, Japan is made up of a number of islands and soon there was a pressure to expand and settle people in neighbouring lands. The easy victims were nearby China and Korea.

This policy led to war with Russia in 1904–5 when both countries had ambitions towards Manchuria, a northern Chinese province. In the fighting, to the amazement of the rest of the world, the Japanese completely defeated the Russians on land and at sea. They wiped out a Russian fleet at the Battle of Tsushima in 1905, one of the greatest naval victories ever seen. Japan had arrived as an important nation.

● **Japan and the First World War**

Most countries involved in the First World War came out poorer than they went in. The Japanese, however, made gains. Their factories produced many war goods and they built ships for the Allies. Their own army and navy were not involved in the heavy fighting that proved so costly to nations in Europe, so they suffered few casualties.

After 1918 they captured and took over all Germany's colonies in the Pacific. They also occupied Kiaochow, a Chinese port which the Germans had controlled previously.

Japan was building an empire.

● **Japan and the great slump**

In the late 1920s the great slump in trade hit Japan as well as other industrialized nations. The sale of Japanese manufactured goods fell and there was unemployment. Another

B *Sun Yat-sen and his wife with soldiers in Western uniforms*

difficulty was that Japan was short of raw materials like oil, iron ore and rubber, which were not found in its own islands. In the early 1930s Japan started to solve its problems by becoming more aggressive, pushing hard to get these things from other lands.

● **China – the background**
At the start of the twentieth century China was a great empire ruled over by an Empress. However, in the age of imperialism much of China's trade and wealth were owned and controlled by several European countries.

Many Chinese found this humiliating. They hated the foreigners who had come into their land and they belonged to the Chinese National People's Party, the Kuomintang. Their motto was 'Asia for the Asians'. In 1911 their leader, named Sun Yat-sen, led a revolution and set up a new Chinese Republic. He was the first president.

But matters were no better for the ordinary Chinese peasants. Over the next twenty years they lived in a country controlled by powerful warlords, who kept private armies and fought with each other. It was an age of lawlessness.

C *Chiang Kai-shek in 1930*

By 1931 there were two important leaders in China. One was General Chiang Kai-shek, who succeeded Sun Yat-sen as leader of the Kuomintang. The other was Mao Tse-tung who founded and led the Chinese Communist Party. The trouble from China's point of view was that these two groups fought each other as violently as they fought with any outside enemy!

In October 1934 the fighting grew so bitter that Mao took his Communists – men, women and children – on 'The Long March' to escape trouble. Thousands of them trekked for 8,800 km from south to north China on a journey that lasted over a year. Many died on the route but the remainder founded the Communist state of Yenan, near Mongolia.

● **Manchuria, 1931**

In September 1931 Japanese troops in Manchuria announced that they were going to take over the whole of the province. The area belonged to China but was rich in coal and iron ore. It was a fine prize for Japan and by December was completely occupied. The Japanese renamed the province 'Manchukuo' and turned it into a colony of what was to be their new Far Eastern Empire.

Both China and Japan were members of the League of Nations and here was a good test case for an organization which had been set up after 1919 to prevent future wars. The League debated what had happened. There was lots of talk of aggression, unfairness and illegal behaviour. But the Japanese ignored it all. To them, possession of Manchuria meant that the land was theirs and nobody was going to move them. And, of course, there was nobody strong enough to try.

Inside Japan, the army grew more important because it had organized the whole operation successfully. They had shown that aggression could pay. Outside Japan, people realized that the League of Nations could not force countries to obey its orders. In 1933 Japan withdrew from the League.

One important result of that kind of behaviour was that other nations might be encouraged to copy it.

● **War with China, 1937**

Japan's military leaders were well satisfied with their success and followed it up in 1937. Realizing that they had the forces and the power to beat the Chinese they struck again. This time they launched attacks at a large area of China, hoping to occupy and control

Japan and China in the 1930s

D *Mao Tse-tung, leader of the Chinese communists, on the Long March, 1934*

the country and make it all part of their empire.

Japanese forces moved out from Manchuria, aiming at the interior. The Chinese fought hard for their native land, under the leadership of General Chiang Kai-shek, but they were not so well equipped as their attackers. The Japanese made good use of tanks and artillery, well supported by their growing air force which carried out heavy bombing raids on towns and cities. Chinese forces had to retreat.

By the last months of 1938 Japanese troops had occupied some of the richest and most important areas of China. Millions of people were now under their control. □

Exercises

1 Correctly match up the two halves of the following sentences and copy them into your book.
   (a) The Battle of Tsushima . . . Germany's colonies in the Pacific.
   (b) After 1918 the Japanese took . . . at the start of the 20th century.
   (c) An Empress ruled over China . . . the leader of the Kuomintang.
   (d) The 'Long March' started . . . was a naval victory for Japan.
   (e) Chiang Kai-shek was . . . in October 1934.

2 Arrange these events in their correct order:
   (a) Sun Yat-sen's revolution in China;
   (b) the Long March;
   (c) the Japanese invasion of Manchuria;
   (d) the Battle of Tsushima;
   (e) the American naval expedition to Japan.

3 Give reasons why Japan wished to conquer other lands
   (a) between 1850 and 1910;
   (b) in the late 1920s.

4 Look at map A.
   (a) Which countries did the Japanese occupy?
   (b) Why were the Japanese successful with their expansion plans?

5 It is 1938. You are a foreign correspondent in China for *The Daily News*. Write two articles for your paper on 'China Today'. In your first article give the background to life in China and in your second article explain how the Japanese occupied large parts of China.

(*A further question appears on page 218.*)

Hitler comes to power in Germany

● Hitler's background

Adolf Hitler was the son of an Austrian customs officer and was born in 1889. At school he showed some ability in art, but little else. After the deaths of his parents he lived for six years in Vienna, having no job, but scraping a living. He became interested in politics and began to form his ideas.

In 1914 he joined the German army at the start of the First World War and served as an infantryman on the Western Front. He now had regularity and discipline in his life. Hitler rose to the rank of corporal and was awarded the Iron Cross while acting as a company runner (messenger). At the end of the war he was in Germany convalescing, because he'd been gassed in 1918.

After the war he went to Munich and joined the newly formed National Socialist German Workers' Party – the 'Nazis'.

● The Nazis

Many Nazis were ex-servicemen who held strong beliefs. One was that the Treaty of Versailles was unjust because it made the Germans accept the blame for the war – and they didn't believe they deserved that. They had no time for the Weimar Republic which had tamely accepted the treaty. Another belief was that the Germans were a superior race and that other races must not be mixed with them. In particular they hated Jews who, they claimed, had helped Germany to lose the war. They also hated Bolshevism, so often fought with Communists at political meetings.

The Nazis formed their own small army, the SA, known as the 'Brownshirts', to protect their meetings. These men carried banners showing the party emblem, the swastika.

A *Hitler used mass rallies at Nuremberg to rally support, to unite his followers and to speak out against Germany's enemies*

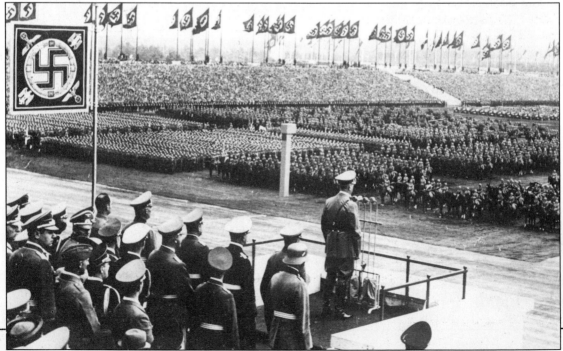

84

Hitler comes to power in Germany

Hitler showed his abilities in this new party. He did not look an outstanding figure, but had great powers as an orator (a speech-maker). His listeners were spellbound, hanging on every word as he made violent attacks on opponents. Soon he was the leader – *Der Führer* – and developed more of his ideas. He had no time for rule by democracy, through a parliament, as Britain had. Instead, he believed in having only one party and inside that party having one man as leader and controller.

● *Mein Kampf*

After the Munich *putsch* (page 70) when the Nazis tried unsuccessfully to seize power in Bavaria, Adolf Hitler was imprisoned in the Landsberg fortress. While there he wrote a book entitled *Mein Kampf* ('My Struggle'). This was his version of his life story and set out all his beliefs. The book became a kind of bible for the Nazis.

Although sentenced to five years imprisonment Hitler was released after serving ten months.

● **The Nazis come to power**

After Hitler's release from prison the Nazi Party made little headway. They still held meetings at which opponents were denounced – and beaten up if present. But as late as 1928 they had little support at elections. Less than one million voted for them in that year out of a total of 30 million votes cast. They appeared to have little future.

But then came the great slump in world trade. Germans could not sell their industrial products and unemployment grew. Americans who had invested in Germany now took out their money, so many firms collapsed. In those desperate times people turned to a party which offered to help them out of trouble.

Between 1929 and 1932 the Nazi vote at elections soared. They found support from manual workers who wanted jobs, from the middle classes who feared for their savings and from the rich who were scared of Communism. In July 1932 the Nazis received 13.75 million votes and became the largest single party in the Reichstag (the German parliament). Shortly afterwards the German President, Hindenburg, asked Hitler to become Chancellor (Prime Minister) of the nation.

It was a time of violence, as an English writer remembered:

---

1 Almost every evening, the SA men came into the cafe. Sometimes they are only collecting money; everybody is compelled to give something. Sometimes they have come to make an 'arrest'. One evening, a Jewish writer who was present ran into the telephone box to ring up the police. The Nazis dragged him out, and he was taken away. Nobody moved a finger. You could have heard a pin drop till they were gone.

● **The Nazis in power**

Hitler now had what he had longed for – power. The opponents of the Nazis were now ruthlessly removed. By the Enabling Act, 1933, other political parties were banned and when President Hindenburg died in 1934 Hitler became President and Chancellor in one.

The Nazis put into practice what they had promised for so long. Communists, Jews and other 'enemies of the state' were imprisoned. Concentration camps were opened for the prisoners. Nazis held all the important positions in national and local government

B *Hitler Youth on parade. All German children over ten years of age had to join the Hitler Youth. The Nazis then taught them Nazi ideas*

and they made a particular point of capturing the minds and imaginations of the young. An organization known as the Hitler Youth was set up to do this.

Hitler once declared:

> **2** When an opponent says, 'I will not come over to your side', I calmly say, 'Your child belongs to us already . . . you will pass on. Your descendants, however, now stand in the new camp. In a short time they will know nothing else but this new community.'

Newspapers and radio were taken over by the state and Joseph Goebbels, an ardent Nazi, was appointed 'Minister for National Enlightenment and Propaganda'. After this the people of Germany heard only one point of view.

They had fallen into the web of a dictatorship, which held them fast.

● **The Night of the Long Knives**

Hitler was always an opportunist. That means that he took full advantage of any situation that arose and got out of it what he could for himself. When some important Germans, including army generals, became worried about the growing strength of the SA – Hitler's brown-shirted army – Hitler decided to remove some of those who had helped him to power.

He called in the black-shirted SS – his protection squads, made up of secret police – and gave them the task. On the night of 30 June 1934 – the 'Night of the Long Knives' – hundreds of SA men were rounded up and over 150 were shot. Hitler later made his explanations to the Reichstag:

> **3** I ordered the leaders of the guilty shot. If someone asks me why we did not use the regular courts I would reply: at that moment I was responsible for the German nation; . . . it was I alone who, during those twenty-four hours, was the Supreme Court of Justice of the German People!

● **The Nazi Programme**

Other Germans quickly learned the lesson. Obey the Führer. Don't do anything the Nazis might think is wrong. Their programme, laid down in 1920, announced:

> **4** None but members of the nation may be citizens of the State. None but those

C *Jewish store branded by Nazis*

of German blood may be members of the nation. No Jew, therefore, may be a member of the nation.

Laws were passed to take away rights from Jews. By the end of 1935 Germans did not use Jewish shops, and Jewish doctors and lawyers were prevented from working. Many were driven from their homes and some from Germany. They were not allowed to marry Germans.

The great persecution had started.

● **Hitler's position**

By 1935 there were fewer unemployed in Germany and industry was recovering. One reason was that Hitler had started to build up the nation's armed forces again. He felt that his position in Germany was safe, so he was now able to turn his attention to other countries. ☐

Exercises

1 Copy and complete these sentences using your own words.
   (a) During the First World War Hitler . . . .
   (b) The first Nazis were. . . .
   (c) In Germany, the effects of the Great Slump were. . . .
   (d) Joseph Goebbels was. . . .
   (e) The SS were. . . .

2 (a) What was the full name of the Nazis?
   (b) What was their emblem?
   (c) On which pictures can you see this emblem?

3 Read the chapter carefully then copy and complete this grid (yours will be bigger).

Hitler's Ideas	
For	*Against*
Germans	Jews
Dictatorship	Democracy

4 Describe what you can see in picture C. Explain in your own words what Hitler's attitude to Jews was.

5 Write a brief essay on 'The Rise of Adolf Hitler'. These points may help you: early life; the Nazis; Germany in the 1920s; Hitler becomes Chancellor; Hitler's opponents; why people supported Hitler.

Depression in Britain

● Britain in the 1920s

In 1914 Britain had been one of the world's greatest nations, immensely rich from trade. British merchant ships carried goods on all oceans, protected by the might of the Royal Navy. But the First World War proved to be very costly for Britain. Overseas markets were lost and the country went heavily into debt, especially to the Americans. So in one sense Britain came out of the war as a loser.

A large part of Britain's prosperity before 1914 had come from its older industries. These had brought wealth during the nineteenth century when Britain's coal, cotton goods, shipbuilding and iron and steel were all in great demand abroad. However, after 1918 other nations started to grow as rivals in trade. Electric power and oil were used to replace coal. Asian countries produced cotton goods. A number of nations built their own ships instead of buying them from British yards.

As British industry declined there were fewer exports, so unemployment soon grew. The figure went past one million in 1921. Industry was forced to sack workers or put them on short time. Many people in work had to suffer wage cuts.

● The General Strike, 1926

The greatest trouble occurred in the coal industry. As soon as European mines moved back into full production after the war British miners felt the pressure of competition. The price of coal went down – and so did wages.

There were arguments between mine owners and their workers. Trade union leaders wanted the government to give help, which they did. But then a report was published in 1926 which recommended changes in the mining industry. One suggestion was that miners should have smaller wages and work longer hours. They responded angrily with the motto:

> **1** **Not a penny off the pay,**
> **Not a minute on the day.**

To support the miners a General Strike began on 4 May 1926. For nine days public transport, power supplies and much of industry came to a halt. However, thousands of workers did not go on strike and others feared that there might be revolution. Volunteers tried to keep businesses and transport running and eventually, on 12 May, the strike broke up. But the miners stayed out till the end of the year, when they were forced back by hardship.

A *Unemployment in Britain, 1922–34*

Percentage of unemployed workers, 1934:	
Jarrow	67.8
Merthyr	61.9
Maryport	57.0
Abertillery	49.6
Greenock	36.3
London	8.6
Birmingham	6.4
Coventry	5.1
Oxford	5.1
St. Albans	3.9

Unemployment figures	
1922	1,543,000
1925	1,226,000
1928	1,217,000
1930	1,917,000
1931	2,630,000
1932	2,745,000
1933	2,521,000
1934	2,159,000

Depression in Britain

● The great slump hits Britain

The effects of the Wall Street crash soon reached Britain, causing many worries. The unemployment figures rose even more rapidly – by 1931, they were over two million. At that time a Labour government was in power with James Ramsay MacDonald as Prime Minister. As Britain's financial crisis grew worse, he decided to form a national government, made up of various political parties, to tackle it. Import taxes were raised and government spending cut. The worst of the crisis passed but the level of unemployment reached a peak of three million in 1933.

● The depths of unemployment

The great industries which brought wealth to Britain during the Industrial Revolution were built up in certain main areas. Lancashire had cotton mills. South Wales and the north-east of England had many coal mines. Ships were built on Clydeside and Merseyside, Tyneside and Belfast. So in between the wars, these were the places worst hit.

The plight of the miners was pointed out in a broadcast made by the Prince of Wales in 1928:

---

2 **Picture for a moment an unemployed man in, say, the Rhondda Valley or in Durham. He has been without work for months, perhaps a year or more. . . . And day after day the father tramps the one narrow winding street of the valley town –**

B *Jarrow approaches London. In 1936 a deputation of unemployed workers marched from that depressed town in the north-east to ask the government and Parliament for help. Here they halt near Bedford for a meal of corned beef and potatoes*

---

the same little post-office, the same half-empty shops, the same chapel, and the ever grim overhanging hills. Now this sort of thing, in different forms, is going on in mining villages throughout the country.

Matters grew worse after 1931 when the great slump hit Britain. In certain areas of northern England, in Northern Ireland and in South Wales, thousands of families suffered as factories and mines closed down, or worked on short time. These were known as the 'depressed areas' and for many people there life was a constant struggle against poverty.

The national government took steps to help people. Money, known as 'the dole', was paid out each week to the unemployed. A family consisting of father, mother and three children would receive about £1.50 per week and this enabled them to exist on

C *Housewife using electric washing machine, 1937*

simple food and no luxuries. Some were very angry that a 'means test' was introduced to make sure that benefit was given only when people had used up their own money, including their savings.

The greatest damage done by unemployment was the feeling of despair brought to certain areas. Where there was no work – and no chance of work – people lost hope. Some men were unemployed for years and spirit left them so they became as depressed as the surroundings they lived in:

---

3 When a man fell out of work he would, on the first day, dress in his Sunday suit with collar and tie. He shaved, pinned on his ex-serviceman's badge and, head held high, lined up at the labour exchange. He kept up his spirits by joking with his mates. . . .

As the weeks passed, the unemployed man changed. He stopped dressing up. He acquired a characteristic slouch. . . . He left the stubble on his cheeks.

As the months passed his hands grew white – softer and whiter than those of his wife. . . .

● **The new industries**
However, the story of gloom was not told everywhere in Britain. Although the old industries were in decline, new ones were developed. These offered good prospects for employment to some areas where the rate of unemployment was low.

There was, for example, a great leap forward in the production of motor vehicles in the period between the wars. The number of private cars increased from 300,000 in 1919 to three million twenty years later. Thus there was plenty of work for craftsmen

Depression in Britain

and engineers in the Midlands, where places like Coventry, Birmingham and Oxford were thriving.

Electric power was installed in many places and this gave employment to thousands of men. The system of the National Grid, allowing electricity to be distributed all over the country, was started in 1926.

There was more housebuilding in the 1930s and as the general standard of living rose, people began to have gadgets like electric cookers and carpet sweepers in their homes.

Around the edge of London many factories sprang up, offering work to many people. They produced a variety of household goods. Because of their position, their products could be transported and sold easily.

● **The position by 1939**

The national goverment tried to encourage industry and trade to what were called the 'special areas'. Firms were encouraged to go to places badly hit by the depression and set up new works there.

After 1936 when Hitler's Germany started to expand in power Britain slowly turned to re-armament and this provided some work. Yet by 1939 there were still 1.35 million people without work. The figure did not fall dramatically until the next year, 1940, after the evacuation from Dunkirk. Then, when the nation faced disaster, work was found for all!   □

Exercises

1 Copy and complete this paragraph by using words from the **word list**.
Before World War 1, Britain had been a great . . . nation, but after . . . its old . . . suffered. As a result, there was . . . scale . . . in the 1920s and. . . . This occurred in areas where . . ., cotton, and . . . were the . . . industries.

> **word list:** coal; large; 1930s; main; 1918; shipbuilding; trading; unemployment; industries

2 Explain the meaning of the following:
 (a) 'put them on short time';
 (b) 'feel the pressure of competition';
 (c) a national government;
 (d) the 'dole';
 (e) 'depressed areas'.

3 Compare the washing machine in picture C with those of today.

4 Study the charts in diagram A. Write a paragraph about unemployment in Britain using these clues to help you: declining industries; Wall Street crash; depressed areas; new industries; increased production; special areas; standards of living.

5 Using all the information provided in this chapter, write three brief radio scripts on 'Work in Britain 1926–36'. The first should deal with 'The General Strike', the second with 'Unemployment', and the third 'New Industries'. Include interviews in your scripts.

The Spanish Civil War

● The problems of Spain

In the past, Spain has had a long and glorious history. During the sixteenth and seventeenth centuries it was one of the most powerful countries in Europe. The Spaniards created a great overseas empire in south America and the Far East and grew rich from trade. However, by the start of the twentieth century most of that empire had either become independent or had been taken by other nations. Spain lost much of its past importance and was no longer a great power. The Spanish played no part in the First World War.

During the 1920s Spain was divided by several differences. There was argument over the power of the Roman Catholic Church. Communists and Socialists wanted changes in society, with land being given to the poor. There were also anarchists who disliked any form of government. Opposing them were Spaniards who did not want change. Some of these formed a Fascist group called the Falange.

In 1931 King Alfonso III of Spain abdicated and the nation ceased being a monarchy. After that Spain became a republic, ruled over by a president.

A *Nationalist troops prepare to attack Madrid, 1936*

Soon there were riots, attacks on churches, and strikes. A country in that state was ripe for trouble.

● The start of war

The trouble occurred in 1936 when a general election was held, and was won by parties of the left – Communists, Socialists and Liberals – called the Popular Front. This victory worried many right-wingers who feared that there might be a revolution of the type seen in Russia. In July units of the Spanish army rebelled. They had as their leader General Francisco Franco and were supported by many people of the middle class and by landowners.

Units of the army crossed from Spanish Morocco in North Africa and invaded Spain. Before long, the rebels, who were called Nationalists, occupied a large area of the west and north of their own land. Opposing them were the government forces – the Republicans – who were in the east and south of the country.

Both sides then began fighting a particularly bloodthirsty civil war. The Nationalists hunted out thousands of their opponents and put them to death. In return, the Republicans were extremely harsh in attacks on the Church, killing over 6,000 nuns, monks and priests.

Up to that point the war was Spanish, involving only Spaniards, but towards the end of 1936 foreign countries began to be involved. That is why the civil war became a very important event in the world history of the 1930s.

● The dictators step in

Hitler in Germany and Mussolini in Italy both sent armed forces to take part in the war. Franco appealed to them for help and they saw the chance of fighting against Communists. In the case of Mussolini there was the chance to claim that Italy was playing an important part in world affairs. For Hitler there was an opportunity to try out some of his forces, especially the newly formed Luftwaffe (Air Force).

Over 60,000 Italian troops were sent to Spain by early 1937 and the Italian navy used ships to help General Franco's men. The Germans transported war materials to Spain together with the Condor Legion, which consisted of aircraft, tanks and artillery.

On several occasions these forces were able to help the Nationalists win battles. For the foreigners there was the chance to gain battle experience and the German Air Force made particular use of that.

Help was also given to General Franco by Oliveira Salazar, the Prime Minister of Portugal, who sent 20,000 troops.

Both Hitler and Mussolini hoped for a Nationalist victory so they could have a Fascist ally in Europe.

● Help for the Republicans

Britain and France wanted to stay clear of

B *While France Sleeps*

Area taken by Nationalists by 1937
Area taken by Nationalists by 1938
Area taken by Nationalists by Feb. 1939
Area taken by Nationalists by Mar. 1939
■ • Cities taken by Nationalists

C *The Spanish Civil War*

someone else's war and believed in 'non-intervention'. They claimed that the quarrel concerned Spaniards and not foreigners. This was a time when they were anxious not to upset the dictators, so they allowed no official help to be sent. In general their sympathies were with the Republicans because they disliked the way that Hitler and Mussolini were helping the other side. Yet they feared the outbreak of another great European war if too many nations became involved.

Russia, nevertheless, did send aid to the Republicans. Tanks, fighter planes and military advisers went to Spain because Stalin believed he should support Communists fighting against Fascists. Later, Russian aid grew less because the Nationalists blockaded ports, preventing supplies from reaching their enemies.

● The International Brigades

Although the governments of Britain and France refused to become mixed up in the war, hundreds of their citizens did. From Europe and America there were many sympathizers with the Republicans. They wanted to do something to stand against the growing power of Hitler and Mussolini so they joined regiments that were known as the 'International Brigades'. They made their way unofficially to Spain as volunteers and then fought against the Nationalists.

● The fighting

General Franco set up his capital and headquarters at Burgos. The Government had theirs in Madrid. Gradually, through 1937 and 1938, Franco's men drove the Republicans back into a smaller and smaller area. The Nationalists were better equipped and organized. They had better discipline and this brought them success on the battlefield. Consequently, by the end of 1938 the Republicans had little hope of victory.

Much of the war was waged in open country, across olive groves where lines of trenches were dug. In towns, the two sides fought bitterly for the possession of streets, even individual houses.

Both sides fought savagely, showing little mercy to their opponents. Franco's soldiers shot any prisoners they believed to be Communists:

---

1 The victims were handcuffed and hobbled [had their legs tied together], but not tied together in a single chain, and thus had relative privacy for their confessions. The squads waited impatiently for the unusually long confessions to be made. As the first victims were shot, a hysterical panic seized the remainder. Men began running, only to be shot down like animals.

D *Defeated Republicans are led across the frontier into France*

The Spanish Civil War

The Republicans made attacks on the Church and its priests, because they supported the Nationalists:

---

2 **After the surrendering soldiers had come out, the crowd set fire to the building in order to dislodge the priests. A machine-gun was set up commanding the entrance to the church, and as the terror-stricken priests emerged they were shot down.**

● **The end**

By early 1939 Republican forces were almost beaten. Thousands of them fled across the border to France. General Franco's army occupied all the main cities of Spain and other governments soon recognized him as the new leader of the nation.

Small groups of Republicans fought on here and there, but were eventually beaten.

At the final count, probably half a million people had died and the country took years to recover. The conflict was the forerunner for the big war that was soon to begin. □

Exercises

1 Re-arrange these sentences so that they make sense and copy them into your book.
  (a) The rebel forces under General Franco . . . some aid from Russia.
  (b) In 1931 the King abdicated . . . Spain was no longer an imperial power.
  (c) The Republicans received . . . helped the Nationalists.
  (d) German and Italian forces . . . were called the Nationalists.
  (e) By the start of the 20th century . . . and Spain became a republic.

2 Arrange these events in their correct order:
  (a) thousands of Republicans fled to France;
  (b) the Popular Front won the General Election;
  (c) Italian troops were sent to Spain;
  (d) The Falange was formed;
  (e) King Alfonso III abdicated.

3 (a) What did the Spanish Communists want?
  (b) What did the right-wingers want?
  (c) What action did these groups take after the 1936 election?

4 (a) Explain the meaning of cartoon B, 'While France Sleeps'.
  (b) Which side would the cartoonist support?

5 Explain the meaning of the following:
  (a) the Popular Front;
  (b) the Nationalists;
  (c) the International Brigades;
  (d) the Condor Legion;
  (e) the Republicans.

6 Why were the Nationalists successful?

7 Why was the war important for the future of Europe?

(*A further question appears on page 218.*)

The League of Nations

A *The League of Nations in session in Geneva*

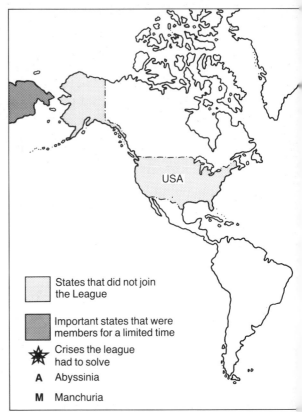

States that did not join the League

Important states that were members for a limited time

Crises the league had to solve

A   Abyssinia

M   Manchuria

Covenant
Each member of the League of Nations promised to bring its quarrels to the League before going to war; to keep international law; and to respect treaties in order to keep international peace

Organization
1 *Assembly* – delegates to all the member states met once a year
2 *Council* – representatives of the Great Powers discussed serious problems
3 *Secretariat* – permanent officials based in Geneva

Flashpoints
1 Disputes between Greece, Italy, Greece, Turkey, French invasion of the Ruhr
2 Japanese invasion of Manchuria in 1931
3 Italian invasion of Abyssinia 1935

Work
1 Discussed and settled arguments between countries
2 *Court of International Justice* interpreted international law
3 Was responsible for national minorities, mandated territories and disputed areas
4 *International Labour Office* dealt with social, health and working conditions
5 Tried to control the drug trade
6 Tried to control the arms race

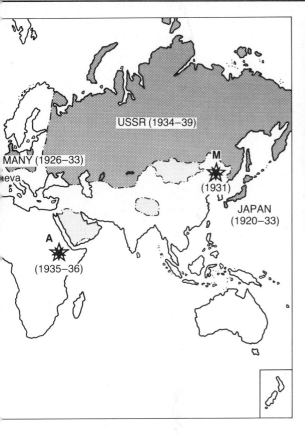

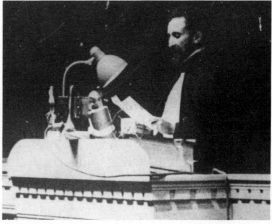

B *Haile Selassie, Emperor of Ethiopia, speaks to delegates at the League of Nations after his country has been invaded by Italy*

Reasons for its weakness
1 USA not a member
2 Germany and Russia not members after the war
3 Countries not willing to give power to League
4 League unwilling to go to war
5 League would only use economic sanctions against offending nations
6 Defeated countries (Germany) associated the League with Peace Treaties

Problems
1 National minorities in Europe
2 Jews and Arabs in Palestine
3 The Saar territory
4 The free city of Danzig

(*A question on the League of Nations will be found on page 218.*)

Steps to war

● German re-armament

Once Hitler felt that his position was secure inside Germany he set about strengthening the nation. To do this he had to break the terms of the Treaty of Versailles, which he hated so much. He started to re-arm and in 1935 brought in conscription for young men.

Then he invited a close Nazi colleague, Hermann Goering, an air ace of the First World War, to build up the Luftwaffe (the German Air Force). The next stage was that in June 1935 Britain and Germany signed an agreement on the size of their navies and Germany was allowed to build submarines again.

German industry turned more and more to the production of weapons of war. Outside observers could feel that trouble was building up.

● The Rhineland

By the terms laid down at Versailles the Rhineland, which was part of Germany, was demilitarized, which means that armed forces were not allowed there. However, in March 1936 Hitler ordered his troops to march back in and occupy the zone. As they tramped into various towns they were welcomed by the local people. Girls in Düsseldorf lined the streets and sang:

---

1 Welcome to the Rhine. Welcome in our hearts. Soldiers, we will show you we are worthy of you.

In Britain and France some angry voices were raised against the German action, but others felt that the Treaty of Versailles had treated the Germans unfairly. As a result, neither government was prepared to take firm action by sending in troops to remove

A *The expansion of Germany under Hitler, 1935–39*

the Germans. So nothing was done.

Hitler was relieved and pleased at their weakness. He had proved that he could defy the Treaty of Versailles – and get away with it.

● The Axis

By late 1936 Germany and Italy had drawn closer together in their policies. Both Mussolini and Hitler were dictators who shared some similar beliefs about how their countries should be governed. Thus, in November Mussolini announced that the two nations had reached a kind of alliance called 'The Rome-Berlin Axis'. He claimed that this was the axis on which Europe would revolve against Communism.

In the same month Germany and Japan signed an agreement to work against

"Why should we take a stand about someone pushing someone else when it's all so far away."

B *Cartoon; 'Increasing Pressure'. The figures are, left to right: British Empire, France, North-west Europe, Near East, The Balkans, Czechoslovakia, Austria*

Communism. This was called the Anti-Comintern Pact.

● Appeasement

Neville Chamberlain became Prime Minister of Britain in 1937, at a time when the dictators were growing in power. He used a policy towards them that has become known as 'appeasement'. To appease means to pacify, or satisfy, or quieten. In Chamberlain's view it was essential to keep Europe at peace, even if that meant giving way to what the dictators wanted.

Why did this happen? There were several reasons. First of all, some British politicians feared Stalin's Russia as much as they disliked Hitler's Germany. They believed that the Nazis could be used as a barrier against the Communists. Second, the memories of the terrible First World War were still in people's minds. No one wanted that kind of slaughter of the trenches all over again. Added to that was the new fear of thousands of civilians being killed in air raids. Third, Britain was barely moving out of the effects of the great slump and the costs

of re-arming could have been disastrous to the country's finances.

Britain's possible allies were Russia and France. But the British would not trust the Bolsheviks in Moscow, who had taken themselves out of the First World War. And France in the 1930s had great troubles with Communist and Fascist riots.

Thus Britain and France appeared weak in the face of the dictators. Since those days they have been blamed for appeasement, yet at the time there appeared to be good reasons for trying it.

● Austria

Part of Hitler's policy was to re-unite all German-speaking people. Austria contained six million German-speaking inhabitants. It was also the country of Hitler's birth, so he had a special reason for wanting to unite his homeland with Germany.

For weeks in March 1938 Nazis living in Austria carried out demonstrations and riots demanding Anschluss (Union) with Germany. Then Hitler acted like their saviour. German troops crossed the frontier and marched in to occupy Vienna. The Austrian people as a nation were given no chance of saying whether they approved.

Once again, the Treaty of Versailles had been broken. And once again, no one raised a finger to stop the dictator.

● Czechoslovakia

Czechoslovakia was a new nation, created at the Peace Conference of Versailles. Inside its borders, as well as the Czechs and Slovaks lived three million Germans, in a region called the Sudetenland which had previously been part of the old Austro-Hungarian Empire. By the summer of 1938 Hitler was demanding that these Germans should have 'self-determination'. By that, he meant that they should be included in Germany. As the map shows, that part of Czechoslovakia was now surrounded by Hitler's territories, so the outlook for the Czechs was poor.

Both from Germany and the Sudetenland came loud cries for re-unification. The Czechs turned to France, because the two countries had signed an alliance. But France would not act without Britain's help – and Chamberlain was not prepared to give it.

As the quarrel built up, war fever grew in Europe. In Britain, air-raid shelters were dug and people were issued with gas masks. Chamberlain decided to visit Germany and although he had never flown before in his life, he made three journeys in September, hoping to keep peace. The last one was to Munich where he met with Daladier (the French Prime Minister), Hitler and Mussolini. The Czechs, whose fate was being decided, were not invited to the discussions.

Afterwards, the decision was reached. Germany was to receive the whole of the Sudetenland. The Czechs felt betrayed and were horrified because their nation had been butchered.

Chamberlain came home to a hero's welcome. 'I believe it is peace for our time,' he told the cheering crowds. Appeasement had worked on this occasion. His thoughts had been shown during an earlier broadcast:

---

2 How horrible, fantastic, incredible it is that we should be digging trenches and trying on gas masks because of a quarrel in a faraway country between people of whom we know nothing.

Some Britons, though, were unhappy with the government's behaviour. Winston Churchill said in the House of Commons, referring to Chamberlain's three visits:

---

3 At Berchtesgaden . . . £1 was demanded at the pistol's point. When it was given, £2 was demanded at the pistol's point. Finally the Dictator consented to take £1.17s.6d. [£1.87½p.] and the rest in promise of goodwill for the future. . . . We are in the presence of a disaster of the first magnitude.

● **Britain re-arms**
By now it was obvious that Hitler had not finished, so Britain and France stepped up their re-armament. More money was spent on the armed services and Britain pushed on with the building of fighter aircraft. Civilians were prepared for war through an organization called ARP (Air Raid Precautions). Shelters were dug or built. Everyone was instructed in the use of gas masks.

C *German soldiers enter the Sudetenland, October 1938*

D *British Prime Minister Neville Chamberlain favoured appeasement. The* Daily Express *reports his home-coming from Germany*

Hitler still had designs on what was left of Czechoslovakia which possessed the giant Skoda armaments factory as well as large supplies of iron and coal. On 15 March 1939 he sent his troops to occupy Prague, the Czech capital. The nation formed at Versailles less than twenty years earlier lost its independence.

By that stage it was obvious that appeasement had failed. A tougher line would be needed when Hitler inevitably chose some other part of Europe and demanded land there for Germany.

Where would it be?

Exercises

1 Re-arrange the words in these sentences so that they make sense and copy them into your book.
  - (a) From produce and weapons 1935 began to Germany re-arm
  - (b) Rhineland marched 1936 soldiers German the into In
  - (c) people speaking German wanted to re-unite all Hitler
  - (d) parts of Germany claimed Czechoslovakia
  - (e) for 1938 early Britain was By war preparing

2 Complete these sentences by using words from the **word list.**
  After Hitler's position was . . . in Germany he started to . . . lands lost through the Treaty of. . . . Britain and . . . did not prevent him from doing this. By the end of 1938 he had . . . the Rhineland, . . . Austria to . . . and taken part of. . . .

word list: re-occupied; Versailles; Germany; France; safe; joined; regain; Czechoslovakia.

3 Explain the meaning of these words:
  - (a) demilitarized
  - (b) conscription
  - (c) dictator
  - (d) re-unification

4 (a) What were Hitler's reasons for acting in the way he did?
  - (b) Why do you think Britain and France tried to appease Hitler?

5 Look at cartoon B and answer these questions.
  - (a) Which country is represented by the large leaning figure?
  - (b) Why is the figure shown wearing a military uniform?
  - (c) Whose hand is pulling the lever?

(*A further question appears on page 218.*)

Off to war again

● The background

You remember that the Treaty of Versailles took some territory from Germany and gave it to Poland. This was to enable Poland to have an outlet to the Baltic Sea. The strip of land was called 'The Polish Corridor' and at the coastal end was the port of Danzig, which enabled the Poles to trade freely.

However, this corridor of land divided East Prussia from the rest of Germany. From the start Hitler would not accept the agreements made at Versailles and he was determined to take back the corridor of land when he had the chance. After his success in Austria and Czechoslovakia he felt safe in putting pressure on the Poles to hand the territory back to Germany.

● Enough is enough

But by the spring of 1939 Britain and France decided that Hitler had gone far enough. They had tried appeasement and had given way to him several times – but his appetite was not satisfied!

It was obvious to the British and French governments that Poland would be the next victim, because of what the Poles had gained at Versailles. On 31 March 1939 Neville Chamberlain explained matters to the House of Commons:

---

1 . . . in the event of any action which clearly threatened Polish independence and which the Polish Government accordingly considered it vital to resist with their national forces, His Majesty's Government would feel themselves bound at once to lend the Polish Government all support in their power. They have given the Polish Government an assurance to this effect. The French Government have authorized me to make plain that they stand in the same position.

Nothing could be clearer, but by now the German leader was making his plans and would not stop.

About a fortnight later Russia asked France and Britain to sign a treaty offering each other military help if needed. But the two western powers declined because they disliked Communism and were suspicious of Stalin.

● The Russo-German Pact

At this stage Hitler believed that Britain and France would not intervene if he invaded Poland. Yet he feared what the Russians might do, so he decided to make a deal with them. In August he sent the German Foreign Minister, von Ribbentrop, to meet the Russian Foreign Minister, Molotov, for talks.

A *A cartoon to show the Russian–German agreement of 1939.*

The world was astounded when the two sides signed a non-aggression pact on 23 August. No one could believe that the Bolsheviks and the Nazis, who hated each other, could come to an agreement. What was not known at the time was that the two sides had also written in a secret section to the treaty. In this they agreed to share out Poland between them when it had been defeated.

Thus Hitler, in a clever move, had avoided the old German fear of fighting on two fronts at once. He still hated the Russians as much as ever but was prepared to use them for his own ends.

● The attack on Poland

The way was now open for Germany to invade Poland. The usual pattern was followed. First of all there was a big propaganda campaign, in which Hitler used newspapers and radio to attack the Poles.

Then a plot was hatched to put the blame for war on the Poles. Some prisoners were taken from a concentration camp, dressed in German army uniforms, then shot near a frontier post on the Polish border. An announcement was put out that the Poles

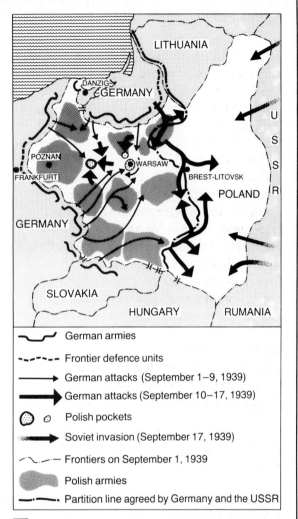

German armies

Frontier defence units

German attacks (September 1–9, 1939)

German attacks (September 10–17, 1939)

Polish pockets

Soviet invasion (September 17, 1939)

Frontiers on September 1, 1939

Polish armies

Partition line agreed by Germany and the USSR

C *The German invasion of Poland, 1939*

B *The British bulldog watches as Hitler, the burglar, breaks into Poland*

had killed them! And that was enough to set the ball rolling.

At 4.45 a.m. on Friday 1 September 1939 Hitler's forces invaded Poland, entering from Germany and from East Prussia. Tanks and motorized infantry rolled across the frontiers, while overhead the Luftwaffe launched an all-out attack on ground targets.

● Britain goes to war

There was still a belief in Hitler's mind that

Britain and France would not move to help a country that lay on the opposite side of Europe. This time he was wrong. Each government sent an ultimatum to Germany, ordering it to withdraw from Poland, but by that time the German forces were smashing their way forward.

The British ultimatum ran out on Sunday 3 September. At 11.15 a.m. that day Mr Chamberlain broadcast:

2 This morning the British Ambassador in Berlin handed the German Government a final note stating that unless we heard from them by eleven o'clock that they were prepared at once to withdraw their troops from Poland, a state of war would exist between us. I have to tell you now that no such undertaking has been received and that consequently this country is at war with Germany.

The French declared war on the Germans at 5 p.m. For many people it was like 1914 all over again.

● **The Polish campaign**

On paper the Poles had a large army and in terms of the fighting of the First World War they could do quite well in battle. But times had changed. The Germans were prepared for a new type of warfare.

They had 'Panzer divisions', equipped with tanks and armoured cars. With these they launched fast, sweeping attacks to break the enemy's defences. Supporting them were aircraft, specially used for ground attacks. This type of warfare was called Blitzkrieg – 'Lightning War' – and it soon defeated the Poles. The Poles were strong in cavalry but their armoured forces and aeroplanes were small in number.

D *Children were evacuated from big cities to the countryside to be safe from air raids. They each had a label, their clothes, and gas mask (in white box)*

Off to war again

Most of the campaign was over in less than three weeks. As the Poles were being pushed back, the Russians, carrying out the terms of their secret treaty with the Germans, came across the border from the east. On 1 October German troops fought their way into Warsaw and all resistance soon ended.

Poland, a nation with a proud history, was divided up between Germany and the USSR. Hitler was now able to turn his attention westward, to the frontier with France.

● The phoney war

In military terms the French and the British should have attacked Germany right from the start of the war. That would have caused trouble for Hitler on two fronts, but the chance was wasted. Instead, all was quiet on the Western Front, while the Germans proceeded to swallow up Poland in the east.

British and French commanders reckoned in the 1930s that any future war against Germany would again be slogged out mainly by infantry and artillery, as it had been in 1914. The French had built up defences along their frontier with Germany – millions of tons of concrete and steel had been used to form the Maginot Line, which they believed the Germans could not crack.

On their side, the Germans built a Siegfried Line, to prevent French attacks.

For months the two sides faced each other at the border. A British Expeditionary Force (BEF) went to France as their fathers had gone 25 years before. They served side by side with the French.

But nothing happened. Few shots were fired and the period became known as the 'phoney (false) war'. It lasted through a long, hard winter and people began to wonder when one side would make a move.

They found the answer in April 1940. ☐

Exercises

1 Order of events: these five events are mentioned in the chapter. Write them out in the correct order.
   (a) Russo-German pact signed
   (b) France declared war on Germany
   (c) Ribbentrop sent to Moscow for talks
   (d) the building of the Maginot Line
   (e) German forces invade Poland

2 Look at cartoon A.
   (a) Who is figure A and who is B?
   (b) Which symbols are they swallowing?
   (c) What is the meaning of the cartoon?

3 (a) Look at cartoon B. Explain what event the cartoon represents.

   (b) Explain why this event was so important.

4 What was the phoney war?

5 Look at picture D. Describe what you can see and say why this precaution was taken.

6 In 1939 each country had reasons for its action. Write a few sentences to explain each of the following points of view:
   (a) a German, on why Germany invaded Poland;
   (b) a Russian, on why the USSR signed a pact with Germany;
   (c) a Briton, on why Britain went to war.

(*A further question appears on page 219.*)

Blitzkrieg in the west

● Denmark and Norway

The 'phoney war' lasted into the spring of 1940. In fact, on 5 April Neville Chamberlain claimed in a speech that Hitler 'has missed the bus'. He was proved wrong only four days later. On 9 April German forces suddenly invaded Denmark and Norway. They quickly seized harbours and airfields, helped by some Norwegian Nazis.

By attacking Norway, Hitler hoped to safeguard the supplies of iron ore that reached Germany from Sweden. The response from Britain and France was too little and too late. A combined force of British and French troops went to help the Norwegians but they lacked good equipment. Also, they were heavily hit by attacks from the Luftwaffe.

In the early days of May the Germans had a tight hold on Denmark and Norway.

● Chamberlain out; Churchill in

What happened in Norway led to the overthrow of Neville Chamberlain. He obviously lacked the drive and toughness needed to lead the country in war. Eventually even some of his own party turned against him. One of them, during a debate, quoted Oliver Cromwell's words, used nearly 300 years before:

> **1** **You have sat too long here for any good you have been doing. Depart, I say, and let us have done with you. In the name of God, go!**

Only one man could now command the loyalty of all British people. This was Winston Churchill, who had been First Sea Lord. On 10 May he was summoned to Buckingham Palace where the king asked him to take on the task of leading the nation.

Churchill could not have been given the job at a more difficult time, because that very morning the Germans had launched an all-out Blitzkrieg on France.

● Blitzkrieg in the West

In the First World War the Germans used the Schlieffen Plan to try to reach Paris. In 1940 they devised a plan to cut off British and French armies in northern France.

First, they invaded Belgium and Holland, intending to draw British and French armies forward to help those countries. Then, from 12 May, they struck in the area of Sedan, at the top of the Maginot Line. Fierce strokes launched by tanks and Stuka dive-bombers soon cracked a way through the defences. By using fast-moving Panzer divisions the Germans advanced swiftly and reached targets they had never achieved in the First World War. General Rommel, commanding Panzers, later wrote:

> **2** **. . . On we went, at a steady speed, towards our objective. Every so often a quick glance at the map by a shaded light and a short wireless message to Divisional**

A *'All Behind You, Winston'*

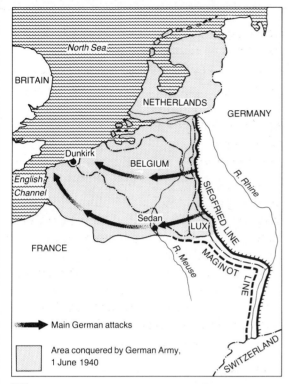

B *German 'Blitzkrieg', May–June 1940*

Labels on map: North Sea; BRITAIN; NETHERLANDS; GERMANY; Dunkirk; BELGIUM; R. Rhine; English Channel; SIEGFRIED LINE; Sedan; LUX; FRANCE; R. Meuse; MAGINOT LINE; SWITZERLAND. Legend: Main German attacks; Area conquered by German Army, 1 June 1940.

H.Q. to report the position and thus the success of the 25th Panzer Regiment. . . . We were through the Maginot Line! It was hardly conceivable. Twenty-two years before we had stood for four and a half long years before this self-same enemy and had won victory after victory and yet finally lost the war.

The Dutch and the Belgians were soon overwhelmed and surrendered, while the French and British armies were forced to retreat. The German left-hook reached the Channel coast on 20 May and it seemed that all of the British Expeditionary Force and many French divisions had been trapped and would have to surrender.

● Dunkirk

By 26 May the Germans had captured Boulogne and Calais and only one Channel port remained open. This was Dunkirk. The British army fell back on the town and, with French forces, held the Germans at bay. Then 'Operation Dynamo' began.

The operation had been planned for some time to meet this kind of emergency. Lord Gort, commanding the BEF, received a telegram from the British government:

> **3** . . . only course open to you may be to fight your way back to west where all beaches and ports east of Gravelines will be used for embarkation. Navy will provide fleet of ships and small boats and RAF would give full support. As withdrawal may have to begin very early, preliminary plans should be urgently prepared.

From 26 May to 4 June hundreds of boats, ranging from destroyers to motor launches evacuated the British army and thousands of their allies. The men were taken from docks and beaches. All the time, the ships were under heavy German attacks by land and sea.

Although losses of men and equipment were heavy, over 330,000 Allied soldiers were rescued by the efforts of the Royal Navy and the Merchant Navy. People spoke of the 'miracle of Dunkirk'.

Afterwards, the resistance of France gave way. Mussolini brought Italy into the war against France on 10 June, then eleven days later the French sought an armistice. Hitler arranged for it to be signed in the same railway coach used for the German surrender in 1918.

● The Battle of Britain

At that stage Britain stood alone against the

Axis powers. The Germans controlled the European coastline from the North Cape of Norway down to the Spanish border. Many people believed that Britain would have to surrender, or come to terms with Hitler. He wanted to make a deal, agreeing not to interfere with Britain's empire overseas if the British would not interfere with his gains in Europe.

In spite of its position, Britain decided to fight on, inspired by the leadership of Churchill. The Germans made plans to invade the island that was such a thorn in their flesh. 'Operation Sealion' was intended to land the triumphant German army on the British coast, from where they would advance to take London. But first, the RAF had to be defeated, to leave the skies free for the main attack. Goering's Luftwaffe was called in to do the job.

From July till October one of the greatest air battles ever known, 'The Battle of Britain', raged in the skies over and around southern England. Day after day formations of German bombers and fighters attacked airfields, factories and ports. They were met by the Spitfires and Hurricanes of the British Fighter Command, which were outnumbered but managed to hold off the enemy.

On 20 August Winston Churchill referred to the bravery of the pilots during a speech.

---

4 **The gratitude of every home in our island, in our Empire and indeed throughout the world . . . goes out to the British airmen. . . . Never in the field of human conflict was so much owed by so many to so few.**

By the end of September the Luftwaffe had failed to win and the proposed invasion was put off. To cut his losses, Goering ordered night bombing to be stepped up.

● **The blitz**
Heavy bombing raids were made on London by day and night. As the winter approached bombers flew from France, Holland and

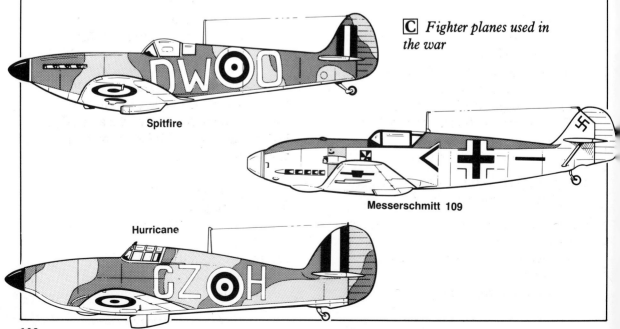

C *Fighter planes used in the war*

Spitfire

Messerschmitt 109

Hurricane

Blitzkrieg in the west

D *Two women emerge from their Anderson air-raid shelter after their houses have been destroyed in the blitz*

Belgium to attack the capital with high explosive and fire bombs. The raids were known as the 'Blitz' and tested civilians, but their spirit did not break.

The Germans then selected other cities to raid, especially ports and centres of industry. Among them were Bristol and Liverpool, Plymouth and Birmingham. One of the worst hit was Coventry where much of the city centre was devastated. The early months of 1941 brought no respite and the Blitz did not end until May when the nights grew shorter. Overall, 40,000 Britons were killed and 50,000 injured.

By then it was obvious that Britain was not going to give in to the power of aerial bombing. But Hitler had already lost interest in conquering the stubborn island. Instead, he was nearly ready to launch his next Blitzkrieg – in another part of Europe. □

Exercises

1 Copy and complete these sentences.
   (a) In April 1940 the Germans invaded Norway because. . . .
   (b) Neville Chamberlain lost support in Parliament because. . . .
   (c) The Maginot Line was. . . .
   (d) At Dunkirk thousands of Allied soldiers. . . .
   (e) 'Operation Sealion' was. . . .

2 Copy map B. Write a few sentences to explain what the map shows.

3 Re-arrange the following events in the correct order:
   (a) German forces reach the Channel coast;
   (b) France surrendered;
   (c) the end of the Blitz;
   (d) 'Operation Sealion' was put off;
   (e) the German invasion of Denmark.

4 Imagine you were a civilian in the Blitz. Write a letter to your relatives in the country telling them about the air raids. Use the pictures and information in the chapter to help you.

5 What was important about:
   (a) Blitzkrieg?
   (b) Winston Churchill becoming Prime Minister?
   (c) the evacuation from Dunkirk?
   (d) British success in the Battle of Britain?

Attack on Russia

● **Hitler and Russia**

Ever since writing *Mein Kampf* Hitler had made no secret of his hatred of the Russians. He only signed the non-aggression pact with them in August 1939 so that he could have a free hand to attack Poland. Early in 1941 he spoke to some German generals and showed his opinion of the Bolsheviks:

> **1** **The Communists never have been and never will be our friends. The fight which is about to begin is a war of extermination. If Germany does not embark upon it in this spirit she may well defeat the enemy but in thirty years from now they will once again rise up and confront her.**

Russia offered good prizes for the Germans. The vast lands of the east were the *lebensraum* (living space) needed for expansion. In the Ukraine were great wheatlands which could provide food for the people of Germany. And the oilfields of the Caucasus offered fuel for Hitler's military machine.

With so much at stake, he had no hesitation in preparing a giant military operation against an old enemy.

● **The Balkans campaign**

Mussolini wanted to follow Hitler's road to greatness by attacking other lands. He invaded Greece in October 1940, but the Italian army ran into early trouble. First of all they found it hard to advance, then suffered several defeats.

All this time Hitler was planning his invasion of Russia. His generals pressed ahead with preparations for beating the largest country in the world.

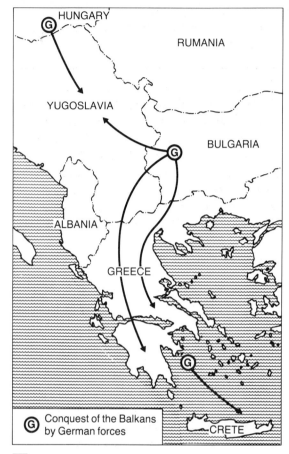

A *The Balkans campaign*

However, when the Italians ran into difficulties with the Greeks, Mussolini asked for German help. Hitler then obliged him for two reasons. First, he would be able to get his ally out of trouble. Second, he would be able to take more countries into his own control and have a long frontier for his forthcoming war with Russia.

First he persuaded, or forced, three countries – Bulgaria, Hungary and Rumania – to become allies of Germany. Yugoslavia refused to join so in April 1941 Hitler launched 'Operation Punishment'. The

German forces took about one week to overrun the Yugoslavs.

The methods to be used were discussed beforehand:

2 **Politically it is especially important that the blow against Yugoslavia is carried out with pitiless harshness and that the military destruction is done with lightning rapidity. . . . The main task of the Luftwaffe is to start as early as possible with the destruction of the Yugoslav air force ground installations and to destroy the capital city, Belgrade, in waves of attack.**

As the Germans reached Greece and crossed its frontiers British troops had already been sent from the Middle East to help the Greeks. But the power of the Luftwaffe once again assisted the Germans to a rapid victory. Some British and Commonwealth forces tried to hold out on the island of Crete, to the south of Greece, but the Germans launched a brilliant airborne assault and once again were victorious.

Nothing seemed able to stop Hitler's progress, as he was now master of the main part of Europe.

● **Barbarossa**

Barbarossa ('Red Beard') was the nickname of a mediaeval German emperor who fought against invaders from the east. His title became the codename for the planned attack on Russia. The invasion was to be a three-pronged drive, aiming at Leningrad in the north, Moscow in the centre and the Ukraine in the south.

The new phase of the war began on 22 June 1941 when the German army (the

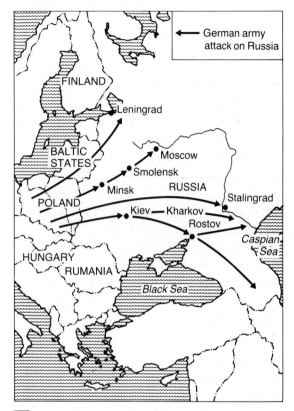

B *Operation Barbarossa, 1941*

Wehrmacht) began to hammer the Soviet forces. At first all went well for the Germans as Blitzkrieg tactics brought success. The Panzer divisions drove forward, closely supported by the Luftwaffe, which destroyed hundreds of Russian aircraft on the ground.

The British were pleased to have a new ally, even if they were Communists! Winston Churchill said: 'Any man or State who fights Nazidom will have our aid. . . .'

The Russians were soon in great difficulty, as one of their generals later pointed out:

3 **Railway junctions and lines of communication were being destroyed**

by German planes and diversionist groups. There was a shortage of wireless sets at army headquarters, nor did many of us know how to use them. . . . Orders and instructions were slow in arriving, and sometimes did not arrive at all . . . Sometimes on narrow roads, bottlenecks were formed by troops, artillery, motor vehicles and field kitchens, and then the Nazi planes had the time of their life. . . . Often our troops could not dig in, simply because they did not even have the simplest implements. Occasionally trenches had to be dug with helmets, since there were no spades.

Russians everywhere were told to use 'scorched earth' methods. This meant they destroyed buildings and crops as they retreated so that the advancing Germans

C *Heavy German infantry cross a river by using rubber crafts*

would find nothing to help them. Stalin ordered:

4 **Whenever units of the Red Army are forced to retreat, all railway rolling stock must be driven away. The enemy must not be left a single engine, or a single railway truck, and not a pound of bread nor a pint of oil.**

D *'Scorched earth': the Russians destroyed these submarines so that they could not be used by the Germans*

Attack on Russia

By September the Germans were approaching Leningrad in the north. In the south they had captured the city of Kiev. Their main prize, Moscow, was not very far away on the central front. They felt that victory was near because they had taken over one million Russian prisoners. However, there were several things they had not allowed for. One was the vast number of men that Russia could call on. Another was the immense size of the country, so that even an advance of 50 miles did not carry the Germans very far.

● **The coming of winter**

The Russians fought desperately for their homeland and their stubborn resistance slowed the Germans down as winter approached. The cold of the Russian steppe lands was far more bitter than anything many of the German soldiers had ever known in their lives before. One of them wrote:

5 Those Arctic blasts that had taken us by surprise in our protected positions scythed [cut] through our attacking troops. In a couple of days there were one hundred thousand casualties from frost-bite alone. . . . A couple of days later our winter clothing arrived. There was just enough for each company to be issued with four heavy fur-lined greatcoats and four pairs of felt-lined boots. Four sets of winter clothing for each company! Sixteen greatcoats and sixteen pairs of winter boots to be shared among a battalion of eight hundred men!

Equipment froze, so that vehicles could not be used and aircraft could not take off to support the army. Men froze to death. Then, right at the end of the year the Russians launched a counter-attack that pushed the Germans back from their capital.

Hitler's plan for a quick victory had failed. □

Exercises

1 Correctly match up these pairs and copy them into your book.
   (a) living space (i) 'Red Beard'
   (b) Molotov (ii) 'My Struggle'
   (c) Bulgaria, Hungary, Rumania (iii) *Lebensraum*
   (d) Barbarossa (iv) allies of Germany
   (e) *Mein Kampf* (v) Soviet Foreign Minister

2 Explain the meaning of:
   (a) *lebensraum;*
   (b) 'Operation Punishment';
   (c) Barbarossa;
   (d) 'scorched earth';
   (e) stubborn resistance.

3 Why, according to the Russian general's evidence (document 3), were the Russians unable to stop the Germans?

4 Why did the Russians destroy parts of their own country?

5 You are a German soldier. You have been captured by the Russians. Write describing your experiences from the invasion in June to your capture in December 1941. Use all the evidence in the chapter.

Japan and Pearl Harbor

A *A British cartoonist's view of Japan's 'rising sun'*

● The lead-up to war

In the 1930s Japan was the strongest power in Asia and was angry that some western nations owned territories in the Far East. A Japanese officer gave his views on the subject:

> **1** 450 million natives of the Far East live under the domination of less than 800,000 whites. Once you set foot on the enemy's territories you will see for yourselves, only too clearly, just what this oppression by the white men means. Imposing, splendid buildings look down from the summits of mountains or hills on to the tiny thatched huts of the natives. Money squeezed from the blood of Asians maintains these small white minorities in their luxurious mode of life – or disappears to the respective home countries. Is this really God's will?

All through the 1930s Japan's aggressive policy towards China had worried nations like Britain and the USA. What worried them also was that Japan had allied itself with Germany and Italy, to make the Anti-Comintern Pact.

Talks were held between the Americans and the Japanese in 1941 to try to sort out these difficulties. But the meetings brought little result as neither side would give way.

On 17 August 1941 the Americans sent a warning note to the Japanese government:

> **2** If the Japanese Government takes any further steps in pursuance of a policy . . . of military domination by force or threat of force of neighbouring countries, the Government of the United States will be compelled to take immediately any and all steps which it may deem necessary toward safeguarding . . . the safety and security of the United States.

● Japanese preparations

The Japanese leader, General Tojo, decided to take the risk of attacking his main opponent, the United States. If the American fleet in the Pacific could be put out of action nothing would be able to stop the Japanese advance. Japan would have the kind of success in Asia that Germany had gained in Europe. So, under top security, a Task Force was prepared. Its main weapon was carrier-borne aircraft, flown from six aircraft carriers, which practised time after time in making attacks on ships.

At the end of November 1941 this Task Force left Japan and sailed in secrecy hundreds of miles across the Pacific. Their target was the main American naval base at Pearl Harbor, in the Hawaiian Islands.

All this time the Japanese kept up their talks with the American Government.

● **Pearl Harbor**

On the morning of Sunday 7 December 1941 the American Pacific Fleet lay at anchor in Pearl Harbor. The USA was at peace and the crews were waking or resting before starting the day. On nearby aerodromes scores of planes had been parked in the open.

Suddenly and without warning the sky was filled with dozens of Japanese aircraft which swept in to attack ships, grounded planes, oil tanks and buildings.

The aeroplanes came from the Japanese Task Force which had approached

undetected to within 300 miles of Pearl Harbor before launching the attack. The first wave roared in just before 8 a.m. and over the next two hours eight American battleships were sunk or heavily damaged, 188 planes destroyed and 2,400 men killed.

The surprise was so great that some Americans having breakfast were totally puzzled:

---

3 **Then a neighbour rushed in.**
'**The Japanese are bombing Oahu!**' **she cried.**
'**Oh, no, it's only a practice. Don't get excited,**' **we said.**
'**If you don't believe it,**' **she exclaimed,** '**turn on your radio and hear for yourselves!**'
I did. '**Keep calm, everybody. Oahu is under attack. This is no joke. The emblem of the Rising Sun has been seen on the wings of the attacking planes.**'

B *The USS* Arizona *after the Japanese attack on Pearl Harbor, 7 December 1941. Over 2000 Americans were killed*

Later, the Japanese declared war on the USA. The whole balance of power in the Far East had been changed at a stroke. The war had become world-wide and America, the most powerful of all nations, had been drawn into the fight.

The American President, Franklin D. Roosevelt, spoke next day to Congress:

4 **Yesterday, December 7, 1941 – a date which will live in infamy – the United States of America was suddenly and deliberately attacked by naval and air forces of the Empire of Japan. The United States was at peace with that nation and . . . was still in conversation with its government and its Emperor, looking forward toward the maintenance of peace in the Pacific. . . .**

C *A newspaper headline tells of the events at Pearl Harbor*

● Japan cuts loose

At the same time, the Japanese invaded territories of the Dutch and British Empires in the Far East. Landing on the coast of Malaya they advanced rapidly towards Britain's greatest base in the Far East – the port of Singapore. British and Commonwealth forces fought back but were neither trained nor equipped for jungle warfare, at which Japanese troops excelled.

The British retreated to Singapore which they hoped to defend like a great fort. However, by February 1942 the city was crowded with thousands of refugees as well as troops. Japanese soldiers attacked powerfully while their air force controlled the skies and bombed heavily. Soon the water supplies were destroyed. The British Commander-in-Chief decided to surrender.

On one day 80,000 British and Commonwealth troops became prisoners-of-war. No other day in the whole of history has proved to be such a disaster for the British army. All over the Far East, local people noticed how an Asian race had decisively defeated Europeans and Americans. That was a lesson they didn't forget.

● The Battle of Midway

Over the following months nothing appeared able to halt the progress of Japanese victories. They sank ships, overran countries and captured islands at will. They even dropped bombs on northern Australia. Their troops were fighting in Burma and near the borders of India.

They had prepared thoroughly for the Pacific War. Over the vast distances there the aircraft carrier became the new 'Queen of the Seas' – and Japan had built many of them.

The first halt to Japanese success did not

D British officers, carrying flags, march with Japanese officers to discuss the British surrender at Singapore, February 1942

come until June 1942. Then, at the Battle of Midway, the Americans hit back. A force including four Japanese carriers met a fleet containing three American carriers. During the ensuing battle one American carrier was sunk. But the Japanese lost all four of theirs – a stunning blow to suffer.

Later, a Japanese officer commented:

> 5 **The Japanese Navy, flushed with victory after the Hawaiian attack, was unaware that operational secrets had leaked out. And so we fell into the trap laid by the enemy, who was forewarned of our movements. A severe defeat followed for the Japanese. Midway was a crucial battle which reversed the whole position in the Pacific War.**

At last there was a glimmer of hope for the Americans and their allies in the Far East. ☐

Exercises

1 Correctly match these dates and events and copy them into your book.
  (a) Battle of Midway   *August 1941*
  (b) Fall of Singapore   *7 December 1941*
  (c) Pearl Harbor   *June 1942*
  (d) USA declares war on Japan
                February 1942
  (e) USA warns Japan   *8 December 1941*

2 Copy and complete these sentences.
  (a) The Japanese disliked Western nations in the Far East because. . . .
  (b) The main weapon of the Japanese Task Force at Pearl Harbor was. . . .
  (c) At Pearl Harbor the US Pacific Fleet was. . . .
  (d) For the British, the surrender at Singapore was. . . .
  (e) The first battle in the Pacific to halt the Japanese was. . . .

3 Look at cartoon A. What do you think *is* the cartoonist's view of Japan's rising sun?

4 Using the information in this chapter and that on pages 80–83 explain why Britain and the USA were worried about Japan.

5 (a) Why did Japan attack Pearl Harbor?
  (b) What happened at Pearl Harbor?
  (c) What were the results of this attack?

(*A further question appears on page 219.*)

Axis powers at their peak

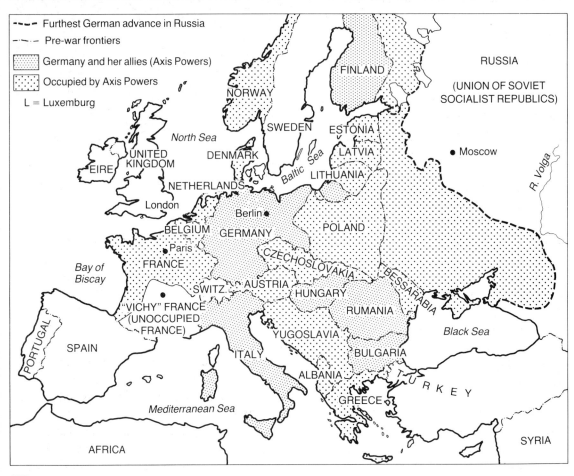

A *The Axis powers at their peak in Europe, 1942*

● **The position in summer 1942**

If you made a graph to show the success of the Axis powers – Germany, Italy and Japan – in the Second World War, you would notice that the peak was reached in 1942. For several months then it appeared that they were going to win and most of the world would fall under their control.

In the Far East the Japanese quickly set up a new empire for themselves. It stretched from the mainland of Asia, through the islands of the Dutch East Indies, down to New Guinea. Also included were many small Pacific islands. They gave this empire the grand title of 'The Greater Asia Co-Prosperity Sphere', which made people think that the Japanese would bring them wealth. But their rule was harsh and the inhabitants of those areas soon found that Japan wanted their riches for itself.

Germany and Italy governed much of Europe and a large area of North Africa. Hitler claimed that he would set up a German state to last a thousand years. By the middle of 1942 his claim seemed justified. Germany had formed a kind of European empire, where it was the chief nation. Most others had either joined or been defeated. There were few neutrals.

● North Africa

When Italy entered the war in 1940, fighting started in North Africa. Both Britain and Italy had empires there so their troops fought against each other in Libya and Egypt. The Italians suffered defeats and Hitler had to send Germans to strengthen them. One German general had a low opinion of his Italian allies, which he told Hitler:

B *An Italian cartoon published during the early part of the war*

---

1 **When he asked me what I thought of them, I retorted: 'I've seen them on the battlefield, not merely in the Officers' Mess.' I told Hitler, 'One British soldier is better than twelve Italians.' I added: 'The Italians are good workers, but they are not fighters. They don't like gunfire.'**

Hitler despatched the Afrika Korps, under the leadership of General Rommel who soon showed himself to be a fine commander. Several victories were won over the British. By the late summer of 1942 Rommel was poised to strike at the Suez Canal in Egypt. He aimed to cut Britain's link with the Far East and capture oil supplies in the Middle East.

● The power of Russia and America

Although the Axis powers looked unbeatable at that time, there were two factors that were to count against them in the future.

One was the immense size of Russia. Napoleon had overlooked that fact in 1812 when he invaded the country and captured Moscow. The Russians merely fell back and waited – then defeated him. Hitler had not

even taken the capital. The Russians withdrew, taking whole factories eastwards, beyond the Ural Mountains. There they were out of reach of German troops and produced munitions for the millions of Russians who came forward to defend their land.

The second factor was the power of the USA. Soon after Pearl Harbor Hitler declared war on the Americans, which meant that he was up against the world's greatest industrial power. While his own industries were under attack from the air, the USA turned out enormous numbers of tanks and guns, ships and aircraft.

● Inside Europe – the Jews

The Nazi Empire in occupied Europe was very efficient. Officials were sent to all the defeated countries to control local industry and farming. The inhabitants had to provide for the German war machine as well as for themselves.

Hitler also put into practice his feelings about how the Jews should be dealt with. The task was passed over to the SS, who were under the leadership of Heinrich Himmler. They called a conference in January 1942 to discuss what they termed

'The Jewish Problem'. Afterwards a report announced:

---

1 In the course of the final solution Europe is to be combed through from west to east. . . . The evacuated Jews will at first be conveyed in train-loads to transit ghettoes [collecting areas] whence they will be further transported to the east. . . .

Therefore at the same time Reinhard Heydrich, nicknamed 'Der Henke' (the hangman), was given the title of 'Commissioner for the Preparation of the Final Solution of the European Jewish Problem'.

Soon after Hitler came to power in 1933, concentration camps had been set up in Germany. They were a hell on earth for the inmates whose 'crimes' varied from theft to

C *Bodies laid out for burial at an extermination camp*

being a gipsy, from speaking against the Nazis to being a Jew. But these would not serve to solve 'The Jewish Problem'. For that, extermination camps were built in Poland, the most infamous being at Auschwitz, Treblinka and Maidenek. Jews were herded together from all the occupied countries of Europe, from France in the west to Russia in the east and were sent in hundreds of trains for 're-settlement'. Most of them believed that they were going to a new life. Instead, they were put to death. The fastest, cheapest, most efficient way was found to be by gassing; the bodies were then burned.

The whole exercise had to become a paying business. An SS officer worked out the costs of keeping, then killing fellow human beings:

---

2 . . . The hiring out of concentration camp inmates to industrial enterprises yields an average daily return of six to eight marks from which 70 Pfennigs must be deducted for food and clothing. Assuming a camp inmate's life expectation of nine months, we multiply the sum by 270; the total is 1,431 marks. The profit can be increased by rational utilization of the corpse, i.e., by means of gold fillings, clothing, valuables, etc, but on the other hand every corpse represents a loss of two marks, which is the cost of cremation.

Estimates have been made of the effects of German policy on the Jewish race. In the countries controlled by Hitler, approximately nine million Jews were living at the start of the war. In six years, some six million had been put to death. This was one of the greatest crimes ever known in the whole of history.

Axis powers at their peak

D *Men of the French Resistance. The 'Cross of Lorraine' seen on one man's armband was their symbol. Men and women in occupied countries tried to free themselves of German control. Capture inevitably meant death*

● **The resistance**

Even though Hitler had defeated a whole string of nations, some of their people fought back. They did this through what was called the resistance movement, or the underground. Its members carried out acts of sabotage, like blowing up munitions trains or burning war supplies. All of these movements had secret radio links with their own countrymen who were continuing the fight from Britain. They passed on information about troop movements and did all they could to hinder the Germans.

Anyone caught taking part in these activities could expect little mercy from the Gestapo, the German secret police. Many of the heroic deeds of these brave people are still remembered in their homelands. ☐

Exercises

1 Copy and complete these sentences using words from the **word list**.
  (a) The 'Greater Asia Co– . . . Sphere' was just another . . . for the . . . Empire.
  (b) Hitler . . . that the . . . State would last for a . . . years.
  (c) General . . . commanded the . . . Korps.
  (d) Thousands of . . . were killed in . . . camps.
  (e) People in . . . countries fought back at the . . . through . . . movements.

> **word list:** occupied; Jews; Prosperity; claimed; extermination; German; Germans; resistance; thousand; name; Japanese; Rommel; Afrika

2 Look at cartoon B. To which countries do soldiers 1, 2 and 3 belong? To which countries do soldiers A, B and C belong and what is happening to them?

3 Consult map A and make a list of those European countries occupied by the Germans and their allies in 1942.

4 Read document 1. What was the German general's view of the Italians?

5 How did the Germans try to solve 'The Jewish Problem'?

6 Imagine you were in the resistance movement and now, many years later, you are writing your autobiography. Describe the part of your life when you were in the resistance and explain what you did.

The defeat of Germany

A *Russian machine-gunners during the fight to drive the Germans out of Warsaw, Poland in 1944.*

● **Three turning points**

The Axis powers reached their highest point of success in mid-1942. Then came three battles which changed the course of the war and they started to decline.

The first was the Battle of Midway in the Far East. The Japanese had to win it to continue their advances, but they failed. Afterwards their fortunes changed.

The other two battles affected Germany and Italy. The first was at El Alamein, in Egypt, where British forces defeated the Afrika Korps in October 1942. The second was at Stalingrad, in southern Russia, where the German Sixth Army was destroyed a few months later.

After those three victories the Allies – Americans, Russians and British – started on the road to final victory.

● **North Africa**

The Afrika Korps under General Rommel hoped to reach the Suez Canal in Egypt by late 1942 and were halted only fifty miles from Cairo. But a new commander, General Montgomery, was appointed to the British Eighth Army and he attacked on 23 October.

After a terrific barrage of artillery fire came the main battle of El Alamein. The Afrika Korps cracked and retreated. They moved quickly westwards with the Eighth Army on their heels. In Britain, people were overjoyed and church bells rang in celebration. Churchill later commented:

1 **It may almost be said, 'Before Alamein we never had a victory. After Alamein we never had a defeat.'**

Then American and British forces landed in French North Africa – Algeria and Morocco – so the Germans were caught between them and the Eighth Army coming from the east. They made a last ditch stand in Tunisia, but by May 1943 Tunis was captured and 250,000 Axis troops were taken prisoner. That was another blow to Nazi hopes.

● **Stalingrad and after**
In summer 1942 the German Sixth Army attacked in southern Russia, aiming to capture Stalingrad. The Russians were determined to hold the city, vital to their defences. By early autumn the Germans had fought their way into the city, but the Russians clung on ferociously to every street and house. Winter arrived with over forty degrees of frost!

Soon the Germans were trapped and gradually the Russians ground them down. In January 1943 the remaining 90,000 surrendered. This was one of the greatest military victories – and disasters – of all time.

A German general described the toughness and determination of Russian soldiers:

2 **The Russian soldier values his own life no more than those of his comrades. To step on walls of dead, composed of the bodies of his former friends and companions, makes not the slightest impression on him . . . without so much as twinkling an eyelid he stolidly continues the attack or stays put in the position he has been told to defend. Life is not precious to him. He is immune to the most incredible hardships, and does not even appear to notice them; he seems equally indifferent to bombs and shells.**

After this the Germans were never able to gain great victories again. The Russians started to push their enemy back.

● **Italy**
After the Axis forces had been driven out of North Africa, British and American troops followed up by attacking Sicily, then Italy. Churchill had called this area 'the soft underbelly of the Axis' and he believed in tackling the weaker enemy first. After that, he believed, Germany might find it impossible to carry on with the war.

B *The D-Day landings, June 1944. Allied troops began the liberation of France*

The Italians soon collapsed. Their government arrested Mussolini and made peace with the Allies. Soon afterwards Hitler sent commandoes who rescued his fellow dictator. Then he poured German troops into Italy, where a hard campaign followed. British, Commonwealth and American troops slowly inched their way northward towards their final target – Germany.

● **Germany's position**
By late 1943 Germany was on the downhill road to defeat, being attacked from four directions. In the east, the Russians were starting to roll back German armies from their lands. In the south, British and American forces were advancing slowly up through Italy. In the west, a vast army was gathering in Britain, waiting to invade France and push the Germans back there. In the skies over Germany day and night bombing were being stepped up.

● **The Russian advance**
All along the front line, stretching for hundreds of miles, Russian attacks probed German positions and forced them to retreat. Nothing that Hitler did could prevent this because he lacked the men and equipment to halt the Russian steamroller.

Thus the Germans fell back, destroying, robbing, burning, slaughtering as they went.

Throughout 1944 the Russians pushed on, driving the Germans out of Hungary, Poland and Czechoslovakia. At the start of 1945 they were at the borders of Germany.

● **D-Day**
On 6 June 1944 – 'D-Day' – thousands of British, American and Commonwealth troops began landing on the coast of Normandy. This was the great Allied attack to drive the Germans back in the west. After

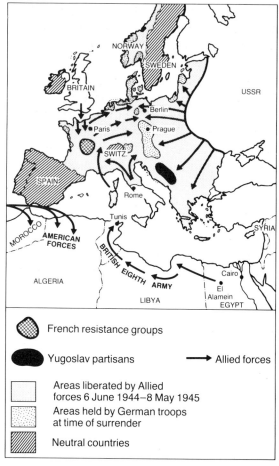

French resistance groups

Yugoslav partisans   → Allied forces

Areas liberated by Allied forces 6 June 1944–8 May 1945

Areas held by German troops at time of surrender

Neutral countries

C *The defeat of Germany*

fierce fighting on the beaches, they gained a foothold in France and the liberation had begun.

The BBC announced:

> **3** **Under the command of General Eisenhower, Allied naval forces supported by strong air forces began landing Allied armies this morning on the coast of France.**

The Allies fought their way across France, pushing the Germans before them. Paris was

The defeat of Germany

liberated and by the end of 1944 they had driven the Germans out of France. The German frontier lay close ahead.

● **The end of the war in Europe**

Early in 1945 Germany was caught in a trap. On one side the Allied forces crossed the Rhine on 29 March and swept forward. On the Eastern Front the masses of the Russian army crossed the River Elbe and aimed for the heartland of their enemy. At the Yalta conference, held in February 1945, the Allied leaders, Churchill, Roosevelt and Stalin, had agreed that the Russians would be allowed to reach Berlin first.

At the end of April Mussolini, the Italian Fascist leader, was killed as he tried to escape to Switzerland. His ideas of a modern Roman Empire died with him.

Hitler was trapped in the Bunker, his headquarters in Berlin. As the Russians arrived he committed suicide on 30 April.

Soon afterwards the Germans asked for an armistice.

Tuesday 8 May was declared VE Day – 'Victory in Europe Day'. All over the Allied world there were scenes of wild rejoicing in towns and cities, villages and hamlets. Most people could hardly believe that the war was over.

In their quiet moments they remembered that there was one enemy still to beat. ☐

Exercises

1 Copy and complete these sentences.
  (a) At Stalingrad the German Sixth Army. . . .
  (b) The Battle of El Alamein was fought in. . . .
  (c) In 1944 the Russians pushed the Germans. . . .
  (d) D-Day was. . . .
  (e) In 1945 both Hitler and Mussolini . . . .

2 Copy and complete this paragraph using the words in the **word list.**
  After 1943 the . . . armies were slowly . . . back. Russian forces advanced from the . . . . American and British forces . . . in . . . in June 1944 and began a slow . . . forward from the. . . . At length, early in . . ., . . . armies entered Germany, . . . committed suicide and the war in . . . ended.

> **word list:** France; rolled; Allied; Europe; east; Hitler; German; 1945; west; landed; drive

3 Explain:
  (a) why the victory at El Alamein was so important;
  (b) why the Germans wanted to capture Stalingrad;
  (c) why the Allies invaded Italy.

4 Using picture B, map C and other information prepare a short radio report on the D-Day landings.

5 Copy map C into your book. Underneath, write a few sentences to explain its meaning.

War at sea and in the air

● Introduction

Fighting on the high seas started on the first day of hostilities and went on till the last. A study of the map shows why the sea was so important to Britain and its allies. For Germany it was less important because men could be transported across land to the main battlefronts.

● Submarines

In the First World War German submarines had successfully attacked Britain's shipping lanes. They used the same tactics again from 1939, with few surface ships but many U-boats. In the year 1940 alone, just over one thousand vessels were sunk, 60% of them by submarines.

After the USA entered the war submarine attacks grew fiercer. U-boats were of bigger and better design and in 1942 over six million tons of Allied ships were sunk by submarines on all waters.

To meet the threat, ships and aircraft were fitted with special undersea detection apparatus. Once they had located the submarines, depth charges were dropped. It was a cat-and-mouse game between U-boats and their pursuers, with each side taking turns in gaining the upper hand.

Not till the last days of the war was the submarine menace beaten.

● The Mediterranean campaign

When Italy went to war in 1940, Mussolini controlled a large fleet, but failed to use it well. The Royal Navy showed aggression and won several battles. At Taranto in November 1940 British torpedo bombers sank several Italian ships. They showed what aircraft could do to warships, a point noted particularly by some Japanese admirals.

Later, there were big battles as convoys

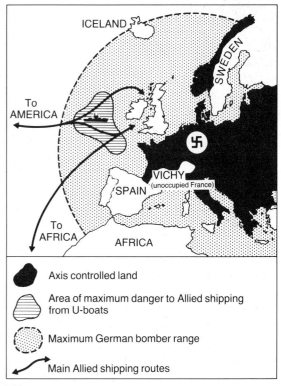

A *The Battle of the Atlantic*

Map legend:
- Axis controlled land
- Area of maximum danger to Allied shipping from U-boats
- Maximum German bomber range
- Main Allied shipping routes

carried supplies to Malta, a small British base in the Mediterranean.

● The Pacific War

The Japanese surprised the world with the power of their weapons and ships in 1941–2. In particular they saw the value of using aircraft carriers in attack. The day of the big-gun battleship was almost over and this was proved early on in the war. At Pearl Harbor, most of the American Pacific Fleet was put out of action. Three days later, two British battleships, *Prince of Wales* and *Repulse* were caught without fighter cover off the coast of Malaya. Both were sunk by Japanese bombers.

The great battles of the Pacific became

B *German civilians wander through the ruins of their town after an Allied bombing raid. The Luftwaffe was unable to give air protection to the Reich.*

contests where the two sides seldom met at sea. Instead, they played a kind of chess game at a range of several hundred miles, with heavily protected aircraft-carriers as their chief pieces. From these 'flat-tops' dive bombers and torpedo bombers were flown off to attack the distant enemy, while fighters were sent up to circle the fleet as protection.

● Russian convoys
Britain and the USA sent supplies and equipment to their ally, Russia, in convoys which sailed round the north of Norway, into the Arctic Ocean. Apart from fighting

German U-boats and bombers they also had to contend with some of the worst weather in the world.

Heavy losses were suffered by ships in those waters. But in spite of this, large quantities of supplies reached Russia through the ports of Archangel and Murmansk.

● How countries used their planes
Aircraft had been so well developed by 1939 that thousands were used in the war. Sometimes a whole campaign was decided mainly by air power.

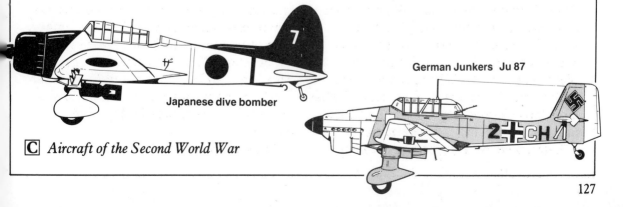

Japanese dive bomber

German Junkers Ju 87

C *Aircraft of the Second World War*

War at sea and in the air

The Germans had the biggest air force in 1939. The Luftwaffe had been built up particularly to work closely with ground forces, hitting anything that stood in the way of their troops. As a result, in the Battle of Britain and the Blitz the Germans had no really heavy bombers to strike at targets. Later in the war the Germans had to build up a large fighter force to defend their homeland.

The RAF was under great pressure during the Battle of Britain. Later, Bomber Command was used to raid targets in Germany. Thousands of heavy bombers were used for that purpose. The raids were usually made at night, to gain the protection of darkness. This, however, led to some inaccurate bombing.

The Russians built thousands of planes, mainly to support their troops on the Eastern Front. They made few big bomber raids on Germany.

The Japanese air force was best known for what it achieved in the war at sea. Many of the early victories scored by Japan were gained by its airmen.

The American air force was built up to become the largest of any nation. In Europe, American heavy bombers were used in daylight attacks of German targets. At first they suffered big losses, but then long-range fighters escorted them and they ranged freely over Germany in the closing stages of the war.

● Bombing Germany

In June 1941 Winston Churchill proclaimed:

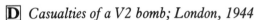

D *Casualties of a V2 bomb; London, 1944*

War at sea and in the air

1 **We shall bomb Germany by day as well as by night . . . casting . . . a heavier discharge of bombs, and making the German people taste and gulp each month a sharper dose of the miseries they have showered upon mankind.**

From 1942 the RAF bombed Germany heavily by night and the US Air Force by day. As a result a number of German towns and cities were devastated. In return, the air forces suffered many losses.

Since the war, the effects of bombing have been examined carefully. Was it worthwhile to attack cities, or should targets like oil supplies and transport have been concentrated on instead?

● **Jets and rockets**
Both Germany and Britain pioneered experiments on jet aircraft. Also, the Germans introduced two 'revenge weapons'. They were the V1, a pilotless flying bomb and the V2, a rocket which could travel at over 5,400 kph. Nothing could stop that! □

Exercises

1 Copy and complete the following sentences using words from the **word list.**
  (a) The . . . was intended to work . . . with German . . . forces.
  (b) The . . . used aircraft carriers in. . . .
  (c) Convoys of . . . reached . . . after sailing through the . . . Sea.
  (d) US bombers made many . . . raids over. . . .
  (e) The Germans introduced . . . flying bombs called . . . and rockets called . . . .

> **word list:** Japanese; V1; ground; Russia; Germany; V2; Luftwaffe; supplies; attack; closely; Arctic; daylight; pilotless

2 Read the chapter again then copy and complete these sentences.
  (a) The sea was very important to Britain because. . . .
  (b) After the USA entered the war. . . .
  (c) The Germans had the biggest air force in. . . .

  (d) Britain and the USA supplied Russia by. . . .
  (e) Germany's aerial revenge weapons were. . . .

3 Make a chart showing how each of the following nations used its airforce:
  (a) USA;
  (b) Germany;
  (c) Russia;
  (d) Britain;
  (e) Japan.

4 (a) What do you think was the reason for Churchill's decison to bomb Germany?
  (b) What were the results of this policy?

5 Imagine that you are (a) a German naval commander in 1939 talking about ways of attacking British shipping. Make a list of the different methods you would suggest; (b) a British naval commander having to protect merchant ships. Make a list of methods you would suggest. Use all the information in the chapter.

The Japanese retreat

● **Introduction**

For the first months of the Pacific War the Japanese success never failed. They occupied large areas of the old empires of Britain and Holland in the Far East and captured American-held islands. They cut Allied supply routes through Burma into China. Their soldiers pressed on towards the frontiers of India. The Philippines, Borneo, Java, Sumatra, all fell to them. They even bombed the city of Darwin in Northern Australia. In the north Pacific they captured the Aleutian Islands. Their men fought in New Guinea.

But they had taken on the world's strongest industrial power. The result was that the Americans slowly but surely built up their strength and started to press the Japanese back. In Burma, British forces held up Japanese soldiers who were trying to invade India.

● **Island hopping**

The US forces used the policy of 'island hopping' in their advance. This meant that they leapfrogged from island to island. Sometimes they by-passed enemy-held positions and kept up the pressure aimed at their final objective – Japan.

This was a costly process because Japanese soldiers fought with a ferocity and determination that surprised American troops. They did not fear death and believed that surrender was dishonourable. One of them noted in his diary:

> **1** **There were about thirty of us wounded soldiers left in the cave. Those who could move assisted others. They all shouted 'Long live the Emperor' before leaving the world. My friend Nagasaka stabbed his throat with a knife, but he did** not succeed in killing himself. I finally decided to assist him so that he could rest in peace. I stabbed my own brother in arms. Who could understand my horrible predicament? I still have two hand grenades; one to destroy myself and one for the enemy.

As the Americans captured islands their engineers rapidly built airfields. Then warplanes were flown in to cover the next stage of the advance.

A *Japanese soldiers with their British prisoners. To surrender was, to the Japanese, a cowardly act and they showed little mercy for their prisoners*

The island battles lasted from 1942 until 1945.

The US forces suffered very heavy casualties in those battles because of stubborn Japanese resistance – at Iwojima (Feb.–March 1945) they had 20,000 casualties; at Okinawa there were twice that number.

● Another enemy

Soldiers fighting in the Far East had two other 'enemies' to contend with. These were climate and disease. In New Guinea, as an American pointed out, there were heat, humidity, rains, malaria, dengue fever, blackwater fever, dysentery, ulcers, typhus, hookworm, ringworm, mosquitoes, flies, leeches, ants and fleas. That was *before* fighting the Japanese! He went on to say that 'disease is an unrelenting foe'.

A British officer involved in the Burma campaign mentioned:

> **2 At this time the sick rate of men evacuated from their units rose to over twelve per thousand per day. A simple calculation showed me that in a matter of months at this rate my army would have melted away.**

● The Burma campaign

After capturing Singapore in February 1942 the Japanese invaded Burma and pushed on towards India, 'the richest jewel in the British Crown'. Fierce jungle fighting followed which showed the toughness of the Japanese soldiers. A British soldier of the Fourteenth Army recounted:

> **3 One particular incident impressed itself upon me – a British officer in the bayonet charge spared and passed a wounded man, who immediately shot him dead from behind. The man was at once killed by the officer's batman [attendant], who was in turn shot by yet another casualty lying, apparently helpless. 'Never pass a wounded Jap,' was now on everybody's lips. 'And one round's no good unless it kills them outright.'**

After that, the 'Forgotten Army,' as the Fourteenth called themselves, slowly drove enemy armies back out of Burma. By the end of the war they had killed 190,000 Japanese, more than were killed anywhere else in the Far East.

● Prisoners-of-war

Thousands of Allied servicemen were taken

prisoner in the Far East during the war. They were despised by the Japanese, who believed that a soldier should die rather than surrender. Terrible conditions were experienced by prisoners-of-war, who were starved, and beaten, over-worked and tortured.

As the Allied forces began to advance and release prisoners, there was great anger over what had been done to these men. Their Japanese and Korean guards had killed or injured thousands who had been fit when they went into captivity. But after months of harsh and cruel treatment, lack of medical care and barely sufficient food to stay alive, some were no more than walking skeletons.

● Kamikazes

The Japanese military code regarded the Emperor as a god. It was an honour to die for him and for the homeland. As Allied forces closed in on Japan several thousand Japanese airmen volunteered for 'kamikaze'

B *A Kamikaze pilot guides his plane into an American aircraft carrier* **C** *(Inset) The result of his suicidal action*

The Japanese retreat

missions. These airmen were 'suicide pilots' who took off in aircraft filled with high explosive. When they found a suitable target, such as an Allied ship or a military base, they would put their plane into a crash-dive. By killing themselves they hoped to destroy hundreds of their enemies.

By the end of the war over 4,600 Japanese pilots had been lost on suicide missions. And in Japan another 5,000 were waiting for any Allied attempts to invade their country.

● **The decline of Japan**
Early in 1945 the Americans had captured a number of islands within air-striking distance of Japan. From these, B29 Superfortress bombers launched heavy raids on Japanese cities, raining bombs on factories and supplies. Also, they dropped thousands of incendiary bombs to cause vast fires among the closely packed and lightly built houses of residential areas.

In one raid on 9 March 1945, 330 Superfortresses attacked Tokyo, destroying over a quarter of a million houses.

Japan's economy was badly hit. Oil supplies grew small, while the production of weapons slowed down disastrously. People suffered from food shortages and US submarines sank many Japanese ships. Gradually, Japan's war effort ran into greater difficulties.

Yet there were still many Japanese who were prepared to fight fanatically to the death when the expected Allied invasion fleets arrived. Estimates were made that up to two million Allied servicemen would be casualties in this operation. □

Exercises

1 Arrange these events in the order of happening:
   (a) 330 Superfortresses attacked Tokyo;
   (b) Japanese invade Burma;
   (c) capture of Singapore;
   (d) the 'Forgotten Army' drove enemy armies out of Burma;
   (e) the Battle of Iwojima.

2 In picture A you can see British soldiers surrendering to the Japanese. Refer to document 1 and 'Prisoners-of-war' and:
   (a) give a Japanese soldier's view of surrender;
   (b) describe how the Japanese treated their prisoners.

3 Describe in your own words in a few sentences the meaning of 'island hopping'.

4 You have been asked to write a report for the Prime Minister, Winston Churchill, on the Burma Campaign. You may wish to use the following points:
   (a) the extent of Japanese occupation in 1942;
   (b) fighting in the jungle;
   (c) the success of the Fourteenth Army;
   (d) prisoners of war.

5 Look at pictures B and C and read the paragraph on 'Kamikazes'. Explain why Japanese pilots took this action and describe the results.

The atom bomb

● **The background**

During the Second World War both the Allies and the Germans made experiments to develop a new type of bomb. It was not a weapon filled with high explosive. Instead, it used atomic power created from uranium. This was capable of producing a gigantic explosion, because millions of atoms were broken down all together.

Germany's experiments made some progress but by the time of the country's defeat in May 1945 its scientists had produced no bomb.

The Allies, on the other hand, had been successful.

● **The Allies prepare**

The experiments and development were carried out in the USA, far away from where the war was being fought. In December 1941 research was started under the codename of 'Operation Manhattan'. Scientists from Britain, America and Canada gathered to work under top-secret security. Even some of the leaders of the Allied nations had no idea what was going on.

Naturally the work was a long, slow business. The costs ran into millions of dollars but the Americans poured money into this scheme to produce a wonder weapon.

● **The test**

Scientists soon found that if a mass of two pieces of uranium was fired into one at great speed there would be an explosion. It would be so enormous that even the biggest explosive bomb would look like a firework in comparison.

Early in 1945 so much progress had been made that all was ready for a big test. Obviously it had to take place in a lonely spot, far from towns and villages. In July, at a ranch-house near a place called Trinity, out in the New Mexico Desert, the preparations began.

Scientists suspended their bomb inside a steel tower and assembled six miles away to watch the experiment. In the early dawn of 16 July they moved the switch to detonate it electrically.

The explosion was so vast, with fantastic light and colours and heat that even the most experienced scientists were surprised. The steel tower evaporated and underneath, the sand turned to glass in the heat.

They had split the atom.

A watcher described it:

---

1 **There came this tremendous burst of light. The whole country was lighted by a searching light with the intensity many times that of the midday sun. It was golden, purple, violet, gray and blue. It lighted every peak, crevasse and ridge. . . .**

● **Should the bomb be used?**

On that same day the three Allied leaders were meeting at Potsdam, in newly defeated Germany. Churchill, Truman and Stalin were having discussions about the future. A code message arrived for the American President. 'Babies satisfactorily born,' it announced and he realized how successful Allied scientists had been.

But that produced a problem. Should the bomb be used? Germany had been beaten, but in the Far East the Japanese were fighting on. They had suffered heavily and some of the Allies' military men believed the Japanese could not last much longer. Their merchant fleet had suffered heavily and they were short of oil, the life-blood of war. But they still fought fiercely.

The Japanese held many thousands of Allied prisoners-of-war and had treated them badly. And the Americans had not forgotten the treacherous attack on Pearl Harbor nearly four years earlier.

So what should be done? If used, an atomic bomb would harm innocent women and children. But if the Allies had to invade the islands of Japan hundreds of thousands of their soldiers would die or be wounded. Should the Japanese be shown a demonstration explosion of an atom bomb over the sea? Or would that cause them to use prisoners-of-war as hostages, by placing them in cities that might be bombed?

At last, President Truman agreed with those advisers who said that the bomb should be used. Some of them were also thinking that such a mighty weapon would impress those strange allies – the Russians.

● Which target?

A special Task Force of aeroplanes was set up to deliver the new weapon. They were stationed on the small island of Tinian, almost 1400 miles from the Japanese mainland. In their B29 Superfortress

A *(Inset) The first atom bomb explodes on Hiroshima, 6 August 1945. The bomb was code-named 'Little Boy'*
B *The wreckage of Hiroshima after the atomic explosion. 60,000 buildings were destroyed*

bomber planes they made practice flights at dropping a special bomb. It was so new and different that most of the men had no idea what it consisted of – or of what it could do.

At 2.45 a.m. on 6 August the aircraft 'Enola Gay' took off with two escorting observation planes and headed towards Japan.

● **Hiroshima**

They flew towards the city of Hiroshima, arriving there just before 8 a.m., when thousands of people were starting their day. The plane crossed the city at a height of over 30,000 feet and dropped one bomb. Then it turned and flew off at top speed.

The bomb fell for 53 seconds and exploded at about 1800 feet above the ground. What followed was the greatest man-made explosion ever seen up to that time. More than 60,000 buildings were destroyed as a huge fire-storm roared across the city. Possibly 80,000 people were killed and thousands of others injured.

As a giant mushroom cloud rose over the city one of 'Enola Gay's' crew looked down at the scene.

'My God,' he said, 'What have we done?'

Later, a writer answered his question in a book:

2 **The initial flash spawned a succession of calamities. First came heat. It lasted only an instant but was so intense that it melted roof tiles . . . charred the exposed sides of telegraph poles for almost two miles, and incinerated nearby humans so thoroughly that nothing remained except their shadows, burnt into asphalt pavements or stone walls.. . .**

Bare skin was burned up to two and a half miles away.

After heat came the blast, sweeping outward from the fireball with the force of a five hundred-mile-an-hour wind. . . .

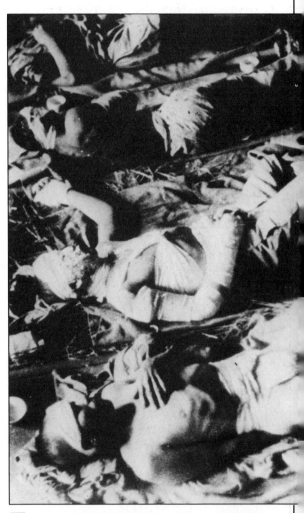

C *Victims of the bomb. 80,000 people died, many thousands more were maimed and affected by radiation*

● **Nagasaki**

Three days later, on 9 August, another bomb was dropped, this time using plutonium instead of uranium. The target on the second occasion was the city of Nagasaki and once again the devastation was enormous. Some 40,000 people were killed and at least as many again were injured. Large areas of Nagasaki ceased to exist.

Also, Japanese scientists became aware of a new hazard. Radiation started to affect hundreds of people:

3 **. . . Doctors here seem to be puzzled by one effect of the bomb which is causing great discomfort and suffering, and turns the skin first white, then red, then black, though there seem to be no visible indications of severe burns. . . .**

● **The Japanese surrender**
President Truman promised that if the Japanese did not surrender, many of their cities would be destroyed by these terrible new bombs:

4 **If they do not now accept our terms, they may expect a rain of ruin from the air, the like of which has never been seen on the earth.**

Faced with this threat the Japanese government decided to give in. The Emperor surrendered on 14 August.

At last the war had finished. But the dangerous atomic age had begun. ☐

Exercises

1 (a) How was the atomic bomb different from other bombs?
  (b) What was 'Operation Manhattan'?
  (c) What did 'Babies satisfactorily born' mean?
  (d) Which President said the bomb should be used?
  (e) What was 'Enola Gay'?

2 Imagine you witnessed the test explosion of the atomic bomb in July 1945. Describe what you saw (document 1 will help you).

3 You have to advise President Truman as to whether or not the atomic bomb should be used. Draw up a list of reasons for using the bomb. Now draw up a list of reasons why the bomb should *not* be used.

4 Look at pictures A, B and C and answer the following questions by referring to the chapter.

  (a) When and from where did 'Enola Gay' take off?
  (b) When did it reach Hiroshima?
  (c) What effect did the explosion have on buildings?
  (d) What effect did the explosion have on people?
  (e) How did at least one of the US airmen react?

5 Where was the second atom bomb dropped?

6 Imagine you had witnessed the test explosion of the atomic bomb in July 1945 and later visited Hiroshima. Describe your feelings. Use the pictures and documents to help with your answer.

7 The atomic bombs forced Japan to surrender. In your opinion, did this justify their use?

The United Nations Organization

In June 1945 representatives of fifty nations met in San Francisco and signed the Charter of the United Nations Organization. The words at the start announced:

1 **We, the people of the United Nations Determined to save succeeding generations from the scourge of war, which twice in our lifetime has brought untold sorrow to mankind, and**

To reaffirm faith in fundamental human rights, in the dignity and worth of the human person, in the equal right of men and women and of nations large and small.

The representatives then worked out the details of organization and the United Nations came into being on 24 October, which is still recognized each year as United Nations Day.

A *Division of labour in the United Nations*

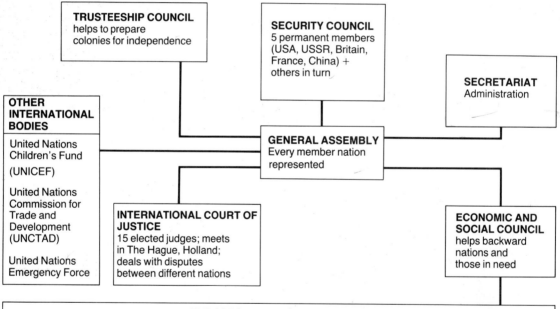

TRUSTEESHIP COUNCIL
helps to prepare colonies for independence

SECURITY COUNCIL
5 permanent members (USA, USSR, Britain, France, China) + others in turn

SECRETARIAT
Administration

OTHER INTERNATIONAL BODIES

United Nations Children's Fund (UNICEF)

United Nations Commission for Trade and Development (UNCTAD)

United Nations Emergency Force

GENERAL ASSEMBLY
Every member nation represented

INTERNATIONAL COURT OF JUSTICE
15 elected judges; meets in The Hague, Holland; deals with disputes between different nations

ECONOMIC AND SOCIAL COUNCIL
helps backward nations and those in need

THE SPECIALIZED AGENCIES, e.g.

The Specialized Agencies do some of the United Nations' most important work. They are concerned with matters like education, health and growing food, especially in the under-developed areas of the world. They have improved standards of farming, medicine and education for millions of people in places such as Africa, South America and the Far East. They have enabled richer countries to help poorer ones. But much remains to be done.

Food and Agriculture Organization (FAO)

World Health Organization (WHO)

United Nations Educational Scientific and Cultural Organization (UNESCO)

The United Nations Organization

● **Keeping the peace**

Since 1945 there have been many times when trouble has broken out in different parts of the world. Then the quarrels have been discussed at the General Assembly or by the Security Council.

Also, a United Nations peace-keeping force has sometimes been organized to deal with trouble spots in the world. Soldiers from member countries have been sent to places where fighting has occurred and they have helped to keep peace there, or at least to stop trouble spreading.

Without these efforts a Third World War might well have broken out several times before now.

B *Keeping the peace – involvement of UN forces*

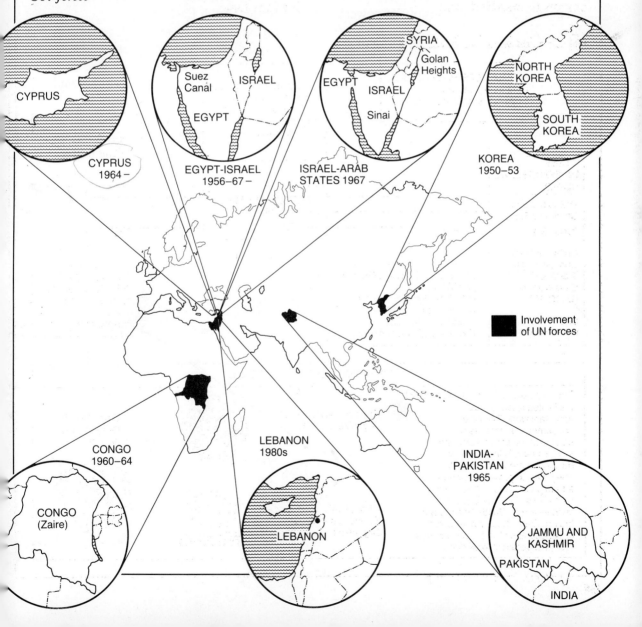

CYPRUS

CYPRUS 1964 –

Suez Canal   ISRAEL

EGYPT

EGYPT-ISRAEL 1956–67 –

SYRIA

Golan Heights

EGYPT   ISRAEL

Sinai

ISRAEL-ARAB STATES 1967

NORTH KOREA

SOUTH KOREA

KOREA 1950–53

■ Involvement of UN forces

CONGO 1960–64

CONGO (Zaire)

LEBANON 1980s

LEBANON

INDIA-PAKISTAN 1965

JAMMU AND KASHMIR

PAKISTAN

INDIA

The end of empire

● Introduction

In 1945, at the end of the Second World War, three European countries had large empires in the Far East. They were Britain, Holland and France. During the war, however, each of those countries had suffered heavy defeats and they lacked the power to go back to the position they had occupied in 1939. The people of Asia wanted their independence, and were prepared to struggle to push Europeans out of power in their lands.

Few Europeans had ever believed that Asiatic people could beat them in war, or overthrow them. But Japan, after attacking Pearl Harbor, had proved this idea to be wrong. Other people in the Far East took note of what had happened.

● The Dutch

The Dutch had been interested in trade with the Far East ever since the early seventeenth century. They developed a very profitable business in spices, silks and precious stones with islands such as Java, Sumatra and the Moluccas. Later, oil was discovered and rubber trees were grown, bringing more wealth. By the twentieth century Holland had a very rich empire in Asia, in what were called the Dutch East Indies.

During the war these Dutch territories were quickly overrun and occupied by Japanese troops. The Japanese were desperate to take as much oil, rubber and other raw materials as they could, for themselves.

When peace came in 1945 there was a

A *Colonial South-East Asia in 1945*

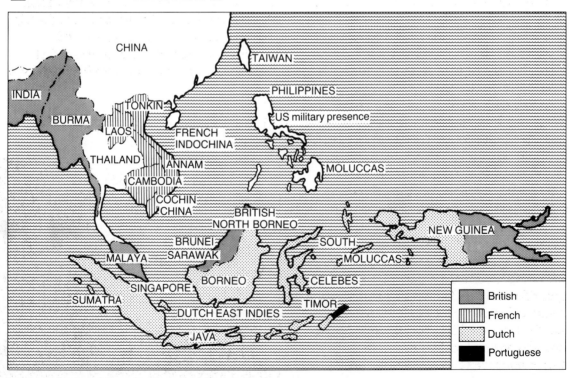

struggle between the Dutch and the people who had been part of their empire. The Dutch wanted to govern the colonies all over again. But the inhabitants of those islands were determined to have freedom. They were led by Dr Achmed Sukarno of the Indonesian Nationalist Party and soon the two sides were fighting.

Battles went on until 1949 when a conference was held in Holland so that both sides could settle down and have talks about their problems.

The Dutch accepted what had obviously happened in the Far East and the old Dutch East Indies were renamed 'Indonesia'. They became an independent republic under the leadership of Dr Sukarno.

● The French

France also had an empire in the Far East at the start of the Second World War. Its territory there was a colony called French Indo-China. After the Japanese went to war in 1941 the French allowed them to occupy the colony. However, the occupation was strongly resisted by Communist guerrilla forces under the leadership of Ho Chi Minh.

When the war finished in 1945 the French wanted to have their empire back again, but Ho Chi Minh's forces did not want that. The Communists set up an independent nation in the north of the country and called it the Democratic Republic of North Vietnam. The French would not accept what had happened and soon there was fighting between them and the Communists.

As the small struggle went on, Ho Chi Minh's forces fought a clever form of guerrilla warfare. Their forces would strike swiftly, then melt away before anyone could pin them down. The French wanted their enemies to stand and fight, but the Communists were too clever for that.

Then in 1954 the Communists, known as the Vietminh, surrounded a large French force at the town of Dien Bien Phu. Although fierce efforts were made to rescue or relieve the French troops they were firmly trapped and beaten. In May 1954 about 15,000 of them were overwhelmed.

After that a conference was held in Geneva to decide the future of Indo-China. It was agreed to divide the country into four areas. Ho Chi Minh became leader of Communist North Vietnam. In South Vietnam a non-Communist government came to power. Two other nations were formed – Cambodia and Laos – and both were neutral. After that, all foreign troops left Vietnam, with the hope that the agreement would last.

That hope was to be in vain.

● The British

In India, the desire to be free of British rule grew between 1919 and 1939. Many Indians appreciated that the British had brought fair laws and justice, wider education and modern transport. But they also saw that Britain had taken much wealth in exchange,

B *Dutch troops fire on rebel snipers in East Java during 1946*

and was responsible for some of India's troubles.

The leader of the freedom movement was Mohondas Gandhi. He hoped, by his policy of 'civil disobedience' (breaking laws by not co-operating, but without violence or bloodshed) to force the British government to grant India its inevitable independence.

But it was not until immediately after the Second World War that Britain agreed. And then they faced a problem – the question of religion.

Religious difficulties

In India there were about 400 million people. Of those, 300 million were Hindus, while nearly 100 million were Muslims. The two religions had disliked each other for centuries.

The Muslims feared that if India became a

C (Inset) One of the most remarkable men of the 20th century, Gandhi was born in 1869. He dressed and lived like a simple Indian peasant, and became known as the 'Mahatma' or 'Holy One'. He had a powerful effect on his followers. A Hindu, he tried to encourage friendship between Hindus and Muslims, but on 30 January 1948 he was assassinated by an extreme Hindu who disliked the way he was so friendly with the Muslims. His death was mourned by millions all round the world

D The aftermath of communal violence in Calcutta in 1946. British troops had to keep order before they eventually withdrew

free country they would be a small group under the control of the Hindus. So they pressed strongly to have a State of their own, where they could live separately under their leader, Mohammed Ali Jinnah. They proposed two areas, one in the north-east and the other in the north-west of India. They would be called 'Pakistan'.

Mr Jinnah pointed out some of the differences between Muslims and Hindus:

> **1 How can you even dream of Hindu–Muslim unity? . . . We have no inter-marriages. We have not the same calendar. The Muslims believe in a single God, and the Hindus are idolatrous [worship idols]. . . . Now again, the Hindus worship animals. They consider cows sacred . . . We want to kill the cows. We want to eat them. . . .**
>
> **There are only two links between the Muslims and the Hindus: British rule – and the common desire to get rid of it.**

The hatred between the two religious groups led to trouble in August 1946. 20,000 people were killed or injured during riots in Calcutta.

Mountbatten's plans

In February 1947 Britain sent Lord Mountbatten to be Viceroy (King's representative) in India. He had served in the Far East during the war, so had a love and respect for the Indian people. His main job was to arrange for the country to be divided up, giving independence to the Hindus and a new State to the Muslims. The time for the change had been set for June 1948, but Mountbatten saw that something had to be done urgently, so the date was brought forward to 15 August 1947.

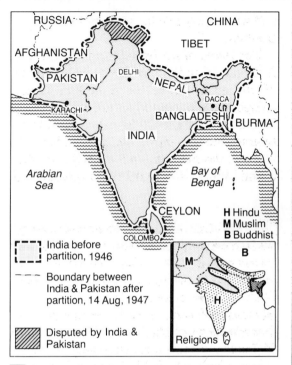

E *The Partition of India, 1947*

The changeover

The time came to move. When all the new lines had been drawn on maps, millions of ordinary people took up their belongings and began to travel to their new homeland. And that was when the killing really started. Hatreds flared up and old scores were settled. Hindus were attacked as they moved towards the new India. Muslims were assaulted as they started the journey to East or West Pakistan.

British and Indian troops travelled to trouble spots, trying hard to keep the peace, but their task often grew impossible because of the numbers and distances involved. Gandhi also made journeys in an attempt to encourage friendship, but when he had moved on the trouble often started again.

The numbers of men, women and children killed is not known exactly – and probably never will be. Estimates of the dead vary between a quarter and a half a million, the great majority being simple peasants and tradespeople who had no quarrel with anyone.

Within a few months the chaos was over and the new nations – India, East and West Pakistan all came into being. To show their liking for the British, they became members of the British Commonwealth.

Since 1948
Since partition, the two nations have existed side by side, although there have often been quarrels between them. In 1971 the Muslims of East Pakistan broke away from those in the West and renamed their State, 'Bangladesh'.

For both India and Pakistan there has been one overwhelming problem since partition. That is how to feed and care for their rapidly growing populations. India has the world's second largest population and their numbers have risen dramatically. The 360 million people of 1951 now exceed 700 million – and they all have to be fed.

F *British troops in Malaya during the 'Emergency'. Here members of the Scots Guards clear an area that is suspected to be the hiding place of Communist bandits*

The income, health, wealth, and expectation of life of the average Indian peasant make even the poorest people in Britain seem comfortably off.

Other areas of the empire
After the partition of India in 1947 Britain had a definite policy of giving up its old empire in south-east Asia. The British knew that there was no going back to the old position they had enjoyed before the war. They withdrew from two other colonial territories during the next year. One was the island of Ceylon, which was soon named Sri Lanka. The other was Burma which became independent and decided not to join the Commonwealth.

There was fighting, however, in Malaya. The British had lost that region to the Japanese in 1942, finishing with the surrender of the great naval base at Singapore. After the war they were faced with a big problem in the area. This was that many Chinese lived in the country and were disliked by the Malays.

In 1948 a kind of civil war started and British troops went into action against local Chinese Communists. For the next twelve years the rebels tied down a force of over 100,000 troops and police, together with a home guard of 200,000 Malays. During the fighting, known as the 'Emergency', great efforts were made to stop food and help being given to the Communist rebels and at length they were beaten.

Malaya became independent and in 1963 Sarawak and Sabah, which were part of the island of Borneo, were joined to it. The new state was called Malaysia. The city of Singapore became a separate state.

Overall, these events were part of the struggle that went on all over the Far East during the chaos that followed a world war.

1 Study map A. Copy the grid into your book, adding in the names of the colonies each nation controlled.

Nation	Colonies
Holland	
France	
Portugal	
Britain	

2 Why . . .
(a) did the Japanese invade the Dutch East Indies?
(b) did Ho Chi Minh oppose the French after 1945?
(c) was a conference held in Geneva in 1954?
(d) did Britain give up its empire after 1945?
(e) did British troops fight in Malaya after 1945?

3 Explain why the Indonesians supported Dr Sukarno.

4 Copy and complete this paragraph by using words from the **word list.**
One of the great . . . in giving . . . to India was the question of . . . . Hindus and . . . disliked each other and . . . to live in . . . states. . . . chose to live in India and the Muslims in. . . . In 1947 thousands were . . . in the fighting between the two . . . groups as people moved to their new. . . .

word list: religion; slaughtered; independence; separate; Muslims; Hindus; religious; difficulties; wanted; Pakistan; homeland

5 (a) When did Britain decide to give independence to India?
(b) Where did rioting lead to 20,000 deaths in August 1946?
(c) Who was the Muslim leader?
(d) Why was Mountbatten sent to India?
(e) What happened to East Pakistan in 1971?

6 According to Jinnah what were the differences and what were the similarities between Hindus and Muslims?

7 Write short paragraphs about the following:
(a) the struggle between Ho Chi Minh and the French
(b) Gandhi
(c) modern India, Pakistan and Bangladesh.

8 (a) What was the 'Emergency'?
(b) How many men were involved?
(c) How did the 'Emergency' end?

9 Imagine you are a newspaper reporter in India in 1947. You have to write an article for your paper about the partition of India. Describe the changeover using the following points as guidelines: people moving to new homelands, religious fights, British and Indian troops trying to keep the peace, Mohondas Gandhi, the new countries, British Commonwealth.

10 *Discussion:* Why do you think some people (a) support, (b) reject non-violence?

Cold War and the Berlin Airlift

● **Germany in 1945**

Nazi Germany was beaten in 1945. Russian forces advanced from the East and invaded their hated enemy's territory. American and British armies pushed forward, crossed the Rhine and attacked Germany from the west. By the early months of the year Nazi forces were collapsing and the end came in May.

On the western side, some commanders had wanted to get to Berlin as quickly as possible. That was Germany's capital city and was therefore the greatest prize. However, the Russians arrived first, reaching the outskirts on 20 April. After fierce fighting the Germans were overwhelmed and Hitler committed suicide. The war in Europe was at an end and the Allies celebrated VE Day (Victory in Europe Day) on 8 May.

The Allied armies from east and west had trapped Germany. They met in central Germany and showed great friendship towards each other – at first. They were putting into practice what had been agreed by Roosevelt, Stalin and Churchill in the previous February when they met at the Yalta Conference. Then they had proclaimed that they wanted a world 'dedicated to peace, security, freedom and the general well-being of all mankind'. That sounded very grand.

● **The division of Germany**

At the Yalta conference the Allied leaders had decided to divide Germany up into four zones, or regions, after the war. So in 1945 the defeated country was chopped into four sections – Russian, French, British and American. Each nation sent troops into its zone to control life there.

There was one particular difficulty. It was decided to divide the city of Berlin also into four zones, giving one to each of the great nations. However, Berlin lay deep in the Russian zone, so how were the other three countries to reach their part of the city? The answer was that the Russians allowed them to cross their zone along corridors – road, rail and air – stretching for about 100 miles.

All would be well if the four nations stayed on good terms with each other. But what would happen if they became enemies?

● **The Iron Curtain**

This is just what happened. The Allies soon fell out. All over eastern Europe where Russian forces advanced, Communist governments were set up and other political parties not allowed into power. This occurred in countries like Poland, Czechoslovakia, Hungary, Rumania and Bulgaria.

A *A cartoon showing Molotov, Foreign Minister of Russia (left), and Bevin, Foreign Minister of Britain (right)*

The Russians did this to create a band of friendly nations in eastern Europe near to their own frontier so that another terrible German invasion could not be launched in the future. The western European powers saw matters in a different light. They believed that the Russians wanted to turn the whole of Europe Communist and that they were spreading their ideas by force.

Even during the war the friendship between Britain and the USA on one side and Russia on the other had never been particularly warm. Now it grew colder. An invisible barrier was formed across Europe, splitting the Communists in the east from what became known as the Free World, or the capitalist countries of the west. Travel across the barrier became difficult. Ideas and ways of life were totally different on each side. This 'frontier' became known as the 'Iron Curtain'.

During a speech made in America in 1946 Winston Churchill referred to it:

1 A shadow has fallen upon the scenes so lately lighted by the Allied victory. Nobody knows what Soviet Russia and its Communist international organization intends to do in the immediate future. . . . From Stettin in the Baltic to Trieste in the Adriatic, an iron curtain has descended across the continent. Behind that line lie all the capitals of the ancient states of Central and Eastern Europe, Warsaw, Berlin, Prague, Vienna, Budapest, Belgrade, Bucharest, and Sofia, all these famous cities and the populations round them lie in what I must call the Soviet sphere, and all are subject in one form or another, not only to Soviet influence, but to very high and, in many cases, increasing measure of control from Moscow.

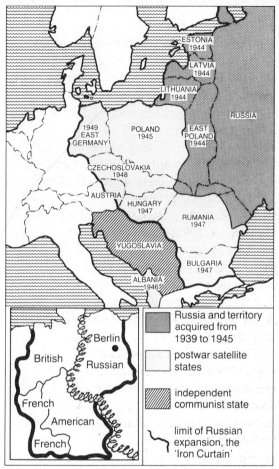

B *Communist Expansion in Europe, 1939–49 (Inset: the division of Germany into four zones)*

● **The Cold War**

A 'hot' war happens when countries fight each other openly. A 'cold' war exists when countries dislike each other. They criticize and are unfriendly. There is little or no trade or travel between them, but the hatred stops short of military attacks.

In 1946–7 the Cold War in Europe really started – and it's never stopped since.

On the eastern side of the Iron Curtain were Russia and the countries of eastern Europe under her control. They were

Communist and had a different way of life from that in the west. Opposite them were the nations of western Europe, supported by forces from the USA which wanted to stop Communism from spreading westwards. Both sides built up powerful forces, either to defend themselves or to frighten their opponents.

The Iron Curtain separating the two sides ran through Germany and that divided country has never been united since 1945.

● The Berlin Airlift
In 1948 the Russians and the western Allies had a disagreement over a new money system for the conquered Germans. The Russians tried to find a way to force the other three nations out of their sectors of Berlin. Their tactics were simple. They closed the road and rail corridors to the capital, thinking that life would become so difficult for the French, British and Americans that they would have to leave the city.

But the air corridors were not closed, so a gigantic operation was mounted by the Americans and the British to supply Berlin by air. A twenty-four hour service of aircraft was set up to carry food, fuel and supplies into the city. Day and night the planes flew in thousands of tons of goods to beat the blockade.

C *The 'Iron Curtain'* **D** *(inset) The division of Europe into armed blocks. The Warsaw Pact nations are controlled by Russia*

NATO
USA, Canada and Iceland

Warsaw Pact

HALT!
ZONENGRENZVERLAUF
UNÜBERSICHTLICH!
LEBENSGEFAHR!

Cold War and the Berlin Airlift

The Russians did not re-open the land routes until May 1949. By then they realized that their campaign had failed – because the western Allies refused to be beaten.

Afterwards the three western Powers set up West Germany – the German Federal Republic – from their three zones. The Russians set up East Germany – the German Democratic Republic – from theirs.

There were now two Germanies.

● NATO

The Berlin Blockade caused great worry to the nations of western Europe, so in 1949 twelve countries joined together in a defensive alliance. It was called NATO – North Atlantic Treaty Organization. Those nations agreed to help each other in the event of an attack from outside – and they kept their eyes on the Russians and their allies on the other side of the Iron Curtain.

The Russians and their friends had a different view of NATO. They believed that the United States and the countries of western Europe were preparing to attack them – or at least be threatening. In 1955 they formed their own organization, called the Warsaw Pact. ☐

Exercises

1 Copy and complete the sentences using the words in the **word list**.
   (a) The . . . reached the outskirts of . . . on 20 April 1945.
   (b) At the . . . Conference in 1945 it was decided to . . . Germany into . . . zones.
   (c) The . . . Curtain divided eastern and . . . Europe.
   (d) A . . . War has separated . . . and the USA.
   (e) The Berlin . . . started in. . . .

   > **word list:** Yalta; western; Russia; 1948; Berlin; four; Russians; Cold; divide; Airlift; Iron

2 Describe what you can see on cartoon A. What *did* happen to Germany?

3 (a) Who met at Yalta?
   (b) What did they decide to do?
   (c) When did the war in Europe end?
   (d) Why was there a Berlin airlift?
   (e) When was NATO formed?
   (f) What is the difference between a 'hot war' and a 'cold war'?

4 'From Stettin in the Baltic to Trieste in the Adriatic, an iron curtain has descended across the continent.'
   (a) Who said this?
   (b) What did he mean by an 'iron curtain'?
   (c) Which western countries border the Iron Curtain?
   (d) Name five countries to the east of the Iron Curtain.
   (e) Who controls these countries?

5 Imagine you were either a resident of West Berlin or a pilot involved in the Berlin airlift. Explain why the airlift was necessary and describe what happened.

6 (a) Why was NATO formed?
   (b) Which countries formed NATO?
   (c) What was the Russian response?

The Chinese revolution

● Introduction

China is a large country and has the world's largest population, which at the last count was reckoned to be about 1,000 million. That means there are almost eighteen Chinese for every person in Britain. The population of China at present is *increasing* by about 30,000 people every day! Compare that with the number of people in your town.

One of the world's great civilizations began in Ancient China. The Chinese discovered or invented things like printing, the wheelbarrow, gunpowder and the compass. They thought little of Europeans when they first met them and wanted to have little to do with strangers they called 'hairy barbarians'. Their dislike grew at the end of the nineteenth century when European nations began a policy of imperialism, seeking colonies and trading posts in the Far East.

● The Second World War

Japan attacked China in the 1920s as part of the policy of extending its empire. The Japanese were better equipped and led than the Chinese and therefore soon made large gains of territory.

A drawback to the Chinese resistance was that it was a divided effort. Two groups fought separately against the Japanese invaders. One was the Communists in the north, under their leader, Mao Tse-tung. The other was the Nationalists (Kuomintang) under General Chiang Kai-shek. Not only did both groups fight against the Japanese, but they also attacked each other! It was small wonder that they had little effect on their enemies.

● Nationalists and Communists at War

The Kuomintang (KMT) were led by Chiang Kai-shek. Born in 1887 he was an army officer who succeeded to the leadership of the Nationalists after Sun Yat-sen's death in 1925.

During the Second World War the Americans did all they could to help the

A *Chiang Kai-shek's troops in the streets of Canton. They were much better equipped than the Communists*

B *An advance by Communist troops. Their tactics enabled them to defeat the Nationalists*

Chinese by sending equipment. Much of this went to Chiang's Nationalists. But he was not prepared to use all of these weapons against the Japanese and kept some of them back for use against the Communists.

General Stilwell of the USA was sent to China. He wrote his opinion of the Nationalists at war, comparing their efforts with those of the Communists:

> **1** **Kuomintang: Corruption, chaos, neglect, taxes, words and no deeds. Hoarding, black market, trading with the enemy.**
>
> **Communist program: reduce taxes, rents, interests, raise production, and standard of living. Participate in government. Practise what they preach.**

For their part, the Communists were led by Mao Tse-tung. They struggled strongly against Japan, but did not really trust the Nationalists. During much of the war the Communists fought more fiercely than their rivals and played a large part in holding back the Japanese, especially in the northern area of China where they had settled after the Long March.

● The Civil War

At the end of the Second World War in 1945 China possessed two powerful armies, one Nationalist and one Communist. Having settled with the Japanese enemy they were now ready to tackle each other.

At first there was a period of negotiation between the two sides in 1946. America tried to keep them at peace and Mao Tse-tung had meetings with Chiang Kai-shek. However, the calm did not last for long. In 1947 fighting broke out as Communist forces started to push down from the north.

Gradually Mao's men grew more popular in China. They were setting out to help ordinary peasants – who therefore helped them. The Communists fought a kind of guerrilla warfare which made them hard to pin down and attack. Through pamphlets and broadcasts their propaganda was good and thousands of Nationalists changed sides during the campaign.

Throughout 1947 and 1948 the war went on, with Communist successes. By the end of 1948 they surrounded Peking, the capital city, and a siege followed. After about two months the city fell and the Communists had taken a great step towards final victory.

As Mao's Red Army pushed on across

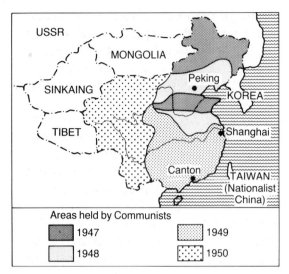

Areas held by Communists

| 1947 | 1949 |
| 1948 | 1950 |

C *The Communist victory*

China, they moved south and the Nationalist resistance crumbled. By October 1949 Chiang Kai-shek saw defeat staring him in the face and left with two million of his Nationalists to live elsewhere. They crossed to the island of Formosa (now called Taiwan), which lies 160 km off the Chinese mainland.

● **The People's Republic**
The People's Republic of China was set up on 1 October 1949. Chairman Mao Tse-tung made a speech near the Gates of Heavenly Peace, Peking:

> 2 We proclaim the establishment of the People's Republic of China. Our nation will from now on enter the large family of peace-loving and freedom-loving nations of the world. It will work bravely and industriously to create its own civilization and happiness and will, at the same time, promote world peace and freedom. Our nation will never again be an insulted nation. We have stood up. Our revolution has gained the sympathy and acclamation of the broad masses throughout the entire world. We have friends everywhere in the world over.

Mao was now in control of China, with its population of 600 million people. In his view there would have to be a Communist revolution in China. The changes would be hard. He said:

> 3 The revolution is, after all, no banquet. It's not quite as dainty an occupation as writing books or painting flowers . . . a revolution is a violent action on the part of one class to overthrow the political power of another.

As part of the revolution there was harsh treatment of landlords and those who opposed the Communists. Thousands were killed or imprisoned as Mao took over and a new age started for China.

● **An age of change**
Over the next few years there was a drive to make China industrialized. At the same time living standards rose for the Chinese people, who made up a quarter of the world's population.

Standing at the head of these changes was Chairman Mao, who was treated as the saviour of his nation. Someone who met him wrote this description of the man who was now such a powerful figure:

> 4 Mao was wearing a light grey tunic, closed at the collar, with baggy trousers to match, heavy brown brogues and cotton socks which fell over his ankles. His tunic

hung in folds around him and he seemed somewhat shrunken and thinner than I had imagined. His hair, meticulously brushed back, was black with scarcely a trace of grey. His face was lined but full and fleshy. He looked younger than his 71 years and showed no signs of tiring as the evening wore on.

America, with its dislike of Communism, refused to recognize Mao's government as the lawful government of China. Communist China was excluded from the United Nations and a place given instead to the representatives of Nationalist China, from Formosa. For its part, Mao's government was determined to oppose the Americans in the Far East. Over the next twenty years it found several opportunities of doing that when American forces were involved in wars in Asia.

For a start, the USA decided to protect Chiang Kai-shek and his Nationalist forces in Formosa (later called Taiwan). The American Seventh Fleet was sent to patrol the waters between the island and the mainland, to stop the Communists invading the Nationalist stronghold. There is little doubt that without the intervention of the Americans, Chiang's men would have been attacked and overthrown many years ago.

Exercises

1 Copy and complete this paragraph using the words in the **word list**.
During the . . . World War there were two . . . of Chinese fighting against the. . . . One group was the . . . and the other group was the. . . . After 1945 they started to . . . each other in a . . . war. At the end of it the Communists were . . . and began a new stage in Chinese. . . .

word list: victorious; Second; Nationalists; civil; Japanese; history; fight; groups; Communists

2 Match these up correctly
(a) Formosa   (i) traders
(b) Mao Tse-tung   (ii) Kuomintang
(c) Europeans   (iii) Communists
(d) Nationalists   (iv) Gates of Heavenly Peace
(e) Peking   (v) Taiwan

3 (a) Copy map C into your book.
  (b) Explain what the map shows.
  (c) Describe in your own words how the Communist forces defeated the Nationalists.

4 Imagine a discussion between a soldier in picture A and a soldier in picture B. Each one speaks about what he is fighting for. Write out their conversation in the form of a dialogue.

5 (a) What did Mao promise the Chinese people in 1949?
  (b) Write briefly on what happened to Chiang Kai-shek after 1949.

(*A further question appears on page 219.*)

The Korean War

● The background

As you can see from the maps, Korea borders on to China. For hundreds of years the Chinese had turned Korea into an area under their influence. However, the Japanese moved in during 1910 and claimed it as one of their colonies. After that they governed Korea.

Just before Japan collapsed at the end of the Second World War in 1945 Russian troops invaded the north of Korea. A little later, US forces arrived in the south. It was agreed that all those Japanese north of the 38th parallel should surrender to the Russians while those to the south would be handed over to the Americans.

At a stroke Korea, which was really one country, had been split into two. Now it was controlled by the world's two greatest powers, who were unfriendly towards each other. They were prepared to use Korea as a battleground for what they believed to be right.

During 1947 the United Nations hoped that elections would be held throughout Korea to provide a single government for the whole country. But the Russians would not allow this in their zone so two sets of elections were held, one in the north and the other in the south. Afterwards, Korea was split into two countries. The Korean People's Republic was Communist and supported by Russia. The Republic of Korea, supported by the USA, was non-Communist. Both sides claimed to be the rightful government of the whole of Korea.

The dividing line between them was the 38th parallel. Then, in 1948–9 the Russians left the north and the Americans left the south.

● The USA in the Far East

After 1945 the USA became closely involved in events in the Far East. The reason for this is simple. Before 1939, Britain, France and Holland had all had empires in Asia but they had lost their power during the Second World War. They had no strength to stop the spread of Communism in that area. The task fell to the Americans, because their nation was now the strongest in the world.

Although some Americans did not want to become involved in other countries'

A *The Korean War up to December 1950*

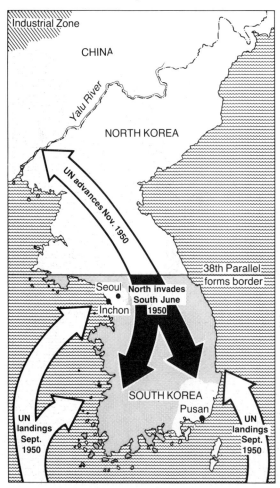

troubles, their government thought otherwise. They made it their policy to oppose Communists wherever they were found.

● The start of the war

The Russians and the Americans were far from friendly with each other by 1950. The USSR gave support to North Korea and was prepared to take on the USA in the Far East. With Russian weapons and encouragement, North Korean soldiers invaded South Korea on 25 June 1950. They were well organized and equipped so they made rapid advances, heading south towards Pusan, the capital.

There was an emergency meeting of the Security Council of the United Nations – which had been set up to deal with problems like this. The Council asked member nations to give help to the South Koreans and before long sixteen countries sent troops, ships and aircraft, which were formed into a UN force.

President Truman of the USA gave his view on what was happening:

---

1 The attack upon Korea makes it plain beyond all doubt that communism has passed beyond the use of subversion to conquer independent nations and will now use armed invasion and war. It has defied the orders of the Security Council of the United Nations issued to preserve international peace and security.

● The War, Part 1

The greatest number of men in the UN force came from the USA and the commander was an American, General Douglas MacArthur. He had served in the Far East during the Second World War and knew the area well.

By the time the combined force had arrived in Korea the Communists from the

north had overrun much of the South. Therefore MacArthur decided on a remarkable and unusual attack. Instead of meeting them head-on he landed thousands of men at Inchon, in the rear of his enemy. After fierce fighting they captured Seoul and threatened to cut off the Communists from their bases.

The war suddenly took a new turn as the North Koreans fell back to the 38th parallel. At that stage the task of removing the invaders had been completed but the UN forces did not stop there. The Americans

B *The Korean War up to the cease-fire*

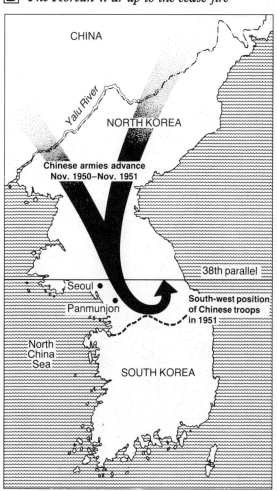

pushed on into North Korea, determined now to overthrow the government there and hold elections for a united Korea.

MacArthur's forces were very successful as they raced forward. Before long they were approaching the Yalu River which marked the border with China.

Then the war entered a new, dramatic and highly dangerous phase.

● **The War, Part 2**

As the UN forces drew near to the Yalu River the Chinese Communist government in Peking became worried. They did not want the Americans who had supported Chiang Kai-shek to be so close to their border so they sent thousands of troops called 'volunteers' across the Yalu River to help the North Koreans.

These soldiers were experienced in fighting and swept back General MacArthur's army which had been on the verge of victory. Their methods of warfare were unusual but highly successful. To unsettle their enemy they charged into battle blowing bugles and banging cymbals. They were not afraid of suffering casualties and so hundreds would die or be wounded to achieve a small advance.

As the UN army was being driven back General MacArthur called for a desperate measure. He believed that if the Chinese were to be stopped, their bases in China should be bombed. There was even talk of using atomic weapons. MacArthur and his President, Harry S. Truman, saw matters from different viewpoints. For Truman, the main threat from Communism came in Europe. For MacArthur, the greatest troubles were in Asia. The general commented:

|C| *US infantrymen in Korea*

> 2 It seems strangely difficult for some to realize that here in Asia is where the communist conspirators have elected to make their play for global conquest . . . that here we fight Europe's war with arms while the diplomats there still fight it with words; that if we lose the war to Communism in Asia the fall of Europe is inevitable. . . . There is no substitute for victory.

Because of these differences of outlook the President dismissed his general in April 1951 and peace talks began between the two sides. Yet these dragged on for another two years, with outbreaks of fighting in between, before an armistice was finally signed in July 1953.

The Korean War

D *A group of North Korean prisoners*

By then there had been almost two million servicemen and civilians killed in the savage war.

Since that time the two Koreas, North and South, have continued to exist in an unfriendly way, glowering at each other across the 38th parallel. Russia lost interest in the war before the end and withdrew much of its support for the North. The Chinese, though, proved to the world that they could and would fight to protect their border.

But overall, the Communists had suffered a defeat and the UN forces, mainly American, had won a victory. ☐

Exercises

1 Re-arrange these jumbled sentences and then copy them into your book.
   (a) the north in the Americans and the Korea in the Russians were of south In 1945
   (b) the Second USA War was a Far World in the powerful After the East nation
   (c) war in The Korean started in 1950
   (d) The General was MacArthur Force by UN commanded
   (e) The 'volunteers' sent North Chinese to Koreans the help

2 Copy out these sentences and say whether they are fact or opinion.
   (a) After 1910 the Japanese claimed Korea as one of their colonies.
   (b) North Korean soldiers invaded the South on 25 June 1950.
   (c) General MacArthur was the best general in the USA.
   (d) Chinese soldiers beat their enemies by using unusual fighting methods.

3 Copy maps A and B into your book and explain what each map shows.

4 (a) Why did Truman support the United Nations?
   (b) Did all Americans support Truman?
   (c) Why did Truman disagree with MacArthur?

5 Using the information in the chapter write brief paragraphs on:
   (a) the causes of the Korean War;
   (b) the war itself;
   (c) the results of the War.

6 Explain the meaning of the following:
   (a) 38th parallel;
   (b) subversion;
   (c) conspirators;
   (d) global conquest;
   (e) diplomats.

Space exploration

● Space

Men and women have always been fascinated by space, because of its immense size and mystery. Ever since Copernicus (1473–1543) showed that the planets revolve round the sun people have looked out at them and wanted to travel through the universe.

● Rockets in war

The first difficulty for any would-be space traveller is to get outside the pull of the earth's gravity. Experiments were made over many years before 1945 in America, Russia and Germany to develop rockets which could achieve this. Obviously, any nation reaching this aim would have a kind of long-range artillery for use in war.

In 1926 an American, Dr Robert Goddard, made a test-firing of a liquid-fuel rocket which rose more than 7,000 feet into the sky. Then three years later some German experiments were made with a rocket-propelled aeroplane, called the Opel, which managed a short flight.

German scientists were first successful in war. During the Second World War they set up a research station at Peenemunde on the coast of the Baltic Sea and there they developed a rocket for use in action. This rocket really marks the start of the Space Age in which we now all live.

The weapon was tested in 1943 and a film shown to Hitler. He commented:

> **1 If we had had these rockets in 1939 we should never have had this war. . . . Europe and the world will be too small from now on to contain a war. With such weapons humanity will be unable to endure it.**

The V2, or Revenge Weapon was 46 feet long and weighed twelve and a half tons. It rose to a height of fifty miles, at a speed of over 5,400 kph. Nothing could stop it. More than 2,000 of these terrifying rockets were fired against southern England in 1944–5 and caused much damage.

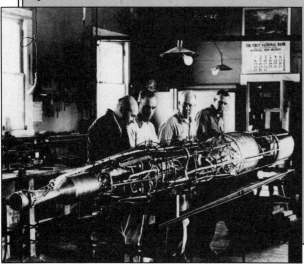

A *Dr Robert Goddard, his assistants and one of his rockets in 1940*

B *German V2 rockets ready for launching at Peenemunde in 1944*

● The rocket in peace

At the end of the war only two countries were sufficiently rich and powerful to do rocket research. They were Russia and the USA, the two new super powers. Since then they have pushed on hard in competition with each other. There are several reasons for this. Each one wants to lead other nations in science. Both can see the value of using space in any future warfare. And each one wishes to be the most advanced country in technology.

Since 1945 the space programme for both nations has been linked up closely with the development of atomic weapons. At first these were intended to be delivered by giant bombers, but then rockets were developed to carry them. By 1953 the two nations had produced an ICBM (Inter-Continental Ballistic Missile), a rocket with a nuclear-powered warhead. Such a weapon could travel over thousands of kilometres at such a high speed that no defence could stop it. In 1957 the Russians claimed to possess a rocket which could reach any part of the world. On 4 October 1957 the Russians announced that they had fired Sputnik 1 – a small artificial satellite – into space on a rocket.

Russia had gained a great lead in the space race.

Then there was strong competition between the USSR and the USA with two aims in view. One was to fire rockets into space, reaching the moon and other planets. The other was to put human beings into space.

● People go into space

Once again, the Russians were successful. Yuri Gagarin became the first man in space when he orbited the earth in April 1961. An American, John Glenn, equalled this feat

C *The American spaceship Apollo II landed on the moon on 20 July 1969. The three astronauts aboard were Neil Armstrong, Edwin Aldrin and Michael Collins. Here, Edwin Aldrin steps from the Lunar Module 'Eagle' on to the moon.*

almost a year later. Then, in 1963 Valentina Tereshkova was the first woman in space when she made 48 orbits in the spaceship Vostok VI.

At that, the Americans pulled out all the stops to take the lead in space travel. President Kennedy gave a challenge to the USA, hoping to push on their efforts:

---

2 I believe that this nation should commit itself to achieving the goal, before this decade is out, of landing a man on the moon and returning him safely to earth. No single space project of this period will be more impressive to mankind or more important to the long-range exploration of

space and none will be so difficult or expensive to accomplish.

All over the world people marvelled at the achievement of the USA, which had gained a lead in what everyone knew was a space race.

● To the moon

So America started her Apollo Program, intending to reach the moon. Thousands of people worked on schemes involving the spending of thousands of millions of dollars. Manned orbits were made of the earth, then of the moon.

At length, on the morning of 21 July 1969 Neil Armstrong, one of the crew of Apollo 11, set foot on the moon and achieved an ambition held by mankind for centuries. At the moment of making history he said: 'That's one small step for a man, one giant leap for mankind.'

Four days later the crew were back safely on earth.

● Since the moon

Other American missions to the moon followed but these were later given up. Both the United States and Russia have maintained their efforts in space since then, but in different ways.

The Russians have fired several rockets deep into space and these have sent back remarkable pictures of other planets such as Mars. Also they have concentrated on putting men into space for long periods of time, some for several months. They have made efforts to build space stations as centres that can be visited by rockets.

The Americans have also made probes

D *The space shuttle Challenger drifting over the earth's surface*

deeper into space. Much of their interest, however, has been to build a re-usable spacecraft, called the 'shuttle'. This is shaped like an aeroplane and after being fired into orbit by means of a rocket, flies back to land safely on earth. On one of the shuttle's journeys in 1983 Dr Sally Ride became the first American woman to go into space.

The two super powers constantly spy on each other from space. Their satellites are always orbiting the world and can take very detailed photos of any nation, showing its military centres and industrial power.

But there are, of course, many peaceful uses of space satellites. The first trans-Atlantic transmissions of television pictures came in July 1962, via Telstar 1. Since then events can be shown live to lands thousands of miles away from where they are happening. Also weather satellites have been used to give good warning of the approach of such dangers as hurricanes in some parts of the world. The earth itself can be inspected from space so that geologists, farmers and foresters can learn much of the treasures at their disposal.

Very recently several European countries have co-operated to put their first rocket into space. But the USA and the USSR have a great lead in rockets for all purposes – in peace or war. ☐

Exercises

1 Copy and complete this grid using all the dates given in the chapter (yours will be bigger).

Date	Country	Development in rocket and space travel
1926	USA	Robert Goddard test fires liquid fuel rocket
1943	Germany	German scientists test rockets
1944 –5	Great Britain	V2 rockets damage cities

2 Write a few sentences on photograph A and on photograph C to explain how they fit into the history of space exploration.

3 Who made the following statements and what did they mean?
   (a) 'If we had had these rockets in 1939 we should never have had this war.'
   (b) 'No single space project of this period will be more impressive to mankind.'
   (c) 'That's one small step for a man, one giant leap for mankind.'
   Which pictures in this chapter are most closely related to these sayings?

4 Imagine that you are one of the following:
   (a) Yuri Gagarin
   (b) Valentina Tereshkova
   (c) Neil Armstrong
   (d) Sally Ride
   Describe your experiences as an astronaut.

5 Write two paragraphs to support the following statements:
   (a) 'The USA and USSR are wasting their money on space programmes.'
   (b) 'Space exploration is of great benefit to mankind.'

(*A further question appears on page 219.*)

Israel and the Arabs

● The background

Jews believe that God promised them a homeland at the time of Abraham, about 3,800 years ago. The land is an area at the eastern end of the Mediterranean and is generally known as Palestine, or Israel. For generations Jews have wanted to return to this promised land.

● Zionists

From the 1880s a movement started among European Jews to return to the promised land which they called Zion. More and more of them travelled to settle in Palestine. The British government approved of this move, but Arabs lived in Palestine and regarded the area as their country

When the colonies belonging to Turkey were taken away after the First World War, the League of Nations gave Britain the control of Palestine and more Jews went to live there. Their numbers rose from 56,000 in 1918 to over 450,000 twenty years later.

The Arabs already living in Palestine were never really asked for their views so naturally this brought problems. On the one hand, they did not like the arrival of so many Jews and felt threatened. On the other hand Jews were determined to move to their promised land. Britain had to sit between them as an umpire. Many Arabs felt that Britain had helped to cause the trouble by promising Palestine to them for fighting against the Turks.

● Nazis and Jews

The Nazi policy of removing Jews (page 120) was put into practice during the Second

A *Jewish irregular soldiers defend a position against Arab troops. The Arabs were better equipped and had regular armies*

World War. By the end of the fighting in 1945 some six million Jews had been put to death in Europe. No race in history had been treated so savagely. Many of the survivors became even more determined to reach Palestine and began to flock there in large numbers.

● The formation of Israel, 1945–8

Their arrival brought more trouble. Soon Arab and Jewish groups were attacking each other and matters grew worse when they attacked British forces who were trying to keep law and order. Both Arabs and Jews were trying to seize power and both believed they were entitled to it.

In 1947 the UN suggested that Palestine should be split between Jews and Arabs but the fighting did not stop. At length Britain withdrew its forces and troubles grew worse.

On 14 May 1948 the Jews proclaimed the State of Israel, which was recognized by the UN. At once, Arab armies invaded across the frontiers of Palestine.

● The Arab war, 1948

A short, savage war followed. To everyone's surprise the Israeli forces fought extremely well, although many had little previous military experience. They were armed with Czech weapons and knew that their whole future was at stake because the Arabs had promised to destroy the new nation and drive all Jews into the sea.

Not only did the Israelis repel these attacks but they also advanced and captured more territory. This was a great disaster for the Arabs.

The war ended in 1949 when a truce was signed. But afterwards the Arab states wanted revenge and showed their dislike by taking steps to make life difficult for Israel.

B *Young Palestinians in a refugee camp*

For example, they refused to allow Israeli ships to pass through the Suez Canal. They also banned trade with Israel.

Some two million Jews, in a land of about 8,000 square miles were surrounded by 40 million Arabs in lands covering 1,600,000 square miles. The future looked bleak.

The two different points of view are shown in the following extracts. The first is from Ben Gurion, Israel's Prime Minister and was made in 1950:

1 In the first year we made the Defence Army: we met and mastered the invaders; we opened wide the gates of the Homeland to all the people of Israel. We enlarged our boundaries, even unto Eilat and the Red Sea, held tight the approaches to Jerusalem and peopled her hills. . . .

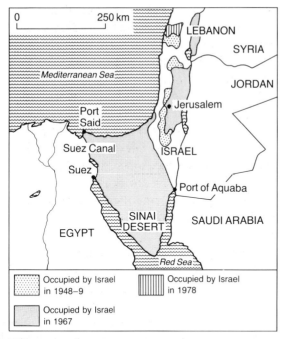

Occupied by Israel in 1948–9

Occupied by Israel in 1978

Occupied by Israel in 1967

C *The Arab–Israeli wars, 1948–78*

Step by step with the ingathering, we must construct the land and make the wilderness to flower. We have doubled the area under the plough, but that is still not a tenth part of the State. . . .

And the second extract comes from a broadcast made by King Hussein of Jordan in 1957. It shows how bitterly the Arabs regarded their failure to destroy the State of Israel in 1949:

2 . . . the disaster which the Arabs suffered in 1949 is not forgotten yet.
We in Jordan have learned from experience to consider every Arab cause the cause of the entire Arab nations, from the Atlantic Ocean to the Arab Gulf, because such causes affect our life.

● **Palestinian refugees**
What made matters worse was that the Israeli victory led to about a million Palestinian Arabs becoming refugees. They lost their homes in Palestine. The UN built large, tented camps to hold them but often they had to live in poor conditions on the borders of Israel or in other Arab countries.

The refugees felt a great bitterness towards the Israelis and vowed revenge against them. They swore not to rest until they had regained their homes. This was the start of a problem that has not been solved today, many years later.

The refugees soon formed their own guerrilla fighting arm, called the PLO (Palestine Liberation Organization). They launched raids across the border at Israeli targets and the Israelis retaliated by attacking their camps.

● **The Suez war, 1956**
Israel was particularly angry that Egypt made attacks on it from Sinai and had blocked the way out for its ships into the Red Sea.

Therefore, during the Suez crisis of 1956 which was carefully planned by Israel, Britain and France working together (page 167), the Israeli Army attacked Egypt. While Britain and France ran into deep trouble with the United Nations over their actions and were forced to withdraw, the Israelis made gains of territory. They won victories which gave them control over the Sinai Peninsula and also an outlet from the port of Aquaba.

The bitterness, especially between Egypt and Israel, lived on.

● **The uneasy peace**
Since then there has been a constant struggle

Israel and the Arabs

between Jews and Arabs, although the UN has appealed for peace. Russia has sent arms, equipment and advisers to Arab countries, while the USA has always been a strong and active supporter of Israel.

● More wars

Three times since 1956 Israel has been involved in big wars with its neighbours. In 1967 and 1973 there was bitter fighting between Israel, Egypt and Syria before the Arabs were defeated and the Israelis gained more territory.

● Camp David and after

In 1979 there was a breakthrough towards peace when Israel and Egypt signed an undertaking. This was the Camp David agreement, reached with the help of the Americans. Both sides agreed to settle their problems peacefully.

However, other Arabs did not agree with this policy and the PLO maintained attacks. War arrived on another frontier in 1982 when Israeli forces struck at PLO camps in the Lebanon. In very bloodthirsty fighting vast damage was done to Beirut, the capital, and many people were killed. PLO soldiers were driven out and forced to go to other countries.

But the problems of the Middle East remained unsolved. ☐

Exercises

1 Copy and complete these sentences.
   (a) The Jews called Israel the promised land because. . . .
   (b) Some Jews called themselves Zionists because. . . .
   (c) Palestinian Arabs were worried by Jewish immigration because. . . .
   (d) The 1979 Camp David agreement was. . . .

2 Copy and complete these sentences by using the words in the **word list.**
   (a) By AD 70 . . . were found in many countries of the world.
   (b) The League of Nations gave . . . control of Palestine in 1918.
   (c) During the . . . World War about six . . . Jews were killed.
   (d) In 1948 the Jews . . . the state of. . . .
   (e) Since 1948 . . . and . . . have fought many. . . .

word list: Britain; wars; Israel; million; Second; Jews; proclaimed; Arabs; Jews

3 Copy map C into your book and explain briefly what it shows.

4 (a) Describe what you see on pictures A and B.
   (b) What arguments would the people in those pictures use to claim that Palestine belonged to them?

5 Compile a timeline on 'Arab and Jew 1948–1980s' showing dates and important events. Refer to other chapters.

6 Write a paragraph on each of the following:
   (a) a Palestinian refugee camp;
   (b) the involvement of Russia and the USA in the Middle East.

(*A further question appears on page 219.*)

The Suez crisis

● **The background**

Britain became interested in Egypt after 1869 when the Suez Canal was opened. The Canal was a direct link, or short-cut to distant parts of the British Empire in the Far East, like India, Hong Kong and Singapore. Also it provided a quicker route to other parts of the empire, such as Australia and New Zealand.

The Canal was built by Ferdinand de Lesseps, a Frenchman, but Benjamin Disraeli, the British Prime Minister, quickly realized its value. In 1875 he arranged for Britain to buy shares in the Canal Company so the government could have some control over how that vital waterway was used. Soon British troops were stationed in Egypt to guard the zone, because Suez was a kind of 'jugular vein' of the empire.

During the Second World War great battles were fought in the Middle Eastern desert for control of the Canal zone. The German Afrika Korps, under General Rommel, made strenuous efforts to reach it and in 1942 were within fifty miles of Cairo. But then the British Eighth Army, led by General Montgomery won the crucial battle of El Alamein and Suez was saved.

● **After 1945**

In 1945 British troops were still stationed in Egypt near the Canal zone. However, times were changing and Britain was no longer the great power it had been in earlier years. All over the world countries were seeking their independence. This same movement affected Egypt.

Some Egyptians were prepared for the British to stay on. Others, though, wanted them to go and several times there were outbreaks of rioting and violence. In 1952 a revolt by the Egyptian army overthrew their

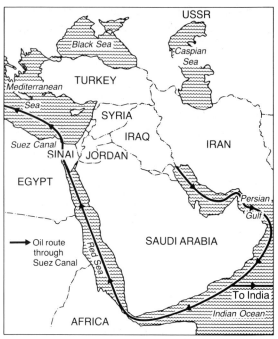

A *The importance of the Suez Canal*

king and later a senior officer, Gamal Nasser, came to power as the new leader of the nation. British troops started to withdraw from the Canal zone.

Nasser wanted reforms for his country, where millions led the life of poor peasants, often close to disease and starvation. Improved schemes of health were required. And in particular he wanted to see more modern methods of agriculture.

● **The Aswan Dam**

All farming in Egypt depends on irrigation from the River Nile and a plan was put forward to build a high dam at Aswan. This would provide water and hydro-electric power to help modernize the country.

The USA came forward with offers of aid in the early stages and work then depended on American dollars. In 1955, however,

General Nasser bought weapons and planes from Czechoslovakia, a Communist country and became very friendly with Russia. This worried the US government and they withdrew their offers of help with the building of the dam.

At that stage Nasser was determined to press ahead with his scheme. In desperation for money he decided to find some inside his own country, so he announced that Egypt was going to take over the ownership of the Suez Canal Company. All of the profits would go towards the building of the dam.

On 26 July 1956 he made a speech to the Egyptian people:

> **[1] The Suez Canal was dug by the efforts of the sons of Egypt – 120,000 Egyptians died in the process. . . . We shall build the High Dam as we want. We are determined. The Canal Company takes £35 million each year. Why shouldn't we take it for ourselves? . . . Thus today, when we build the High Dam we are also building the dam of dignity, freedom and grandeur. We are eliminating the dams of humiliation and servitude. . . . We want to do what we like. We want no partner.**

The speech was guaranteed to gain enormous support from the Egyptian people to whom Nasser was a hero. It also brought him many enemies in France, Britain and Israel. Britain and France feared that Nasser could now control their trade through the Suez Canal, especially their oil supplies. And Israel was the enemy right on Egypt's doorstep.

● **The secret agreement**
The British government were angry that a disagreement between the USA and Egypt

B *Cartoon, 'The Sphinx, Lion and Cockerel'*

had led to trouble for Britain and France. As a result the Prime Minister, Sir Anthony Eden, approached the US President, Dwight D. Eisenhower. He announced that Britain intended to take action against Egypt and asked for American support.

But the US government refused. They were not prepared to intervene.

So Britain and France decided to go it alone. First of all they held secret talks with the Israelis, who were worried by the growing strength of Egypt. The talks were arranged in France, with British and French politicians looking for a way to overthrow Nasser. And they quickly worked out a plan.

● **The war**
The secret plan started to unfold on 29

The Suez crisis

October 1956, when the Israeli army invaded Egypt across the Sinai Peninsula. The next day Britain and France sent an ultimatum to each of the two fighting nations, Israel and Egypt. They ordered both sides to keep their forces away from the Canal area.

Nasser refused to accept these terms so British and French forces went into action. Their planes bombed airfields. Paratroops were dropped on the Canal zone and troops were landed in a seaborne invasion. With their superior firepower they soon occupied important positions in the area.

● **The reaction**

The reaction to the invasion was very hostile.

At a meeting of the United Nations it was condemned. Russia even suggested that it might use force against Britain to compel it to withdraw. The heaviest blow, however, came from the Americans who were old friends. They spoke against the French and British adventure and brought pressure to bear to end it. The US refused support when Britain drifted into a financial crisis.

C *The Suez Canal blocked, 1956*

The Suez crisis

In Britain there was strong reaction, with powerful debates in Parliament. Some people believed that British rights had to be upheld and that the invasion was justified. Others said that British action was illegal and an example of bullying. These opponents used a motto: 'Law not War'.

Meanwhile the Egyptians closed the Canal by sinking a number of blockships.

● The end

With such opposition the small war ended quickly. The force of French and British troops was withdrawn and UN soldiers from several countries arrived to take their place. Their particular task was to clear away the blockships and later the Canal was handed back to the Egyptians who have run it ever since.

The Suez crisis was a great defeat for Britain and a turning point in its history. It proved that the old days of empire had finished and that such strong-arm methods would not work in the future. Many British people were angry with the Americans whose actions had helped to start the trouble, yet who would not give support later on.

President Nasser became a famous figure throughout the Arab world. The Russians gave him finance to carry on with the construction of the Aswan Dam and it was finished in 1970.

The arguments over who was right and wrong still go on. □

Exercises

1 Quick questions.
   (a) When was the Suez Canal opened?
   (b) Who arranged for Britain to buy shares in the Canal Company?
   (c) How does Egypt depend on the waters of the River Nile?
   (d) Which Egyptian officer was leader of the nation by 1956?
   (e) Who was the British Prime Minister in 1956?

2 Explain, using the information and document 1, why Nasser wished to modernize Egypt and why the Aswan Dam project was so important.

3 Imagine you attended the secret meeting between Israeli, French and British politicians to plan the overthrow of Nasser. Give the reasons why each country wished to take action against Egypt.

4 (a) What message did the British and French governments send to Nasser after the meeting with Israel?
   (b) How did Nasser react?

5 Copy map A. Underneath, write a few sentences to explain the importance of the Suez Canal to Britain.

6 Look at cartoon B and answer the following questions:
   (a) Which countries do the sphinx, lion and cockerel represent?
   (b) What is the sphinx holding?
   (c) Why are the lion and the cockerel looking so dejected?

7 Why was the Suez crisis a turning point in Britain's history?

8 What parts did the USA and the USSR play in the Suez crisis?

The wind of change in Africa

● **The background**

You will remember from Chapters 1 and 2 how European countries took most of Africa into their empires at the end of the nineteenth century, in what was called the 'Scramble for Africa'. By 1914 only two territories there – Liberia and Abyssinia (Ethiopia) were independent. Even after the Second World War in 1945 only four African countries governed themselves.

But the world situation changed. Those European nations which had owned empires were no longer powerful. Also, thousands of African people wanted independence and were not prepared to remain as subjects of these faraway countries.

After 1945 the old European empires started to break up as Africans asked and demanded, struggled and fought for their freedom. Such a movement was like a wind that kept blowing so that no one could stop it. The British Prime Minister, Harold Macmillan, referred to this in a speech made in South Africa in 1960:

A *A publicity poster from Uganda*

---

1 **We have seen the awakening of national consciousness in peoples who have for centuries lived in dependence on some other power.**

Fifteen years ago this movement spread through Asia. Many countries there, of different races and civilizations, pressed their claim to an independent national life.

Today that same thing is happening in Africa . . . in different places it may take different forms, but it is happening everywhere. The wind of change is blowing through the continent and, whether we like it or not, this growth of national consciousness is a political fact.

● **Britain in Africa**

Britain had a large empire in Africa, with territories spread over many parts of the continent (page 00).

A strong movement for independence started in the Gold Coast, building up in the early 1950s. Kwame Nkrumah founded a political party there – the Convention People's Party (CPP) and launched a campaign for freedom. At first the British resisted strongly. Nkrumah was put in prison, but later he was released and became Prime Minister. Then in 1957 Britain agreed to the Gold Coast becoming independent, with its new name – Ghana. It was the first British territory to achieve freedom in this way and became an example that others tried to follow.

The wind of change in Africa

In 1959 the British Colonial Secretary, Mr Iain Macleod, described the British view of what was happening:

> **2** **We could not possibly hold by force our territories in Africa. The march of men towards their freedom can be guided but not halted. Of course there were risks in moving quickly. But the risks of moving slowly were far greater.**

Thus freedom movements followed in other parts of Africa. In Kenya this led to violence when some Africans began a secret society called Mau Mau, which made attacks on anyone who helped white people. Mau Mau members believed that British settlers years before had taken the best land area – called 'The White Highlands' – for themselves. There were about 20,000 killings and a long struggle before peace came. Then, Jomo Kenyatta who had been put in prison, accused of leading Mau Mau, was released. Kenya achieved independence with Kenyatta as its first President.

There was also war in Nigeria, which is a large country with over 80 million inhabitants. The cause was the fact that the people there belonged mainly to three tribes, all with very different outlooks, who did not get on well together. After Nigeria became independent in 1960 the old hatreds came to the surface and a civil war broke out seven years later. This happened when the Ibos of the eastern region tried to break away and form their own nation. By the end of the fighting, in which the Ibos were unsuccessful, thousands of people had been killed or had starved to death.

B *Jomo Kenyatta celebrates* Uhuru *(freedom) in December 1963. Notice both European and African dress*

Independence was achieved by other African territories that had been part of Britain's empire – Sierra Leone, (1961), Uganda (1962) and Tanganyika, which became Tanzania in 1964. In each case they established their own governments controlled by Africans, yet kept their links with Britain by staying as members of the Commonwealth.

● Other European nations in Africa
You can see from the map on page 4 that other European states controlled territories in Africa. Because of this they too were affected by the movement towards African independence.

Belgium gave independence to the Belgian Congo (now called Zaire) in 1960. For years the Belgians had done little to teach the people there how to govern themselves when the time came. Therefore there was fighting as Belgian settlers and civil servants poured out of the country in large numbers. Soon afterwards there was a civil war between two groups of Africans in the Congo, with much bloodshed. Then, General Mobutu came to

[C] *Moroccan soldiers guard a public building during the civil war which followed the granting of independence to the Belgian Congo*

power in a nation which has grown richer from its supplies of copper and oil.

The French also started to give up their African territories. President de Gaulle of *France* made this his policy after 1960 and the lands were divided up into about a dozen small, separate states, such as Mali and Chad. In North Africa matters were more complicated. Morocco and Tunisia gained independence in 1956, but there was a long, drawn-out struggle in Algeria. Many French settlers lived there and war broke out between them and local Algerians who sought freedom. After much bloodshed, de Gaulle agreed to independence in 1962.

Portugal was more reluctant to give up its colonies in Africa – Angola in the south-west and Mozambique in the south-east. The Portuguese fought strongly to hold on to them, sending thousands of soldiers to struggle with the black African 'freedom fighters' who wanted to remove them. But by 1975 over three quarters of a million Portuguese settlers left these colonies, which then became independent.

● Southern Rhodesia
Britain found matters more difficult with colonies further south in Africa. Northern Rhodesia and Nyasaland both became independent, with the names of Zambia and Malawi respectively. But Southern Rhodesia was a stumbling block.

There were far more white settlers living there. They owned most of the country's resources and had brought technical progress, but they governed the country without allowing any voting rights for black people. They certainly were not prepared to give up what they had, or to share power with the black majority.

In 1965 the Southern Rhodesian government declared themselves

The wind of change in Africa

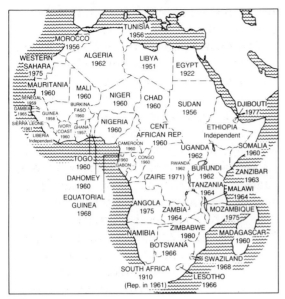

D *African independence*

independent of Britain. Although the British government called this move illegal and placed a ban on trade with them, the Rhodesians went on their own way. As a result, in the 1970s African guerrilla forces inside the country began a struggle for freedom and power and a civil war started.

At length, white Rhodesians had to agree that elections should be held on the principle of 'one person, one vote', regardless of colour. The result was an overwhelming victory for one of the guerrilla leaders, Robert Mugabe, and his party, the Patriotic Front. Mugabe became the leader of the new nation which was renamed 'Zimbabwe'. These developments caused some worried looks from a country which bordered the new Zimbabwe. That country was South Africa, where the black Africans had few rights and little power.

Exercises

1 Answer the questions on the following statements.
   (a) 'The wind of change is blowing through the continent.'
      (i) Who said this?
      (ii) When and where was it said?
      (iii) Which continent is referred to?
   (b) 'We could not possibly hold by force our territories.'
      (i) Who said this?
      (ii) Which territories was the speaker referring to?
      (iii) What risks was the speaker referring to?

2 Copy and complete these sentences.
   (a) In 1914 the following European countries had colonies in Africa. . . .

   (b) In 1965 the following European countries had colonies in Africa. . . .

3 What does it mean?
   These words, names and phrases appear in the chapter. Copy them into your book and explain what each one means:
   (a) national consciousness;
   (b) the White Highlands;
   (c) technical progress;
   (d) freedom fighters.

4 What have been the advantages and disadvantages of European rule in Africa?

5 Explain why South Africa might be worried by what happened in Zimbabwe.

South Africa and apartheid

● The background

The first Europeans to settle at the southern tip of Africa arrived there in the mid-seventeenth century. In those days, before the building of the Suez Canal the sea route to the Far East passed round the Cape of Good Hope. A number of Dutch settlers decided to make their homes in that region and soon began to farm there. They became known as Boers, or Afrikaaners.

As they travelled northwards from the Cape they came into contact with black African tribes. Sometimes they made peaceful agreements with them over territory. On other occasions there were wars in which the Boers, with firearms, were usually successful.

They were very good farmers in the fertile new land, using black Africans to labour for them. Their view of the native tribes was the usual white person's opinion of the time – that they were primitive and not fit to share the country with European settlers, except as unskilled workers.

Greater wealth started to come into the country at the end of the nineteenth century when gold and diamonds were discovered. That brought more and more Africans into the area to work in the mines for the white man.

Between 1899 and 1902 the white settlers fought against Britain in the Boer War, as you learned from Chapter 2. Then in 1910 the Union of South Africa was formed and became part of the British Commonwealth. It was a prosperous and beautiful country, but the Boers were determined to keep the power that they had in the hands of white people. To them, the local black people, coloureds and Indians were second- or third-rate citizens who should not be allowed to take part in the government of the nation.

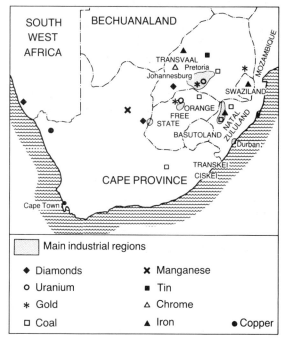

A *South Africa's natural resources*

● The Nationalists in 1948

After the Second World War there were two main groups of white people in South Africa. One consisted of descendants of British settlers who had come to the region after 1815. The other was a larger group which comprised the descendants of the Dutch settlers, the Afrikaaners, some of whose ancestors had been there since the mid-seventeenth century.

In 1948 a general election was held with, of course, only the whites voting. The Nationalist Party, which contained many Afrikaaners, won and began to bring in new policies. Led by Dr D. Malan, they started to pass laws which brought changes to everyday life in South Africa. Since then the Nationalist Party has been so strong that it has never been beaten at an election and has been able to press on with these laws.

South Africa and apartheid

● **Apartheid**

The basis of the new policy was called 'Apartheid', which is an Afrikaans word meaning 'separate development'. The Nationalists believe that blacks, whites, coloureds and Indians should all develop separately. There should be as little mixing of the races as possible. The blacks, who were called Bantus, should have their own states, called 'Bantustans', where they could live. They could come into white areas, but only as workers and servants. In white areas they would have to live in special black townships on the outskirts of cities.

Over the following years apartheid was put into practice and brought great trouble.

It set out to keep most power and land for the three million whites who claim to have created most of South Africa's wealth. To them the eleven million blacks are not suitable to share the government of the country.

Marriage between blacks and whites was forbidden as a punishable offence. Later, not more than ten Africans were allowed to meet together without permission from the police. All Africans had to carry an identity card, called their pass book, to show which racial group they belonged to.

In theatres and cinemas, restaurants and shops, whites and blacks were not allowed to mix. At the seaside there were 'white' and

B *Pass books being burnt in South Africa, 1960*

'black' beaches. Sports teams were organized by colour, not by ability. The education offered to whites was far and away superior to that given to blacks.

● Some incidents

The policy of apartheid has led to great opposition both inside and outside South Africa. For a start, some black Africans joined political parties like the African National Congress to protest against what was being done. But the government treated all opposition as a kind of Communism which had to be put down. There were peaceful protests but often these were met by violence.

In 1960 matters came to a head at a township called Sharpeville, near Johannesburg. On 21 March hundreds of blacks decided to protest against the laws by which they had to carry identity cards. But the police opened fire on them and there was panic in the crowd. Afterwards it was found that 67 had been killed and almost 200 injured.

The effects of the Sharpeville massacre were felt all round the world. There was an outcry in many countries and the policy of apartheid was detested by millions of people.

C *Signs of segregation*

South Africa and apartheid

● **Independence in 1961**

After Sharpeville a conference of Commonwealth leaders met in London. Many were very critical of South Africa and its policies. In 1961 the South Africans decided to leave the Commonwealth and become an independent republic. Then they carried on with their policy of apartheid.

They set up a number of separate states for black Africans within the borders of South Africa and called them Bantustans. But these states were only small areas and the people who lived there had few rights.

● **Events since independence**

Because of its racial policies South Africa has been shunned by many other nations. The United Nations have passed many resolutions condemning apartheid. Most countries refuse to play against its teams at sport and some will not trade.

But the South Africans have not been greatly disturbed by these things. They have certainly altered some laws so that black people now have more rights than they once did. But there is still a long way to go. The South African government argues that black people in their country are better off than others on the African continent. Yet blacks still have only a small share of the nation's total wealth.

Any opponents of the government are liable to be imprisoned under the country's harsh laws. Demonstrations against government policy lead to trouble. For example in 1976, at Soweto, near Johannesburg, police fired at schoolchildren who were making a protest and killed twenty-five of them. Other riots followed in which a total of some 500 blacks died.

South Africa, the richest country on the continent, appears to have a troubled future.

Exercises

1 Complete the sentences using the words from the **word list.**
   (a) . . . settlers in South . . . were known as. . . .
   (b) The . . . Boer . . . occurred between 1899 and 1902.
   (c) . . . are states where . . . people live.
   (d) The . . . book was an . . . card. . . . by black people.
   (e) South Africa . . . the . . . in 1961.

> **word list:** Africa; war; left; Boers; black; carried; Bantustans; identity; Dutch; pass; Commonwealth; Second

2 Why is South Africa referred to as 'the richest country on the continent'?

3 (a) What are Bantustans?
   (b) Why were they set up?

4 Explain, using all the information in the chapter:
   (a) the Boer opinion of native Africans;
   (b) how the Nationalist Party has developed this view;
   (c) how the black people have reacted to apartheid.

5 What action have other countries taken against South Africa to protest at its policy of apartheid?

The Cuban missile crisis

● **The background**

Cuba is an island lying between the Gulf of Mexico and the Atlantic Ocean. At its closest, Cuba's position lies one hundred miles to the south of Florida, part of the USA. The islands of that area of the world – the West Indies – were important to the Spaniards after the remarkable voyage of Columbus in 1492. Afterwards, Spain came to build a great empire in what was known as 'The New World' and Cuba was part of it. This lasted until 1898 when the Spanish Empire broke up and Cuba became independent. For years afterwards, its main crop, which was sugar, was bought by the United States and large American companies gained great power there.

● **Castro comes to power**

In the 1950s Fulgencia Batista was dictator of Cuba. His rule was harsh and many peasants suffered hardship, living in great poverty. A group of rebels led by Fidel Castro set out to overthrow him. These guerrillas fought from the mountains, gradually growing stronger and on 1 January 1959 overthrew the Batista government.

At once they began to bring in reforms. In a speech to the Cuban people, Castro asked such questions as:

A *Fidel Castro, the Cuban revolutionary leader. He and his guerrillas fought to overthrow Batista and set up a Communist state*

---

[1] Do you approve of our having given you honest administration of public funds for the first time in the history of Cuba?

Do you approve of our having tried and executed guilty war criminals by firing squads?

Do you approve of our having put the price of medicine within the reach of the people?

Do you approve of our having given land to the farmers?

Now more than ever, we take for our own the words of our national anthem: 'Hasten to the fight, Cubans, the country is proudly watching: do not fear a glorious death. To die for your country is to live on.'

● **American opposition**

Castro was supported by a number of Communists, so the United States did not show any favours to the new government. The Cuban leader took over the land for the nation and seized some companies belonging to Americans without paying any compensation. Bad feeling between the two countries increased when the USA refused to buy Cuba's sugar crop in 1960. The Americans did this after Castro had signed a trade agreement with Russia.

● The Bay of Pigs, 1961

Several thousand Cuban exiles, supporters of Batista, had fled to Florida, USA, when Castro came to power. The Americans now helped them to prepare for an invasion of Cuba, organized by the CIA (Central Intelligence Agency), which was the US secret service. The new American President, John F. Kennedy, agreed to the scheme and promised support from US ships and aircraft.

On 17 April 1961, 1,500 Cuban exiles landed in the Bay of Pigs on what was intended to be a successful invasion to overthrow Fidel Castro. But the adventure went terribly wrong. The invaders found little support from the people of Cuba and after three days of fighting, they surrendered.

This was a blow to the Americans, especially to President Kennedy.

● The Russians step in

The Russian Prime Minister, Nikita Khrushchev, saw a chance and took it. Through his friendship with Cuba he now had the opportunity of placing weapons near to the United States. So from August 1962 Russian vessels started to arrive in Cuba carrying secret supplies.

On 14 October an American reconnaissance plane flew over Cuba and took photos which were to shake the world. They showed that Russian rockets were being installed within easy range of a number of America's greatest cities. The news was taken immediately to President Kennedy who also learned that Russian

ships were on the high seas, heading for Cuba – and carrying more missiles.

The President spoke to the American nation on 22 October:

---

2 **This urgent transformation of Cuba into an important strategic base – by the presence of these large, long-range, and clearly offensive weapons of sudden mass destruction – constitutes an explicit threat to the peace and security of all the Americas.**

● The crisis

Kennedy had several options in front of him but realized that one false step could lead to deep trouble between the USA and the USSR. Both he and Khrushchev knew that there could be a nuclear war. The American President picked his moves carefully.

He laid down three points. First he announced that any ships carrying weapons to Cuba would be stopped and turned back. Second, he ordered more reconnaissance flights over the island. Third, he said that any attack from Cuba would be treated as an attack from Russia – and that would mean the start of World War Three.

B *Canvas-covered missiles (marked x) on board the Russian ship* Divinogorsk *bound for Cuba*

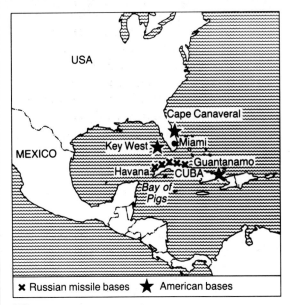

C *The Cuban Missile Crisis*

× Russian missile bases   ★ American bases

on the borders of Russia. If the USA would withdraw those weapons he would move Russian rockets out of Cuba. But Kennedy would not give way and refused to do any deals with the USSR until the Russians stopped their ships which were carrying rockets.

By this time tension was high. Cuba was surrounded by American warships, while a US Task force waited in Florida, ready to invade at a moment's notice. Both sides possessed powerful ICBM's (Inter-Continental Ballistic Missiles) and squadrons of bombers to carry atomic weapons.

On 28 October the Russians suddenly climbed down, much to the surprise of many people. A further message from the Russian leader to the American President stated:

4 **So as to eliminate as quickly as possible the conflict which is threatening peace . . . the Soviet Government . . . has given a new order to dismantle those weapons which you have described as offensive, to crate them and return them to the Soviet Union.**

All over the world, people appreciated what was at stake. They knew that the fate of millions everywhere depended on the decisions taken by two men. They also appreciated that one thoughtless move could lead to tragedy – for everyone.

On 26 October Kennedy received a letter from Khrushchev. In it the Russian leader said:

3 **We and you ought not to pull on the ends of the rope in which we have tied the knot of war, because the more the two of us pull, the tighter that knot will be tied. . . . Let us not only relax the forces pulling on the ends of the rope, let us take measures to untie the knot. We are ready for this.**

The next day Khrushchev sent another letter, offering a deal. He pointed out that American rockets were installed in Turkey,

D *Cartoon: Khrushchev (left) and President Kennedy (right) engage in a trial of strength over the issue of Cuban missiles*

The Cuban missile crisis

The pressure was off and the crisis passed quickly. Russian ships carrying missiles turned round and headed home.

The general feeling was that Kennedy had kept a cool head and had not given way under pressure.

It appeared that Khrushchev had stepped back. In reality, this decision helped to end the Russian leader's career.

Both men realized the dangerous situation that had occurred and how close their countries had been to a terrible struggle. They took steps to improve communications between the USSR and the USA. A telephone link was established between the two capital cities so that in future the leaders could speak to each other swiftly and directly. This 'hot line' has been in existence ever since. ☐

Exercises

1 Copy and complete this grid.

The Cuban Missile Crisis

Date	Development
1 January 1959	Overthrow of Batista Government
17 April 1961	
14 October 1962	
22 October 1962	
28 October 1962	

2 Who said:
   (a) 'We and you ought not to pull on the ends of the rope in which we have tied the knot of war.'
   (a) 'This urgent transformation of Cuba into an important strategic base . . . constitutes an explicit threat to the peace and security of all the Americas.'
   (c) 'Do you approve of our having given land to the farmers?'

3 Explain why Fidel Castro and his followers overthrew Batista's government and make a list of the reforms they introduced.

4 It is April 1961. You are adviser to President Kennedy. Write a brief report urging him to invade Cuba.

5 Look at picture B and answer these questions.
   (a) To which country does the ship belong?
   (b) What was the ship carrying?
   (c) Where was the ship going?
   (d) Who sent the ship and for what reason?
   (e) Who threatened to stop the ship and why?

6 In cartoon D you can see two men.
   (a) Identify the two men.
   (b) What are they about to do?
   (c) What had caused the two men to confront each other?
   (d) Explain the actions taken by both men.
   (e) Give two results of the Cuban missile crisis.

7 (a) What is the 'hot line' mentioned in this chapter?
   (b) Why is communication between the USSR and the USA important?

Vietnam

● The background

By the end of the nineteenth century France had built up an empire in the Far East. The territory it took there was a large area known as French Indo-China, which the French found profitable for trade. France kept the territory until 1941 when the Japanese entered the war. Then the French authorities there were forced to accept Japanese occupation of the country because they had no military power to defend their empire.

Nevertheless, some local people did fight against the Japanese. They were Communists and were led by Ho Chi Minh, who had lived and worked for some years in Europe. They used guerrilla warfare and by the end of the war in 1945 had learned much about methods of military action. They also were now determined to become independent.

● The French in trouble

In 1945 France hoped to restart running its empire in the Far East, where it had left off six years before. But the people of Indo-China (also called Vietnam) did not want their old masters back. Like so many Far Eastern people at that time they were seeking the freedom to govern themselves. As a result, Ho Chi Minh set up a Communist Democratic Republic of North Vietnam, but the French would not recognize the new nation.

Instead, fighting broke out between the French Army, which had poured thousands of men into their old colony and the North Vietnamese soldiers who were known as the Vietminh.

The two armies fought an entirely different form of warfare.

French forces looked for a battle against

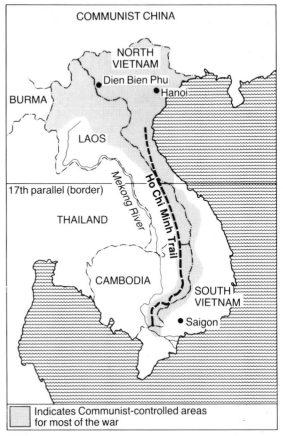

A *The war in Vietnam*

enemies who stood their ground and fought for set positions, like towns, river crossings or forts. They were well equipped and included units of paratroops – *les paras* – and men of the French Foreign Legion.

The Vietminh, on the other hand, tried completely different tactics. Their commander, General Giap, believed in avoiding set battles. His men were trained to hide up during the day, then fight by night. If threatened by a French advance they seemed to melt away into the surrounding countryside. The Vietminh received strong support from the peasants living in villages who gave them food and other supplies.

● Dien Bien Phu

In 1954 French forces occupied the town of Dien Bien Phu, in the north of Vietnam. They hoped that the Vietnamese troops would attack them there and be beaten in a great battle.

They were, however, in for a surprise.

Vietminh troops surrounded the town with thousands of men, dragged in artillery and bombarded the French for days on end. As the net closed tighter the French position became impossible and in May 1954, 15,000 of them were overwhelmed. They had suffered a great humiliation and had to give up their old empire in Indo-China.

Afterwards a peace conference was held at Geneva in Switzerland. As a result the old French colony was divided into four territories. Two of them, Cambodia and Laos, were neutral, while North Vietnam was Communist and South Vietnam non-Communist. A plan was put forward to hold free elections later to unify the two Vietnams.

B *These North Vietnamese carry their remaining possessions through the ruins after an American B-52 bomber raid on their city*

● Enter the Americans

But trouble still boiled. Before long, fighting started in South Vietnam between government forces there and Communist guerrillas, known as the Vietcong. Each side was struggling for power in the country.

America was drawn in because it wanted to stop the spread of Communism in the Far East. At first it sent military advisers to prop up a government that was corrupt but anti-Communist. In return, North Vietnam sent more guerrilla troops south along the 'Ho Chi Minh Trail' to attack them.

After 1964, President Lyndon B. Johnson increased the involvement of the United States because he wanted to hold back Communism in the Far East. From the following year American bombers were sent to launch heavy raids on targets in North Vietnam – and civilians as well as soldiers were killed there. In spite of the bombing the US forces could not defeat an enemy who was skilled in guerrilla warfare.

Some Americans were worried that their government was supporting corrupt governments in South Vietnam, calling them democracies while they were really dictatorships.

C *Women and young supporters of the Vietcong in training. The US army could not defeat the Vietcong which used guerrilla tactics*

Vietnam

● **The world's reaction**

In many countries of the world opposition grew to American intervention in Vietnam. Demonstrators marched through cities to protest. Even in the USA there were outcries against the policy of President Johnson, with chants of:

> [1] Hey, hey, L.B.J.,
> How many kids did you kill today?

Many demonstrators agreed with the North Vietnamese leader, Ho Chi Minh, who wrote in 1968:

> [2] The Vietnamese people have never done any harm to the United States. But the US Government has ceaselessly intervened in Vietnam. . . . The US Government has committed war crimes, crimes against peace and against mankind.

After Richard Nixon became President of the USA in 1968 he made efforts to bring peace. The forces of South Vietnam were built up but many American servicemen were withdrawn. At the same time, talks were held in Paris between representatives of the USA and the Vietcong. By late 1972 many Americans were heartily sick of war.

D *A Vietnamese woman held at gunpoint*

Vietnam

At length, in January 1973 agreement was reached and there was a ceasefire.

● Later events

Although the Americans withdrew, fighting went on in Vietnam. Early in 1975 forces from the North invaded the South and soon defeated their old enemies. By then Ho Chi Minh was dead, but his dream of a united Vietnam had come into being.

Later there was fighting in Laos and Cambodia, the other two territories of the old French Indo-China. In both places Communists seized power but that brought a new form of trouble. The Communists in Cambodia had been helped by China, while those in Vietnam had received aid from Russia. Thus there was rivalry between those two great powers.

In 1979 fighting occurred between Vietnam and Cambodia and later between China and Vietnam. Some people feared that in the future a large-scale war could break out in that part of Asia. ☐

Exercises

1 Copy and complete the paragraph using the words in the **word list**.
In 1945 the . . . wanted to . . . their old Far Eastern . . . in Indo- . . . . However, they were opposed by . . . from the . . . under the . . . of Ho Chi Minh. Years of . . . followed, first with the . . . and later with the. . . .

> **word list:** leadership; French; fighting; Americans; French; empire; restore; China; north; Communists.

2 Match up the heads of the following sentences, (a)–(e), with the correct tails, (i)–(v).
  (a) American bombers launched raids
  (b) Between 1965 and 1973 Vietnam
  (c) There was a ceasefire in
  (d) At Dien Bien Phu in 1954
  (e) After the Americans left Vietnam

  (i) Vietnam in January 1973
  (ii) the French were defeated
  (iii) the north defeated the south
  (iv) became the centre of American effort
  (v) against targets in North Vietnam

3 Copy map A into your book and explain what it shows.

4 Describe and explain what you can see in pictures B, C and D.

5 Explain:
  (a) why France was unable to regain power in Indo-China;
  (b) why American presidents sent aid to South Vietnam;
  (c) why US military methods were unsuccessful;
  (d) why there was opposition to US policy in Vietnam;
  (e) what has happened in Vietnam since 1973.

6 Imagine you are one of the Vietminh troops in 1954. Describe the methods of fighting you and your fellow soldiers use and explain how you defeat the French at Dien Bien Phu.

EFTA and the Common Market

● **Europe after 1945**

In 1945 large areas of Western Europe had been affected by six years of war. Industry and transport, farming and business had been badly hit. Thousands of buildings had been destroyed or damaged. Tragically, millions of people had been killed, wounded or were refugees. A gigantic effort was needed to restore the continent's life in countries stretching from Germany to France, from Britain to Italy.

Through the programme of Marshall Aid the USA poured billions of dollars into western Europe. This was done for two reasons. First, the Americans saw the need to repair the damage done by the greatest war of all time. Second, they wanted to build up the countries of that area into a barrier against the spread of Communism.

But as European nations gradually got back on their feet, rebuilding industry and transport and restarting their commerce, one important fact became painfully clear. This was that Russia and America were now the world's two super states. Europe, once the most important continent, had lost its position.

● **The Treaty of Rome, 1957**

Some European leaders looked forward to the day when their countries would play an active part in world affairs again. But they knew that they could not do this individually. In 1949 the North Atlantic Treaty Organization (NATO) was formed to defend them against possible Russian attacks from the east. If such a pact could be signed for defence, some argued, surely there could be a similar treaty for trade.

Two leaders in this movement were President Charles de Gaulle of France and Chancellor Konrad Adenauer of West Germany. For generations their nations had been enemies and both had been shattered by two world wars. They both saw the need for co-operation in peace, through trade.

As a step forward in 1951, six European countries formed a common market in coal and steel. They were Germany, France, Italy, Belgium, Holland and Luxemburg. Their organization was called the European Coal and Steel Community (ECSC) and it helped to increase steel and coal production by having no customs barriers to trade in those commodities.

Then in 1957 those six countries went a step further by signing the Treaty of Rome and setting up the European Economic Community (EEC). Through this they did

A *A German poster which states 'Free Pass For The Marshall Plan'*

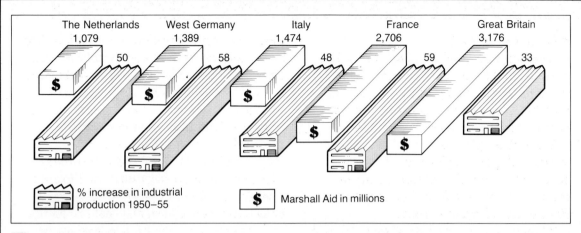

The Netherlands	West Germany	Italy	France	Great Britain
1,079	1,389	1,474	2,706	3,176
50	58	48	59	33

% increase in industrial production 1950–55

$ Marshall Aid in millions

B *Artist's impression of aid given to Europe through the Marshall Plan*

away with paying customs duties on goods traded among them. What became known as the Common Market came into operation.

● **Britain and EFTA**

What was Britain's view of the Common Market? For over two centuries Britain had owned an empire and took more interest in that than in Europe. Winston Churchill once commented: 'We are with Europe, but not of it'.

After 1945 some British people wanted to maintain these old connections, especially with Commonwealth countries like Australia and New Zealand, who were trading partners. So Britain did not join the Common Market.

But the EEC had such success that in 1960 Britain started a rival organization called the European Free Trade Association (EFTA). Seven countries joined – Britain, Austria, Denmark, Norway, Portugal, Sweden and Switzerland. They abolished taxes on all industrial goods they traded with each other.

● **Britain and the Common Market**

Gradually opinion in Britain changed and more people were in favour of joining the Common Market which was doing well. In 1961 the Conservative government under Harold Macmillan applied for membership, but the French leader, General de Gaulle, objected. He believed that Britain was too dependent on the USA. He also claimed that:

> **1** **England is . . . linked by trade, markets and food supply to very different and often very distant lands. She is essentially an industrial and commercial nation, and her agriculture is relatively unimportant.**

Following that, nothing came of Britain's application.

In 1967 Harold Wilson's Labour Government tried to gain entry to the EEC. Britain's trading position had grown worse, while members of the Common Market had continued to expand. But once again de Gaulle refused.

Then after the Conservatives came to power in 1970 they made another attempt to be accepted by the French. In a speech, Sir Alec Douglas-Home said:

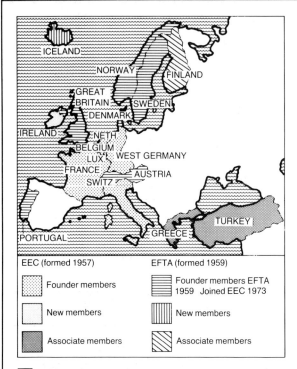

EEC (formed 1957)

∴	Founder members
	New members
▨	Associate members

EFTA (formed 1959)

☰	Founder members EFTA 1959 Joined EEC 1973
⫼	New members
⧄	Associate members

C *EEC and EFTA*

> **2** Whether we join or not, this Community will grow stronger and stronger, and if we are outside our freedom will be less, not more. It is as sovereign members of the Community that we shall be in a position to safeguard the future of Britain – all of Britain – in the years to come.

By that time General de Gaulle had retired and his successor, Georges Pompidou, was in favour of British entry. As a result there were talks and negotiations. Britain joined the Common Market on 1 January 1973. Denmark and Eire also joined, so the 'Six' became the 'Nine'.

In 1975 Britain's new Labour government, which had once been against membership, held a referendum, or free vote among British people to see whether they wanted their country to stay in the Common market. They voted in favour by a majority of two to one and Britain has remained a member ever since.

● **The Common Market since 1975**
The EEC was started to keep trade but it has other tasks. A European Parliament has been set up and all member countries send representatives there to discuss matters affecting them. The British representatives are called 'Euro-MPs'. There is a Council of Ministers who deal with such matters as the very thorny problem of how much each nation should pay towards running the Common Market. Also there is a Court of Justice to which people can appeal, if they feel that the laws of their own land are unjust.

So each country belonging to the EEC has its own government and laws and customs. Yet it also has the strange position in which another Parliament is dealing with some of its affairs. A number of people in Britain have found that hard to accept.

From Britain's point of view there have

D *Konrad Adenaeur (left) and Charles de Gaulle (right) did much towards improving French and German friendship after the war. De Gaulle did not wish Britain to join the EEC*

been changes in the pattern of trade since joining. Obviously now Britain buys and sells far more than it once did to other members of the EEC, like Germany and Italy. Its old trade with Commonwealth countries such as Australia and New Zealand has declined.

There has been a great deal of argument over how much each member nation should pay and receive from the Community. Here, Britain feels that it has been unfairly treated because, with West Germany, it is the largest contributor. Many British people believe that mainly agricultural nations, like France, have received too much in order to encourage their farmers. As a result, it is argued, vast supplies of butter, wine and milk have been produced and put into cold storage because they are not required.

Western Europe has drawn closer through the EEC and several other members have joined in recent years – can you find their names? But there is at present not the unity of government and armed forces which would be needed to make Europe a super power to rival Russia or America.

Exercises

1 Quick questions.
  (a) Who poured vast sums of money into Western Europe after 1945?
  (b) What do the initials NATO mean?
  (c) When was the Treaty of Rome signed?
  (d) When did EFTA start?
  (e) Which French President opposed Britain's entry into the EEC?

2 Look at the cartoon 'Free Pass For the Marshall Plan'.
  (a) Name some of the flags you can see.
  (b) What was the Marshall Plan?
  (c) Give two reasons why the USA wished to help Western Europe.

3 Copy and complete the chart.

Initials	Meaning	Established	Purpose
NATO	North Atlantic Treaty Organization	1949	To defend Europe against Russian attack
ECSC			
EEC			
EFTA			

4 (a) Copy map C into your book.
  (b) Under your map write down in two columns the member countries of the EEC and EFTA.

5 Fact or opinion? Which of the following statements are fact and which are opinion?
  (a) By the Treaty of Rome, 1957, members of the EEC did away with customs duties on goods traded amongst them.
  (b) Europe, once the most important continent, lost its position after 1945.
  (c) Most people in Britain had little interest in joining the EEC.
  (d) Britain's trade would have improved faster if the country had not joined the EEC.
  (e) Most British people today would prefer Britain to leave the EEC.

6 Write down the advantages and disadvantages of Britain being a member of the EEC.

(*A further question appears on page 219.*)

Hungary, Czechoslovakia and Poland

GERMANY
POLAND 1947
CZECHOSLOVAKIA 1948
AUSTRIA
HUNGARY 1949
RUMANIA 1947
YUGOSLAVIA 1945
BULGARIA 1946
ALBANIA 1946

Russian satellites with dates of complete Communist control

Communist but expelled from the Cominform

Russian   British   ▬▬ Iron Curtain, 1949

American   French   ▬▬ Germany, 1945

A *Central and Eastern Europe since 1945*

● Eastern Europe after 1945

In the last stages of the Second World War, during the period 1944–5, Russian troops advanced deep into Eastern Europe, driving the Nazi armies before them. They overran countries stretching from Latvia in the north to Rumania in the south. Thus when the Germans surrendered, the Red Army occupied territory from Berlin eastward to the Russian frontier.

The Russian leader, Joseph Stalin, had worked out a policy of how he was going to treat the conquered lands. His first principle was to set up friendly governments in them so that Russia could rely on their obedience. Then he would be able to use them as a kind of shield protecting Russian frontiers against any possible future attack by the Germans or any other nation in the west.

Elections were soon held in the Russian-occupied countries. What often happened was that Communists from those countries who had lived in the USSR during the war were brought back. Before long, with the aid of Russian officials, they had pushed other parties out of power. Sometimes their opponents were thrown into prison – or they disappeared. From 1945–8 Bulgaria, Yugoslavia, Hungary, Rumania, Poland and Czechoslovakia all became Communist-dominated. The same thing happened in the eastern zone of Germany where the Russians faced the western powers across the 'Iron Curtain'.

Gradually the 'Cold War' developed in Europe. On occasions there were outbreaks of trouble between the two sides. Stalin, the dictator of Russia, appeared firm in his hatred of the Americans and fear of the Germans.

● The death of Stalin, 1953

Joseph Stalin died in March 1953. He had been one of the most ruthless dictators of all time and ruled Russia with a rod of iron. The Tsars of old had never had such power. Any opposition was stamped out by his secret police and even those close to him never knew when they might fall out of favour and be removed. During the last months of his life some of his doctors were arrested and accused of taking part in a poisoning plot.

After the death of Stalin Russian policy changed, as if a heavy burden had been lifted off the nation. Nikita Khrushchev came to power in 1955 and soon life was easier. Some political prisoners were released and the new leader actually denounced Stalin during a famous speech made in the next year.

Khrushchev even suggested that the Russian people could have had a higher standard of living by competing with the capitalist countries of western Europe and America in trade. He said:

---

[1] We want to compete with the capitalist countries in peaceful endeavour . . . let us see who produces more per head of population, who provides a higher material and cultural standard for the people.

As a result of the new policies those countries in eastern Europe which were under Russia's control also wanted some freedom. They were its satellite states, like

planets round the sun, but now wished to have some say in running their own policies. Since 1955 three have tried to gain some independence, but on each occasion the Russians have stepped in to prevent it.

● 1956 – the Hungarian uprising

The first nation of eastern Europe to try for greater freedom was Hungary. There were demonstrations against those politicians who had supported Stalin and eventually the Prime Minister, Imre Nagy, asked Russian troops to leave in November 1956. This brought a sharp reaction from the USSR. Khrushchev could see that if Hungary pulled out of the Warsaw Pact the whole Russian defensive system might collapse, leaving the country open to another invasion.

As a result, Russian forces were sent into

[B] *Stalin's statue was pulled down in Budapest on 2 November 1956, when Hungarians rebelled against Russian influence in the country*

action against the Hungarians. Their tanks fought on the streets of Budapest in a short, bloodthirsty campaign before the rebellion was stopped. Over 200,000 Hungarians fled from their homes to the west and about 30,000 others died in the revolt. Afterwards Nagy was taken prisoner and shot by the Russians.

Khrushchev hoped that the other satellite countries would learn from the example of what had happened in Hungary. But he was wrong.

● **Czechoslovakia, 1968**

In January 1968 Alexander Dubcek became Secretary of the Czechoslovak Communist Party. He tried to bring in a 'socialist, democratic revolution', promising a change in people's lives. There was freedom for the press and that led to criticisms of Russia.

Such freedom worried the USSR and other nations in the Warsaw Pact.

In August 1968 Warsaw Pact forces, led by Russians, invaded Czechoslovakia, claiming they had been asked in! The Russian News Agency, Tass, reported:

[2] Party and governmental leaders of the Czechoslovak Socialist Republic have asked the Soviet Union and other allied states to render the fraternal Czechoslovak people urgent assistance, including assistance with armed force. The request was brought about by the threat which had arisen to the socialist system existing in Czechoslovakia. . . . Nobody will ever be allowed to wrest a single link from the community of socialist states.

[C] *A Soviet tank in the centre of Prague, during the occupation of Czechoslovakia, August 1968*

The last sentence is the clue to why the Russians intervened. There could be no chink in the armour of protecting nations near their frontiers.

There was little fighting, but Dubcek was quickly overthrown. The new-found freedom soon disappeared.

● **Poland, from 1979**

After 1945 Poland became a satellite state of the USSR, with a Communist government firmly fixed in power. Much of the country's economic life in farming and industry was linked to what Russia needed and wanted it to produce. The standard of living for most Poles was low compared with the countries of western Europe.

Poland's trade suffered badly in the 1960s and 1970s and large sums of money had to be borrowed from abroad. At length some workers formed a trade union, named 'Solidarity', which aimed to fight for better conditions of pay and employment for its members. This spelt danger to Communist thought, where trade unions were not allowed.

Another point is that the vast majority of Poles are Roman Catholics. A Polish cardinal became Pope, as John Paul II, and the devotion of the Polish people was remarkable. Many of them disliked the godless Communism of Russia.

In 1981 Solidarity launched strikes, supported by thousands of workers. The country seemed to be approaching a civil war and many people watched anxiously to see how Russia would respond. But the Polish government reacted sharply and put the country under martial law. Lech Walesa, the leader of Solidarity, was put under house arrest. The authorities were not prepared to allow Poland to drift away from its close ties with Russia. ☐

Exercises

1 (a) Copy map A into your book.
  (b) Shade in all those countries under Russian control.
  (c) Underline the names of countries invaded by Russian troops.

2 Look at picture B and answer the following questions.
  (a) Whose statue was pulled down?
  (b) Where was the picture taken?
  (c) Why was the statue pulled down?
  (d) What action was taken by the Russians?
  (e) What did Khrushchev hope to achieve?

3 Explain why the Russians invaded Czechoslovakia.

4 You have been sent to interview Lech Walesa. Ask him about Poland's recent history, the Polish standard of living, 'Solidarity' and the Polish government's reaction to it.

5 Explain the meaning of:
  (a) 'Iron Curtain';
  (b) 'Cold War';
  (c) capitalist countries;
  (d) satellite states;
  (e) independence.

China since the Cultural Revolution

● The Great Leap Forward

After the Communists under Mao Tse-tung took power in 1949 they made great efforts to industrialize China. They knew that if their nation was to stand beside the great powers of the world there would have to be a rapid growth of factories and production. So they followed a kind of Russian Five Year Plan and made some remarkable achievements – from 1952–7 the production of coal and machine tools doubled, while the output of steel increased 400 per cent.

A *There is no labour shortage in China. The people have worked together, as in this canal project, to improve their standard of living*

B *A huge parade during the Cultural Revolution. Notice the 'little red books'*

However, these changes often made life difficult for peasants in the countryside. The population of China was increasing rapidly so the peasants had to work harder to produce more food. But in return, many felt that few benefits in the form of manufactured goods came their way.

Chairman Mao wanted the Chinese to discuss these matters openly. In 1956 he invited people to talk. He said:

---

1 Let a hundred flowers bloom and a thousand schools of thought argue.

There was a great response, with much criticism of what was being done. So in 1958 Mao announced the Great Leap Forward.

In the countryside the lives of millions of ordinary Chinese were reorganized. Villagers became part of the work-force of 26,000 huge farms, called communes, each of which contained up to 50,000 people. They ate together in large halls, their children were put in crèches while the mothers were employed and there was a drive to work harder to raise production. Millions of acres of land were reclaimed and farming became more productive.

Yet many peasants felt overworked. Mao claimed that his nation was 'walking on two legs', one being machinery and the other one human muscle power. The Great Leap Forward came to an end about 1960 because many peasants did not take to the life of the great collective farms. They wanted the chance to work on their own small patches of land as well.

● **Splitting with the USSR**
Both China and the USSR were Communist powers in the 1950s. For many years the

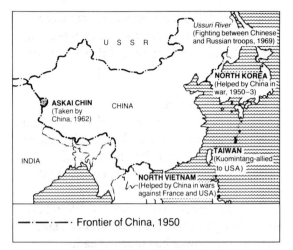

| C | *Chinese expansion after 1949* |

Map labels:
- U S S R
- *Ussuri River* (Fighting between Chinese and Russian troops, 1969)
- NORTH KOREA (Helped by China in war, 1950–3)
- ASKAI CHIN (Taken by China, 1962)
- CHINA
- INDIA
- TAIWAN (Kuomintang-allied to USA)
- NORTH VIETNAM (Helped by China in wars against France and USA)
- — · — · — Frontier of China, 1950

● The Cultural Revolution

By 1966 Chairman Mao believed that the revolution he had brought to China was not going in the right direction. Therefore he launched a campaign that became known as the 'Cultural Revolution'. Thousands of young people, called Red Guards, were sent all over the country to bring in the true revolutionary spirit.

They drove out western ideas. They drove out of office any government official who did not seem keen enough to follow Mao's teachings. Most of them carried a little red book, containing Mao's sayings. Mao said that experts were a danger and had drifted away from the people:

2 **From entering primary school to leaving college is altogether sixteen or seventeen years. I fear that for over twenty years people will not see rice, mustard, wheat or millet growing; nor will they see how workers work, nor how peasants till the field.**

He believed that officials, factory managers and lecturers should go into the countryside to work. His little red book stressed the need for them to serve the people and criticize themselves. Mao said:

3 **We must drive actors, poets, dramatists and writers out of the cities and push them all off to the countryside. They should all periodically go down in batches to the villages and to the factories. . . . Whoever does not go down will get no dinner; only when they go down will they be fed.**

Russians had given encouragement and supplies to the Chinese and some people believed that the two nations might grow closer in their policies in the Far East. However, the opposite happened.

When Nikita Khrushchev became premier of the USSR in 1957 he tried to reach agreements with the Americans. In the opinion of Chairman Mao he was too soft with them. By 1959 relations between the Russians and the Chinese had grown distinctly cool. Mao complained that the USSR was turning back to capitalism and soon afterwards the Russians stopped sending advisers and economic aid to China.

Later, matters grew worse. As the map shows, the countries share a very long frontier of over 8,800 km. Some border areas were claimed by China and Russia and in the late 1960s both moved in troops who faced each other across disputed land. In 1969 some fighting actually broke out, although it did not last for long.

No one knows what future relations will be between the two countries.

China since the Cultural Revolution

The Red Guards certainly caused a stir in China. Many of them were students from colleges and schools who gave up their studies for long periods to go demonstrating, or helping in farming or industry. This meant that their formal education suffered. All over the nation trade and production fell and there were outbreaks of violence as those who were attacked fought back.

Through the Cultural Revolution, Mao hoped to shake up those officials who were not changing quickly enough to his way of thinking. He hoped to get the young on his side and stressed the idea that the individual must give way to the community. In 1957 he wrote:

---

4 The young people are the most active and vital force in society. They are the most eager to learn and the least conservative in their thinking. This is especially so in the age of socialism.

By the time the Cultural Revolution came to an end thousands of officials had lost their jobs. Revolutionary committees were set up everywhere to run the country and Mao's position in China had been strengthened. Many of his opponents were removed. Lin Piao, who had once been a close comrade, disappeared in mysterious circumstances in which it was said that he had died in an air crash.

● China after Mao

In the early 1970s a powerful figure in China was the Prime Minister, Chou En-lai. After the break with Russia he encouraged Chinese industry to expand to produce its own materials. China even built and exploded its own atomic bomb in 1964 and since then production of coal and oil, steel and electric power has raced ahead.

Both Chou En-lai and Mao Tse-tung died in 1976. By then, China was a full member of the United Nations (1971) and was the world's third super power.

Since Mao's death some of the old opponents of the Cultural Revolution have come back to power. They have been keen to hold talks and trade with western nations. Some of Mao's ideas have been set to one side. His widow and three of his supporters, nicknamed 'The Gang of Four' have been blamed for leading the nation in the wrong direction.

The future of a country which contains one quarter of the world's population is obviously going to affect everyone's lives by the end of the century. □

Exercises

1 (a) When did Mao announce the Great Leap Forward?
  (b) Why was there a split between Russia and China?
  (c) What was the 'little red book'?
  (d) Who were the 'Gang of Four'?

2 (a) Read extracts 1, 2, 3 and 4 and compile a list headed 'Mao's ideas for China'.
  (b) What do you think of his ideas?

3 Write a few lines on each of the following:
  (a) the Great Leap Forward;
  (b) the Cultural Revolution.

The Japanese revival

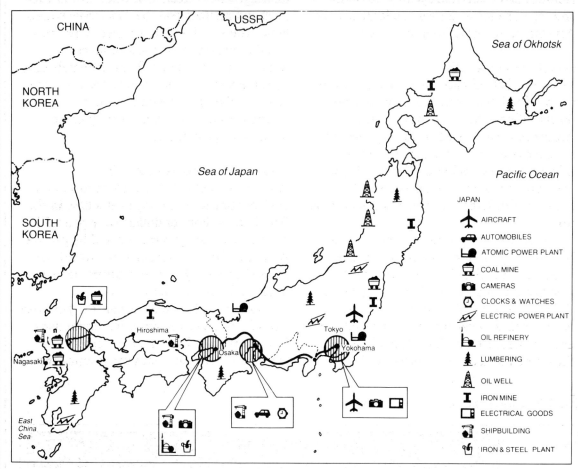

CHINA
USSR
NORTH KOREA
SOUTH KOREA
SOUTH KOREA
Sea of Okhotsk
Sea of Japan
Pacific Ocean
Hiroshima
Nagasaki
Tokyo
Osaka
Yokohama
East China Sea

JAPAN

AIRCRAFT
AUTOMOBILES
ATOMIC POWER PLANT
COAL MINE
CAMERAS
CLOCKS & WATCHES
ELECTRIC POWER PLANT
OIL REFINERY
LUMBERING
OIL WELL
IRON MINE
ELECTRICAL GOODS
SHIPBUILDING
IRON & STEEL PLANT

A *Modern Japan*

● Japan in 1945

In 1945 Japan was a defeated nation. After the early successes of the Pacific War, from 1941–2, the Japanese had been slowly crushed by the immense military and economic strength of the USA. By the end of the war several cities, including the capital, Tokyo, had been devastated by fire-bomb raids from US aircraft.

The dropping of atom bombs on Hiroshima and Nagasaki had been the final steps in a humiliating defeat. Japanese pride had been badly hurt when the Emperor announced over the radio that the nation would have to surrender to its enemies, the Americans and the British.

When the first Allied units landed in Japan to take over the country they found a nation devastated by the effects of war. Many Japanese could barely believe that they had lost. They were humiliated by the surrender and the fact that their Emperor, Hirohito, could no longer be regarded as a kind of god.

Ships had been sunk, food and raw materials were in short supply. Many factories had been destroyed by bombing and Japan had lost control of a large part of Asia that it had held from the 1930s.

● Help from the USA

Japan was helped back on to its feet by the nation which had been mainly responsible for its defeat – the USA. At first, the Americans made sure that the Japanese war machine could not work again. Several military leaders, including General Tojo, were brought to trial and executed. A number of different political parties were set up.

The Americans poured money into Japan because they did not want it to turn towards Communism. Also they gave land to farmers who had previously only leased it as tenants.

But the event which started the Japanese on the path to prosperity was, strangely enough, another war! This time, however, they were not actively involved in the fighting. The Korean War broke out in June 1950 and immediately the Americans placed large orders with firms in Japan. They were asked to provide stores and supplies, vehicles and munitions. These demands gave a great boost to Japanese industry which was able to build up factories with new machinery and introduce the very latest methods of production.

● Japanese industry takes off

After the end of the Korean War in 1953 the USA continued to use Japan as a base in the Far East. Millions of dollars were poured in by the American government and by private American firms. In response the world was amazed by what Japanese industry achieved over the following twenty years.

Thousands of people flocked into Japanese cities from the countryside and found work in a boom time. In particular, Japan expanded industries that were running into

B *The world production of cars, 1983*

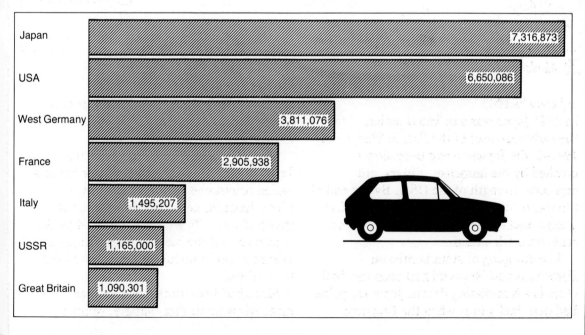

Japan	7,316,873
USA	6,650,086
West Germany	3,811,076
France	2,905,938
Italy	1,495,207
USSR	1,165,000
Great Britain	1,090,301

trouble in other industrialized countries, like Britain. Steel output rose. Shipbuilding expanded. And Japan did extremely well in the production of motor cycles, cars and commercial vehicles. The latest methods of mechanization were used and Japanese goods sold all over the world. Cameras, radios, televisions, videos and computers were found in many lands as Japanese industries continued to expand.

Some people in the USA and Europe became very worried because Japanese goods seemed to drive others out of the market. They were reliable, well and cheaply produced. European nations particularly found the pace of competition very hard to match. In some cases those nations found that their old industries were driven out of

the market. The next time you walk along a street, look at the countries of origin of the motor-bikes that roar past. Then remember that in 1950 they were nearly all produced by British firms.

By 1968 Japan's exports equalled Britain's. In 1975 it had the world's largest and most successful shipyards. By then it was the world's third largest industrial producer, exceeded only by the two super powers, the USA and the USSR. All of this progress has been achieved with only small quantities of raw materials found in Japan. Most has to be imported, as well as all of the oil used by its industry.

No other nation since 1945 has attained such rapid and overwhelming success economically. There are several reasons why

C *Honda motor cycles awaiting export. Japanese competition – good products at lower prices – has affected many European industrialized nations*

The Japanese revival

this has happened. One is the fact that Japan has spent very little on its armed forces – it has never been allowed again to build itself up into a warlike nation. The USA gives protection, with American soldiers, ships and aircraft, so the Japanese have been able to focus all of their attention on beating their rivals in industry.

But another reason is Japanese pride in themselves. They called themselves 'Sekai Ichi', which means 'the world's best'. Certainly they have achieved this in a kind of economic miracle since 1945.

● **Other areas in the Far East**

Japan showed the way of progress to other nations in the Far East. Some of them have also started to compete in the production of goods to be sold abroad. Many of these places have much lower costs than European countries because labour is so cheap.

Many goods on sale today announce 'Made in Taiwan'. The Chinese Nationalists living there ever since the Communist revolution in China during 1948–9 have now entered the world of trade. Their prices are often lower than those demanded for goods produced in Europe or the USA. Another competitor in world trade is South Korea where, for example, shipbuilding and repair yards are doing well. A third competitor in the Far East is Singapore, which offers goods at low prices.

These new nations compete for trade, producing articles cheaply and these are often bought readily by customers in Britain. However, British industries can thereby be harmed in the long run, because they will be faced with unemployment. Governments all over Europe and in the USA have to decide which is better for their people – cheaper prices or greater production. □

Exercises

1 Make a list of ten Japanese products which can be bought in Britain.

2 Write a paragraph on 'Japan since 1945' using the following points:
   (a) Japan in 1945;
   (b) American aid to Japan;
   (c) Japanese industry since 1945;
   (d) Sekai Ichi;
   (e) Japan and its industrial competitors.

3 Draw a chart to represent the figures shown in diagram B. Divide the countries into groups, for example those producing between 1 million and 2 million cars.

4 (a) How has Japanese progress affected other countries in the Far East?

   (b) Why do British people often prefer to buy goods from Taiwan and Korea rather than those made in Britain?
   (c) Do you think British people should 'Buy British'? Give reasons for your answer.

5 What do you understand by the following terms:
   (a) economic strength?
   (b) prosperity?
   (c) boom time?
   (d) industrialized countries?
   (e) economic miracle?

6 Look at picture C. Write a few sentences to explain how it illustrates the history of Japan since 1945.

The Irish Question

● The background

What is often known as 'The Irish Problem' or 'The Irish Question' has gone on for centuries. At the root of the trouble is the fact that for hundreds of years Catholic Ireland was ruled over by Protestant England. The Scots, Welsh and English were treated as foreigners who had no business in a land that didn't belong to them.

The people of Ireland suffered poverty and hardship in the nineteenth century. In many cases they did not own their land but had to rent it from English landlords. And in 1845–6, when the potato crop failed, thousands starved to death in a great famine. Thousands of others emigrated, seeking a new life, going to places such as America or Australia. In 1841 there were just over eight million inhabitants of Ireland; seventy years later the total was less than four and a half million. Many Irish people blamed the British for doing too little to relieve disasters.

By the end of the nineteenth century there was a strong move among the Southern Irish for two things. First, they wanted Home Rule, which was the right to govern themselves, separated from the rest of Britain. Second, they wanted land reform, which meant that Irish farmers should own the land they worked, not have to rent it from English landlords.

But in the north of Ireland lived many Protestants who were glad of their links with the United Kingdom. They had complete loyalty to the crown and wanted to maintain it.

● Ireland, 1900–14

Between 1900 and 1914 the struggle for Home Rule and Land Reform continued.

A *A barricade erected in Townsend Street, Dublin during the Easter Rising of 1916*

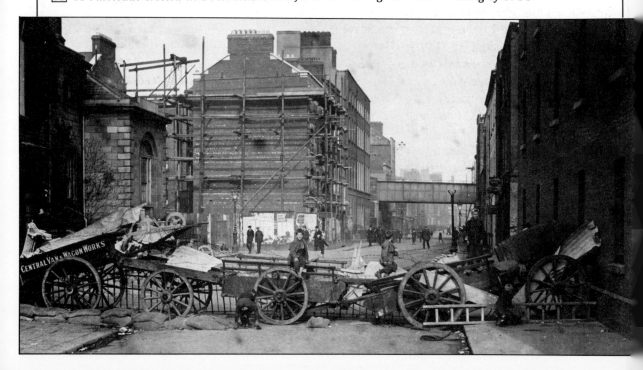

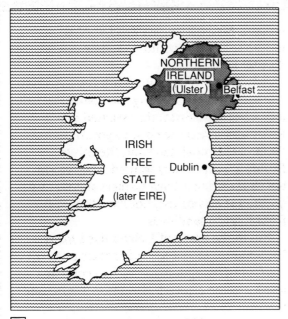

B *The Division of Ireland, 1922*

C *The anti-Catholic slogan on this banner illustrates the extraordinary 'Orange' (Protestant) enthusiasm in working-class Belfast, 1974.*

But the British Parliament would not agree and so there were burnings and murder, imprisonment and eviction.

In 1912 a Bill to give Home Rule was introduced into Parliament but caused bitter argument in Ireland. Protestants in the north reacted strongly against it, while in the south, men were prepared to fight for it. A civil war appeared to be close.

Then, in 1914, the quarrel was set to one side when the Great War started.

● The Easter Rising, 1916
It was generally agreed that the Home Rule Bill would be shelved until after the war. However, some Irishmen were not prepared to wait, and at Easter, 1916, there was an uprising in Dublin. Members of the Irish Sinn Fein Party declared themselves independent of the United Kingdom.

British troops moved in to put down the revolt and there was fierce fighting.

Afterwards some of the ringleaders were shot and Irish people thought of them as martyrs, trying to gain freedom.

● Ireland, 1918–45
After 1918 there was increasing trouble between the British and the Irish until 1922. Then a treaty was signed which separated Ireland into two parts. In the north, six counties stayed with the United Kingdom and were generally known as Ulster. The rest of Ireland became a self-governing dominion, known as the Irish Free State, which was still part of the British Empire.

However, this arrangement did not please many Irishmen in the south and Catholics in the north, who wanted a United Ireland, with its government in Dublin.

Gradually the links between Britain and Ireland grew weaker, until 1937 when the Free State was renamed Eire and broke away into independence.

During the Second World War, Eire remained neutral, refusing to enter the war against Hitler's Germany. Ulster, on the other hand, was a part of the United Kingdom and took part in the war.

● Ireland since 1945

Since 1945 the world's attention has often been concentrated on Ireland. This has been caused mainly by the troubles of Ulster, in the north. In that province live about a million people, with Protestants outnumbering Catholics by roughly two to one. Generally, the Catholics want to be part of a United Ireland, while the Protestants wish to remain attached to the United Kingdom. These differences of religion and outlook have caused trouble between the two groups ever since 1922.

Violence broke out on a big scale in 1969, with many Catholics believing that they had been badly treated over such matters as housing and jobs. The Protestants, however, believe that the Catholic minority are disloyal to the crown and do not act as good citizens of the United Kingdom.

Both sides have their own secret 'armies' which carry out shootings, burnings and bombings. British troops were sent to the province in 1969 to keep order but have been unable to prevent many acts of violence that have occurred since then. Many Catholics view them as an occupying force of foreigners.

Groups like the Catholic Irish Republican Army (IRA) and the Protestant Ulster Volunteer Force (UVF) have maintained a steady rate of violence against their

D *Troops in the Lenadoon estate of Belfast, July 1972*

opponents. In addition, the IRA have launched a campaign of bombing of targets both military and civilian. The end result is that since 1969 over 2,000 people have died and many thousands of others have been injured in a type of 'war' that has split the citizens of Ulster into two groups.

Sometimes the violence has been carried across to the mainland of Britain. Several well-known people have been killed or wounded in a campaign launched by extremists of the IRA. The most sensational killing of that type occurred in 1979 off the coast of Southern Ireland when Earl Mountbatten, who had brought independence to India and was a relative of Queen Elizabeth II, was blown up in his small boat. But death or injury has also come to ordinary people who have been victims of bomb blasts.

● **The future?**
As far as Britain is concerned the Irish Question is still one of the greatest problems facing the nation. Although it has lasted for so long, a solution will have to be found over the next few years.

What are the options? One is that Ulster will remain part of the United Kingdom, governed by a Protestant majority. The Catholics and Nationalists who want to be joined to Eire will not accept that.

Another is that Ulster will become part of a United Ireland, so the Protestants will be a minority in the new nation. Protestants and Loyalists who want to keep their links with Britain will not accept that.

A third is that Ulster should become a small, independent state with no links to any other country. It would be difficult to persuade people on both sides of the argument to agree to that.

Today's younger generation will have to come up with a solution that is acceptable to both sides. Until then, the killings and bombings will continue. ☐

Exercises

1 Why are the following dates important in Irish history:
   (a) 1845–6?
   (b) 1912?
   (c) 1916?
   (d) 1922?
   (e) 1969?

2 Copy and complete this grid.

Picture number	Event
A	Easter Rising, 1916
C	
D	

3 What did the chapter tell you about the following:
   (a) the background to the Irish problem?
   (b) Home Rule?
   (c) the Easter Rising?
   (d) the Irish civil war?
   (e) Ireland since 1945?

4 Read the section 'The future?' again. What options are open to those who look for a solution to 'The Irish Question'?

5 Imagine you are either (a) Catholic or (b) Protestant and explain your solution to the Irish problem.

American domestic problems

● **Introduction**

Although the USA is the world's richest and strongest country, with a higher standard of living overall than anywhere else on earth, the nation has had some deep troubles at home since 1945. These have led to great bitterness among the people involved.

● **McCarthyism**

As Communism grew stronger in the world after 1945 many Americans had fears that there were 'Reds' inside their country. They believed that some of these people were in positions of power and could undermine the USA. A senator from Wisconsin, Joseph McCarthy, seized on these fears and began a 'witch-hunt' to search for Communists.

From 1950 to 1954 McCarthy led investigations into people's lives and backgrounds. He was made chairman of a Senate Committee which could call witnesses and enquire into the past of prominent Americans. Soon he was seeing 'Reds' everywhere in public life. Civil servants, lecturers and film stars all became objects of his questioning. Looking back, it is obvious that accusations were unfair and untrue, but at the time many people believed them.

At length he even denounced General Marshall, who was a trusted American soldier and many then doubted McCarthy's claims. When they saw him on television they realized that his methods of bullying with half-truths were wrong.

In 1954 the US Senate criticized McCarthy and he lost his power. Yet by then scores of Americans had lost their position or their reputation through appearing before his committee.

● **Civil rights**

The Americans have a Constitution which

A *Joseph McCarthy's view of the 'Red'*

sets out in writing the duties and rights of all its citizens. The Fifteenth Amendment to the Constitution says:

⬆1 **The rights of the citizens of the United States to vote shall not be denied or abridged [altered] by the United States or by any state on account of race, colour, or previous condition of servitude [slavery].**

This means that all American citizens, whatever their colour, are regarded as equal in their right to vote. But ever since the end of the American Civil War in 1865 negroes had been treated as second-class citizens in many parts of the USA. Most of them lived in the southern states, where their ancestors had been slaves. And there, racial discrimination was shown towards them. In some areas they were not allowed to travel on public transport with white people, or use the same cinemas or restaurants. They did not have equal opportunities of education.

However in the 1950s and 1960s steps were taken towards obtaining civil rights. Under successive Presidents – Eisenhower, Kennedy, Johnson and Nixon – laws were passed to bring some equality.

In 1954 the US Supreme Court ruled that black pupils should be allowed to attend any school. But there was great resistance to this ruling in the southern states and sometimes police and troops had to escort black children into schools.

Black people were angry. One of them, Dr Martin Luther King, believed in peaceful protest and led demonstration marches. He remembered words that his mother had taught him when he was a boy:

---

2 You must never feel that you are less than anybody else. You must always feel that you are somebody and you must feel that you are as good as anybody else.

Luther King became known across the world for his aims and methods, which were based on his deep Christian beliefs. But his words and actions brought hatred from those who disapproved of what he was trying to do. Tragedy came in 1968 when he was in Memphis, Tennessee. He was shot dead by a white man.

Other black people reacted more violently against what they saw as injustice in almost every part of their daily lives. In 1965 there were riots in the Watts district of Los Angeles, with 35 deaths. More violence followed in other parts of the USA.

Some black men and women were attracted to the Black Power movement. This wanted to end the fact that blacks had to depend on whites for everything from jobs

B *The Ku-Klux-Klan is a secret society dedicated to removing all 'un-American' people. Most of its energies are directed against black people but its enemies include Catholics, Jews, socialists and non-English-speaking immigrants. The Klan's stronghold is the southern states. Its activities include beatings-up, tar-and-feathering and lynching. Nearly 5 million Americans joined between 1920 and 1925*

to dignity. One of its leaders, Stokely Carmichael, said:

---

3 . . . We have to stop being ashamed of being black. A broad nose, a thick lip, and nappy hair is us, and we are going to call that beautiful whether they like it or not.

● **The death of President Kennedy**
One of the most popular presidents since 1945 was John F. Kennedy, a Democrat who came to office in 1960. Then he was the

American domestic problems

youngest president in American history. He became a world figure in 1962 at the time of the Cuban missile crisis. Many people believed that he acted with tact and understanding then and helped to avert a world war.

In November 1963 he visited Dallas, Texas on a general visit when an assassin shot him dead. The motives of the killer, Lee Harvey Oswald, were never discovered and the death of Kennedy is still one of the great unsolved mysteries of modern American history.

● **Vietnam**

The Vietnam War was not supported by all Americans. In fact, a strong protest movement against taking part in the war grew in the USA while Lyndon B. Johnson was president in the late 1960s.

The 'Protest People' were able to see events shown on television. They saw the massive bombing of North Vietnam and many believed that their nation was waging war against civilians. They also realized that the high costs were a drain on the American economy. There were large demonstrations against the war and thousands of young men refused to go to the Draft – which meant to join the armed services.

When Richard Nixon became President in 1968 and announced that American forces would be withdrawn from Vietnam there was great relief for millions of people in the USA. By 1972 he had met his promise.

● **Watergate**

Richard Nixon visited Mao Tse-tung in 1972 and took much credit for bringing together the USA and China, two of the world's greatest powers. Then a cloud appeared on the horizon and led to his downfall.

The President had been worried for some time that government information was being

C *A mixture of protest: Civil Rights and anti-Vietnam war marches in 1966*

D *An anti-war placard. The bayonet sliced through the word 'America' suggests that the country is being torn apart by internal troubles*

'leaked' to newspapers by someone who held an official position, so he allowed secret agents to try to find who was responsible. But they used illegal methods and tried to carry out a burglary at the Democratic National Committee's headquarters in the Watergate Hotel, Washington. The agents were discovered and arrested.

For a long time President Nixon acted as if he had known nothing of what was going on. Then, at length, the American courts forced him to release tape-recordings of conversations he'd had with his officials. These showed without doubt that the President had known about the burglary.

The 'Watergate Scandal' broke Richard Nixon. He resigned in August 1974, the first American President ever to do so. □

Exercises

1 Answer the following questions:
   (a) Who was President of the USA at the end of World War II?
   (b) Which US President resigned?
   (c) Which US President was killed in Dallas?
   (d) Who is the President of the USA today?

2 Copy and complete these sentences by using the words in the **word list**.
   (a) The USA has the highest . . . of . . . in the world.
   (b) Joseph . . . was chairman of a . . . committee.
   (c) In the 1950s and 1960s black people in the USA sought . . . .
   (d) President Kennedy was leader of the . . . Party.

   (e) The . . . scandal ended President . . . career.

   > **word list:** civil; living; rights; McCarthy; standard; Senate; Democratic; Nixon's; Watergate.

3 What do you understand by these phrases? Write out your explanation and say which illustration is linked to your answer:
   (a) standard of living;
   (b) the Fifteenth Amendment;
   (c) the Protest People.

4 Explain the significance of pictures A, C and D, in US history since 1945.

5 What was the 'Watergate Affair' and what were its consequences?

Latin America

A *Central and South America*

● Latin America

Going south from the United States, the American continent stretches on for some five thousand miles before finishing at Cape Horn. This area is generally known as Central America, as far as the nation of Panama. After that it becomes South America. In those zones are twenty-two separate states and the general name given to them all is Latin America.

They are called this because the settlers from Europe who landed there, after Columbus's remarkable voyage in 1492, came from Spain and Portugal. Both of those nations have languages which originate from Latin. Those early settlers brought their own languages to what was often called 'The New World' and Spanish and Portuguese are still spoken today by most of the inhabitants of Latin America.

In that vast area of the world are great riches. Some of the early European settlers grew wealthy from silver and gold. But there are mineral resources, like copper, oil and tin. South America also has some of the most amazing geographical areas of the globe, ranging from the Andes mountains to the Amazon jungle.

● Some problems

Ever since most of the inhabitants of Central and South America broke away from their Spanish rulers at the beginning of the nineteenth century, they have been faced with a number of problems. Two of these are particularly seen still at the present day.

One is connected with the way they make a living. Most of them rely on exporting raw materials and importing the manufactured goods they need. Those nations have never built up big industries of their own so they have tended to be closely tied to the United States, away to the north. The USA has bought most of their products and has supplied them with most of their manufactured industrial goods.

Venezuela and Mexico provide oil. Brazil grows coffee. Chile has great supplies of copper and nitrates. Bolivia mines tin and Argentina produces beef. During the twentieth century these nations have come to depend heavily on the USA. Thus when the 'great slump' hit the United States in the 1930s, Latin America was badly affected also. Some large companies from the United States have a great deal of power in South America and this is disliked by many of the inhabitants. These companies pay little attention to the needs of the local people.

Another urgent problem facing Latin America is the growth of population. There is great poverty in most of the Latin

American nations, as well as considerable wealth for some few families, but this has not stopped the population explosion of recent years. Brazil, for example, which had just over fifty million people in 1950, contained over 84 million by 1966 and about 120 million in 1980. An estimate has been made that Brazil's population could number 358 million by the year 2010!

The obvious problem is how to feed, clothe and house so many people. Many of them have flocked to the cities, searching for work and so several cities have grown at a phenomenal rate. Among these are Mexico City, Sao Paulo and Brasilia. The main areas of many Latin American cities contain fine roads and modern buildings. But on the outskirts are 'shanty towns' where thousands live in conditions of great poverty.

● The USA and Latin America

Since 1945 the United States has been the world's most powerful opponent of Communism. For that reason it has not been pleased when left-wing revolutions have occurred in Latin America, because it has feared that Russian-inspired ideas could be brought to the American continent. This explains its anxiety when Fidel Castro came to power in Cuba in 1959 and the missile crisis developed there three years later. America was also worried when Salvador Allende, a Communist, became President of Chile in 1970. Three years afterwards, the Americans were relieved when a military revolution overthrew him. (They had sent in money and agents to make sure this would happen!)

There have also been left-wing uprisings in Central America. In El Salvador and Guatemala rebels have attacked government forces and the United States has felt uneasy.

Some of the people of Latin America are pleased to have such a powerful neighbour as the USA offering trade, business and protection. But to many of the poor the difference in wealth between North America and Latin America is unfair and a point of constant argument. They are not happy at the way in which the United States intervenes in their government and their economy.

B *The Brazilian city of Sao Paulo has over 7 million inhabitants*
C *Children in a shanty town outside a big city. Thousands live in great poverty*

● Britain and Latin America

Generally Britain has had good relations with the nations of South America. In the past it has helped them to develop, especially in the building of railways during the last century and has traded regularly with them.

A number of Commonwealth countries are to be found in Central America, especially in the area of the West Indies. Since 1945 they have asked for and received independence, while keeping their links with Britain. Thousands of citizens from such places as Jamaica, Antigua and Barbados have come to settle in the British Isles, searching for work.

The richest and best developed of all South American nations has also had strong links with Britain. This is Argentina, whose transport, banking and business systems were developed by the British in the nineteenth century. The meat trade there, involving the production of beef cattle, was also aided by them.

● Trouble in the South Atlantic, 1982

However, there was one great point of argument between Britain and Argentina. This concerned the ownership of a group of islands which lie in the South Atlantic Ocean, about 400 miles off the east coast of South America. To the United Kingdom they were known as the Falkland Islands and had been settled by British people from the early 1830s. To the Argentinians they were the Malvinas, from which their own people had been driven out at that time.

D *Royal Marines training off Ascension Island. HMS Fearless is in the background.*

Latin America

In April 1982 the military government of Argentina sent troops to take over the islands and claim them as part of the Argentine. Thousands of soldiers poured ashore, overcame the small British garrison and renamed the islands the 'Malvinas'.

Britain complained to the United Nations which agreed that an act of aggression had taken place. However, the Argentinians claimed that they had only taken what was rightfully theirs, so they refused to withdraw.

● The Falklands War

In response, the British government said that such aggression must not be seen to pay. A Task Force was organized and sailed to the South Atlantic. It contained ships of the Royal Navy and merchant vessels including two great ocean liners, to carry marines, paratroops and other servicemen.

When ground forces were landed, hard fighting took place in some of the world's most barren country. Several ships of the Task Force were hit and lost, as well as an Argentinian cruiser. At length, the Argentinian soldiers surrendered and were sent back to their homeland. Britain had won a distant war but its policy was opposed by many South Americans.

The future in that area is still uncertain. British policy holds that the islanders must decide which country they want to belong to; Argentina's view is that the islands are its territory.

So will the trouble occur again in your lifetime?

Exercises

1 Quick questions.
 (a) Which European peoples settled in Latin America?
 (b) What did they call it?
 (c) Which languages did they bring to Latin America?
 (d) How did the Europeans grow rich?
 (e) How many modern states are there in Latin America?

2 Copy map A into your book. Write a list of the countries named on it and beside each write any information you can find in the chapter.

3 Read sections 2 and 3 ('Some problems' and 'The USA and Latin America') and then study the map again. Explain how the USA is linked economically to Latin America but how politically it faces problems there.

4 Imagine you live in a shanty town outside Sao Paulo. Give reasons for your being there and how you would like to change your existence.

5 (a) Explain, as a guerrilla in El Salvador, why you would resist US influence.
 (b) Explain, as a US President, why you would wish to help defeat the guerrillas.

6 Why did Britain and Argentina go to war in 1982? Explain what happened in that war.

7 Imagine you are either (a) a Falkland Islander, or (b) an Argentinian. Explain why you think you should be allowed to live on the Falkland Islands.

Today's giants: USA and USSR

● The best way?

There are a number of different ways of ruling, governing and running a nation in the modern world.

Britain, for example, has a monarchy, where kings or queens succeed to the throne. But in Britain the Queen has little power or say in governing the nation.

That is left to Parliament. In the British Parliament there are several political parties and once every five years at the longest they stand at a General Election. The party gaining the greatest number of seats becomes the next government. At the election the vote is given to nearly everyone who is aged eighteen and over. We call this system democracy.

Many other nations in Europe have similar systems of choosing a government. Some of them, also, are monarchies, but others are republics.

In a republic there is a president as Head of State. Usually he or she is elected for a period of years. For example, the President of the United States is in office for four years and people can decide freely whether to choose him again, or have someone else.

Some nations, however, have less choice. There is one party in power and often no other parties are allowed to exist.

Communist states generally allow no opposition. At elections there is a choice of candidates – but they are all from the governing party. They claim that having several parties represents a class system – and that is outdated. They believe that their system is true democracy.

● Capitalism and Communism

Today, Russia is the world's leading Communist power. Ever since the 1917 revolution the Communist Party has held power there. The state owns business and land, industry and trade and runs it on behalf of the citizens of the nation. Private business does not exist as it does in the west. In this way, the Communists claim, all benefit and no one is exploited.

A *The American system of government*

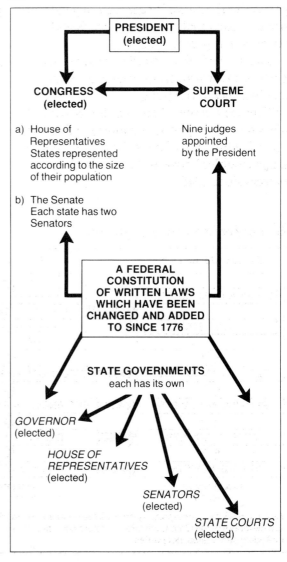

PRESIDENT (elected)

CONGRESS (elected)

SUPREME COURT

a) House of Representatives
States represented according to the size of their population

Nine judges appointed by the President

b) The Senate
Each state has two Senators

A FEDERAL CONSTITUTION OF WRITTEN LAWS WHICH HAVE BEEN CHANGED AND ADDED TO SINCE 1776

STATE GOVERNMENTS
each has its own

GOVERNOR (elected)

HOUSE OF REPRESENTATIVES (elected)

SENATORS (elected)

STATE COURTS (elected)

Since 1945 Communist ideas have spread to other lands, from Poland to China, from North Korea to Cuba.

The world's leading capitalist power is the USA. In a capitalist state individuals are given great freedom to own businesses, land and property. Some inherit it while others have the chance of making fortunes. In some capitalist nations, like Britain, certain means of production are owned by the state, for example, coal mines and railways. But generally, the nation's economy depends on private individuals providing goods and services that people require.

This way of life is found in many other parts of the world, from France to Brazil, and Norway to Australia.

There is a contest between the two sets of ideas on how to govern a country and run its everyday life. This contest lies at the root of many troubles between the two great super powers since 1945.

● **The Union of Soviet Socialist Republics**
The USSR is one of the two most powerful nations in the world and its position has been recognized since 1945. It is by far the largest country anywhere in size and covers almost one-sixth of the land area of the world. Russia is more than ninety times bigger than the United Kingdom and stretches across two continents – Europe and Asia.

It is made up of fifteen different republics, such as Georgia and the Ukraine and has a population of over 270 million people. Such a large country has enormous quantities of natural resources, like oil and gas, coal and forests.

Russia suffered terrible losses during the Second World War, when some twenty million of its people were killed. Ever since then it has decided to guard her frontiers carefully against any future attack. At the same time it has helped to spread Communist ideas across the world. The view

B *The Soviet system of government*

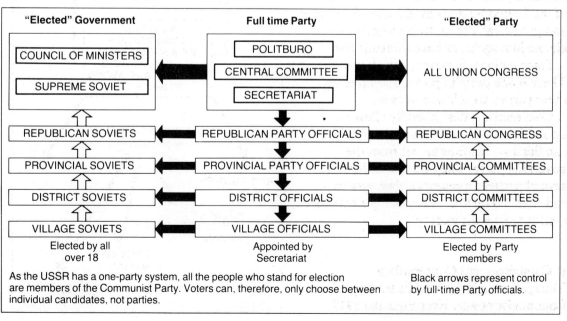

"Elected" Government | Full time Party | "Elected" Party

COUNCIL OF MINISTERS — POLITBURO / CENTRAL COMMITTEE / SECRETARIAT — ALL UNION CONGRESS
SUPREME SOVIET

REPUBLICAN SOVIETS — REPUBLICAN PARTY OFFICIALS — REPUBLICAN CONGRESS
PROVINCIAL SOVIETS — PROVINCIAL PARTY OFFICIALS — PROVINCIAL COMMITTEES
DISTRICT SOVIETS — DISTRICT OFFICIALS — DISTRICT COMMITTEES
VILLAGE SOVIETS — VILLAGE OFFICIALS — VILLAGE COMMITTEES

Elected by all over 18 | Appointed by Secretariat | Elected by Party members

As the USSR has a one-party system, all the people who stand for election are members of the Communist Party. Voters can, therefore, only choose between individual candidates, not parties.

Black arrows represent control by full-time Party officials.

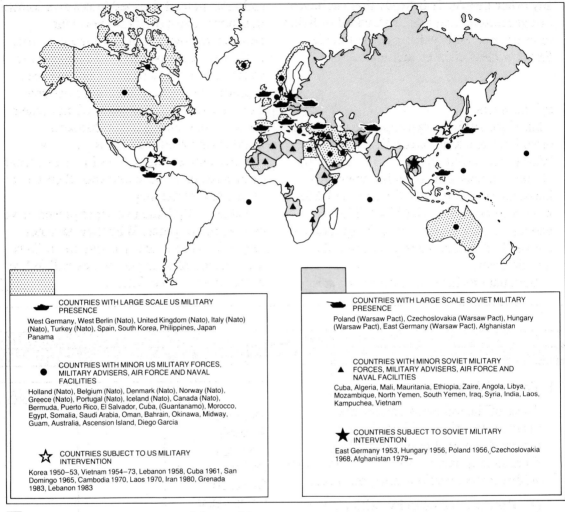

COUNTRIES WITH LARGE SCALE US MILITARY PRESENCE

West Germany, West Berlin (Nato), United Kingdom (Nato), Italy (Nato) (Nato), Turkey (Nato), Spain, South Korea, Philippines, Japan Panama

COUNTRIES WITH MINOR US MILITARY FORCES, MILITARY ADVISERS, AIR FORCE AND NAVAL FACILITIES

Holland (Nato), Belgium (Nato), Denmark (Nato), Norway (Nato), Greece (Nato), Portugal (Nato), Iceland (Nato), Canada (Nato), Bermuda, Puerto Rico, El Salvador, Cuba, (Guantanamo), Morocco, Egypt, Somalia, Saudi Arabia, Oman, Bahrain, Okinawa, Midway, Guam, Australia, Ascension Island, Diego Garcia

COUNTRIES SUBJECT TO US MILITARY INTERVENTION

Korea 1950–53, Vietnam 1954–73, Lebanon 1958, Cuba 1961, San Domingo 1965, Cambodia 1970, Laos 1970, Iran 1980, Grenada 1983, Lebanon 1983

COUNTRIES WITH LARGE SCALE SOVIET MILITARY PRESENCE

Poland (Warsaw Pact), Czechoslovakia (Warsaw Pact), Hungary (Warsaw Pact), East Germany (Warsaw Pact), Afghanistan

COUNTRIES WITH MINOR SOVIET MILITARY FORCES, MILITARY ADVISERS, AIR FORCE AND NAVAL FACILITIES

Cuba, Algeria, Mali, Mauritania, Ethiopia, Zaire, Angola, Libya, Mozambique, North Yemen, South Yemen, Iraq, Syria, India, Laos, Kampuchea, Vietnam

COUNTRIES SUBJECT TO SOVIET MILITARY INTERVENTION

East Germany 1953, Hungary 1956, Poland 1956, Czechoslovakia 1968, Afghanistan 1979–

C *How the super powers control the world*

of the Russian leaders has been that one day the whole globe will become Communist and that they have a duty to speed up the process.

● **The United States of America**

The USA is the richest and most powerful nation in the world. Since 1945 it has been recognized as the leading capitalist nation. It is a large nation, stretching almost 3000 miles from the Atlantic Ocean in the east to the Pacific Ocean in the west.

The USA consists of 50 separate states, with most of them, including Alaska, on the North American mainland. The islands of Hawaii also belong to the Union. The population is about 230 million and they live in a country of great natural resources. From these they enjoy the world's highest general standard of living, with more wealth than any other people. It believes that capitalism brings freedom and a high standard of living to everyone. Thus it has opposed Soviet Russia's ideas all over the globe.

● The rivals

Thus since 1945 the two super powers have often been in a kind of conflict. This 'Cold War' has involved trying to gain the support of other nations and spreading their own ideas. Occasionally the USA and the USSR have been close to a 'Hot War'. This happened, for example, over the question of the Berlin Airlift and also over the Cuban Missile crisis.

Both nations have built up the greatest and most powerful armed forces ever known in history. Because of the enormous destructive power of modern weapons each of the two super powers could destroy the world several times over. They have great supplies of missiles which could destroy cities in a matter of minutes. Giant rockets point at New York – and at Moscow. Bombers are ready to take off at a few minutes notice. Submarines in distant oceans carry missiles which could wipe their enemy off the face of the map.

Yet since 1945 the two super powers have kept a kind of peace. Why they have not fought is a matter of some argument. So is the question of what policy they will follow in the future – your future. □

Exercises

1 True or false?

Three of the following statements were made in the chapter. Find the two incorrect statements and then change them so they agree with the chapter. Copy all five correct versions into your book.

(a) Britain is a monarchy, with a royal family.
(b) Presidents in republics are usually elected for a lifetime.
(c) In Britain some means of production are owned by the state.
(d) The USSR is made up of twenty different republics.
(e) Since 1945 the two super powers have kept a kind of peace.

2 Copy and complete this chart and add any other items to column one if you wish to.

	The USSR	The USA
Monarchy		
Republic		
President		
Political Parties		
Capitalist		
Communist		

3 List those countries mentioned in the chapter which
   (a) have Communist governments and
   (b) have non-Communist governments.

4 Compare and contrast the systems of government in the USA and the USSR.

5 Make a list of as many conflicts you can think of since 1945 which have strained relations between the USA and the USSR.

(*A further question appears on page 219.*)

Further exercises

● **Questions related to specific chapters**

2 Britain and its empire
Who were the Boers? Why did the British go to war with them in 1899? Why did the British win this war?

5 Sarajevo and war
Explain how each of the following has a bearing on the outbreak of the First World War in 1914:
(a) the division of Europe into armed camps;
(b) naval rivalry;
(c) the murder at Sarajevo;
(d) Belgian neutrality.

10 The end of the war
Why did the United States of America not enter the First World War until 1917? Why did it eventually declare war on Germany?

11 The Treaty of Versailles
What were the main aims of the makers of the Treaty of Versailles? How did they try to achieve these aims? How successful were they?

14 Russia's time of trial
Why did revolution take place in Russia in 1917? You may mention, among other things, conditions in Russia and the rise of opposition to the Tsar, Lenin and the Bolsheviks, the war and defeats.

15 Stalin and Russia till 1939
(a) What changes did Stalin make in the organization of Russian farming? Why did the kulaks oppose these changes?

(b) Describe the methods by which Stalin maintained himself in power.

16 Mussolini in Italy
(a) Describe the rise to power of Mussolini in Italy.

(b) How did Mussolini attempt to strengthen Italy and expand its empire before 1939?

19 The New Deal
Describe Roosevelt's achievements as President of the USA up to 1941.

20 Japan and China in the 1930s
(a) Why did the Japanese invade and occupy Manchuria in 1931 and 1932?

(b) Describe how Japan gained territory from China between 1932 and 1938.

23 The Spanish Civil War
(a) Why did a Civil War break out in Spain in 1936?

(b) How did General Franco rise to power between 1936 and 1939?

(c) Explain what part was played in these events by:
(i) Russia;
(i) Germany and Italy.

24 The League of Nations
(a) Describe how the League of Nations came to be set up in 1919.

(b) What were its aims?

(c) Give an account of the structure and organization of the League.

(d) Give as many reasons as you can to explain the failure of the League to achieve its main aim.

25 Steps to war
Imagine that you have attended a debate in the 1930s between a supporter of

appeasement and an opponent of appeasement. Write a summary of the arguments you might have heard first from one side and then from the other.

26 Off to war again

Describe some of the actions taken by Hitler in Germany from the time he became Chancellor in 1933 to 1939.

29 Japan and Pearl Harbor

(a) Name the great British naval base in the Far East that surrendered to the Japanese on 15 February 1942.

(b) Why were the Japanese forces so successful between 1941 and 1942?

38 The Chinese revolution

Write a paragraph in answer to each of **three** of the following:

(a) How successful was Sun Yat-sen's 1911 revolution in making life better for ordinary Chinese peasants?

(b) Why did the Kuomintang collapse against the Communist challenge 1945–49?

(c) How did Mao Tse-tung keep the support of the Chinese peasants for the Communist government?

(d) In what ways was Mao Tse-tung successful in strengthening China's industry?

(e) In what ways did China's world influence increase between 1949 and 1971?

40 Space exploration

Write an account of the conquest of air and space *either* (a) before 1945 or (b) since 1945.

41 Israel and the Arabs

Describe the development of the conflict between the Arab states and Israel using the following outline as a guide:

(a) the persecution of the Jews in Europe;

(b) the British withdrawal from Palestine and the creation of the State of Israel;

(c) the first Arab–Israeli War 1948–49;

(d) the Suez Crisis 1956;

(e) the June War 1967 and after.

47 EFTA and the Common Market

What part have the following played in the economic development of Europe since the end of the Second World War:

The Marshall Plan;

The Common Market (European Economic Community);

EFTA?

54 Today's giants: USA and USSR

(a) Why are Russia and the USA regarded as 'super powers'?

(b) Suggest reasons for the USA and USSR being hostile to each other.

(c) Why is such hostility considered a threat to world civilization?

(b) Describe and explain the events that led to the Cuban crisis of 1962. How was the crisis resolved?

● General questions

1 Answer both sections.

(a) 'From Stettin in the Baltic to Trieste in the Adriatic, an iron curtain has descended across the continent.' (Churchill, 1945)

   (i) Explain what is meant by 'an iron curtain' and explain its purpose.

   (ii) What is meant by a 'cold war'? Why did the 'cold war' develop?

(iii) Why did a 'Berlin crisis' develop in 1948 and how was it settled in 1949?

(b) 'For many years the United States had a clear nuclear lead.'
    (i) Explain what is meant by 'clear nuclear lead'.
    (ii) How did the USSR attempt to combat it?
    (iii) How did rivalry between the USA and USSR result in the 'Cuban crisis' in 1962? How was this crisis settled?

2   Answer both sections:
(a) Explain how each of the following events weakened the German Weimar Republic and helped the Nazis:
    (i) the Versailles Treaty 1919;
    (ii) the inflation of the mark 1923;
    (iii) the world slump after 1929.

(b) How did each of four of the following help Hitler to strengthen his dictatorship in Germany?
    (i) the burning of the Reichstag;
    (ii) the 'Night of the Long Knives';
    (iii) the Gestapo;
    (iv) the concentration camps;
    (v) the Hitler Youth.

3   *Either* Explain what is meant by 'Dominion Status' and show how the idea developed from 1867 to 1931 using the following links:
The Dominion of Canada – Imperial Conferences on other dominions – First World War – League of Nations – Statute of Westminster 1931
   or Describe the changes that have taken place in the British Commonwealth since 1945, mentioning as many as possible of: new dominions; republican status; 'the wind of change'; Rhodesia.

4 (a) What is meant by the 'Great Depression'?
(b) How did the governments of
    (i) the USA
    (ii) Germany
attempt to deal with their difficulties after 1930?

5   Each of these organizations sought to achieve international co-operation. Write a paragraph about each of **three** of them, explaining how the organization was set up, who its members were, what kind of co-operation between nations it sought, how far it has been successful:
(a) the North Atlantic Treaty Organization (NATO);
(b) the Warsaw Pact;
(c) the European Free Trade Area (EFTA);
(d) The United Nations Educational, Scientific and Cultural Organization (UNESCO);
(e) the Council for Mutual Economic Aid (COMECON).

6   Describe and explain the reasons for *either*
(a) German success in the Second World War up to 1942, *or*
(b) German lack of success in the Second World War after 1942.

7   Write an account of the events associated with two of the following places:
(a) Wall Street, 1929;
(b) the beach at Dunkirk, 1940;
(c) the Suez Canal;
(d) Hungary, 1956.
Estimate the importance of the two events you have chosen.

8 (a) In 1918 the British Empire consisted of four self-governing colonies or dominions, the Empire of India, and a large number of colonies and other dependencies. George V was King of the whole empire. Explain the chief differences between the British Empire as it was in 1918 and the Commonwealth as it is today.

   (b) Why have most of the changes taken place since 1945?

9 This question concerns the Second World War, 1939–45. Answer three of the following:
   (a) Explain the German technique of the Blitzkrieg and give examples of its use.
   (b) What was the Maginot Line and why was it a failure?
   (c) Who were the Free French and what was their contribution to the Allied cause?
   (d) Describe and explain the fall of Singapore.
   (e) Describe the Warsaw Rising of 1944. Why did the Russians fail to take the city of Warsaw until the rising was over?

10 After Stalin's death some aspects of Russian policy changed and some remained the same. From the following list, choose two examples to show how Russian policy changed and two to show how it remained the same. Write briefly about each.

   (a) Stalingrad became Volgograd
   (b) In 1956 the Hungarian Rebellion was suppressed
   (c) The Berlin Wall was built in 1961
   (d) Krushchev talked of 'peaceful co-existence'
   (e) Krushchev was allowed to retire in 1964 without being put on trial
   (f) Russia established missile bases in Cuba in 1962.

11 Choose **four** of the following, and write a paragraph about each:
   (a) an air raid;
   (b) 'Digging for Victory';
   (c) rationing;
   (d) 'V' bombs ('Doodlebugs' and rockets);
   (e) D-Day;
   (f) 'Lord Haw Haw';
   (g) the Nuremberg trials.

12 After the initial German dash for Paris had failed in 1914, the War in the West became complete 'stalemate' with neither side able to make any real progress for two and a half years; and the greatest attempt to break that 'stalemate' – by attacking another front at Gallipoli in 1915 – was a disastrous failure.
   (a) Why do you think there was complete 'stalemate' in the West?
   (b) Write a paragraph about trench warfare.
   (c) Write an account of the Gallipoli campaign.

Projects and revision

● **Study techniques**

Your learning style
We all work and learn in different ways. Some people like to work systematically whilst others prefer to adopt a more relaxed approach. There is no best way. You will develop a style which is best suited to you.

Being organized
No matter what your learning style is, you will find that having a plan of work or a timetable is very useful. You will avoid pressure and crises in this way. Having the books and notes you need also reduces stress.

Knowing what to do
A clear idea of the task or exercise you have to complete is vital. Having an objective can motivate you. A lot of objectives will have to be fulfilled during an examination course, for example writing an essay or completing a project.

Knowing how to complete a task
This very much depends on the directions given to you, the amount of information you have and your understanding of it, and the books and notes you have to assist you. If you are unsure you should always seek guidance.

Using resources
Knowing what is available to you and where it can be found should be an essential part of your learning plan. School and class libraries, the local library, newspapers and current affairs magazines will all contain useful and relevant material.

Reading
– Be sure that what you read is relevant to your topic
– Be sure that the book is at your reading level
– Vary the pattern of your reading
– Read quickly to get the main ideas
– Read slowly when you are note-taking

Note-taking
– Notes make your work easier to remember
– Notes help you to clarify and understand your reading
– Notes are useful for easy revision
– You must listen or look for key facts or phrases
– Organize your notes by classifying and numbering

Essay writing
– Make sure you understand the essay title
– Ask yourself what the essay demands of you
– Use many sources of information to prepare your essay
– Prepare an essay plan – introduction, development, conclusion

Project work
– Begin with a general title, for example 'World War Two'
– Read around the title using as many books as you can
– Concentrate on a more manageable topic, for example 'The Outbreak of War in 1939'
– Organize your work and draw up a timetable
– Read and make notes
– Collect materials such as illustrations
– Organize your material and plan the project

Projects and revision

- Write the project and present your material
- Revise where necessary
- Present the project

● **Revision techniques**

You should revise
- because you will be expected to recall details of the course you have studied
- in a planned, systematic way
- with all the material you need close at hand
- in a quiet, warm, well-lit room
- in short, definite, planned sessions
- in a way which allows you to get the best out of your learning style

Guidelines
- Prepare a revision timetable well before the exams start
- Start revising well in advance of the exams
- Divide subjects into topics
- Allocate time for each topic
- Allow for relaxation
- Do not concentrate only on your strong points
- Make an effort to revise your weak points
- Do not leave everything until the last minute
- Make sure you know how the exam is structured
- Make sure you know how many questions to answer

Acknowledgements

The Publishers' thanks are due to the following for permission to reproduce copyright photographs:

Associated Press: pages 66, 117, 141, 188, 191; B T Batsford Ltd: page 176; BBC Hulton Picture Library: pages 8, 18, 20, 21, 22, 38, 41, 49, 50(D), 56, 68, 73, 74, 81, 82, 86, 89, 96, 142(C), 144, 150, 163, 178, 202, 207; Belfast Telegraph: page 203; Bildarchiv Preussischer Kulturbesitz: pages 135(A), 158(B); Brazilian Embassy: page 211(B); British Film Institute: page 72; Bundesarchiv, Koblenz: page 186; Camera Press: pages 151, 172, 183(B), 194, 195, 209, 211(C); Deutsche Presse Agentur: page 162; Edimedia: page 62; David Evans: page 33; Mary Evans Picture Library: page 87; The John Hillelson Agency: pages 83, 94, 175, 183(C), 208; Historical Research Unit: page 17; Robert Hunt Library: page 148; Ikon: pages 10, 57; The Trustees of the Imperial War Museum, London: pages 23, 26, 28, 36, 37, 40, 45, 120, 121, 123; International Institute of Social History, Amsterdam: page 69; Kenya Information Services: page 171; Library of Congress: pages 6, 206; London Express News and Feature Services: pages 99, 101, 106 (cartoons supplied by permission of *The Standard*); Moro, Roma: page 65; NASA: pages 158(A), 159, 160; Novosti: pages 48, 50(C), 122; Photo Source: pages 60, 84, 92, 97, 100, 112(D), 127, 142(D), 179, 184, 192, 200; Popperfoto: pages 52, 75, 112(C), 128, 130–1, 135(B), 136, 168; Punch: pages 13, 14, 54, 102, 114; Roger-Violett: page 58; F D Roosevelt Library: page 78; Society for Cultural Relations with the USSR: page 167; South Wales Echo: page 103; Suddeutscher Verlag: page 64; Syndication International: page 204; Tennessee Valley Authority: page 77; Topham: pages 53, 90, 104, 109, 212; Ullstein Bilderdienst: page 70; United Nations: page 157; UPI/Bettmann: page 76; US Navy: pages 115, 132(C and D), 156

The Publishers would be pleased to hear from the copyright holders of the following illustrations, whom they have regretfully been unable to trace: pages 93, 116, 119, 146, 170, 180.

We would like to thank the following examination boards for the use of their questions in the 'Further exercises' section: ALSEB; EAEB; EMREB; LREB; NWREB; SEREB; SWEB; WJEC; WMEB; YHREB.

Index